The Best
Lawyer in a
One-Lawyer Town

The Best Lawyer in a One-Lawyer Town

A Memoir

Dale Bumpers

The University of Arkansas Press
Fayetteville
2004

Published by arrangement with Random House, an imprint of
Random House Publishing Group, a division of Random House, Inc.

Manufactured in the United States of America

08   07   06   05   04   5   4   3   2   1

Book design by Mercedes Everett

∞ The paper used in this publication meets the minimum requirements
of the American National Standard for Permanence of Paper
for Printed Library Materials Z39.48-1984.

LIBRARY OF CONGRESS CATALOGING-IN-PUBLICATION DATA

Bumpers, Dale.
The best lawyer in a one-lawyer town : a memoir / Dale Bumpers.
p.   cm.
Originally published: New York : Random House, c2003.
ISBN 1-55728-773-2 (pbk. : alk. paper)
1. Bumpers, Dale. 2. Legislators—United States—Biography.
3. United States. Congress. Senate—Biography. 4. Governors—
Arkansas—Biography. 5. Lawyers—Arkansas—Biography.
6. Arkansas—Politics and government—1951– I. Title.

E840.8.B84A3 2004
328.73'092—dc22
2004002969

This book is dedicated to my children, Brent, Bill, and Brooke. Throughout the three and a half years I spent writing this book, I had to constantly remind myself that it was a memoir—not a story about my children and my devotion to them.

Contents

The Best
Lawyer in a
One-Lawyer Town

Chapter 1

He Couldn't Even Walk

M en in Panama hats and corseted women waving fans provided courtesy of the local funeral home were still dripping sweat. The odor of perspiration was pervasive. Most men were in overalls, with the tops of their cans of Prince Albert cigarette tobacco protruding just above the pocket in the front bibs. "Rolling your own" cost about one-fourth as much as Lucky Strikes, Camels, or Chesterfields, the only three brands known in Charleston. Not one of the Prince Albert smokers knew, or would have cared had they known, that Prince Albert was the husband of England's legendary Queen Victoria.

The crowd, estimated at thirty-five hundred, was accustomed to the oppressive heat of Arkansas summers, and nothing could dampen their excitement as they awaited the moment for which they had come. It was 1938, and the worst depression in the nation's history stubbornly held on.

My older brother and I stood by my father, who was dressed in his only summer suit, a seersucker, as he engaged in small talk with friends and total strangers. Everyone shared one thing in common—they worshiped Franklin Delano Roosevelt. I was twelve.

That FDR's train would stop in Booneville had been the only topic of conversation at our house since the first news story two days earlier. He was on a cross-country political tour, and Booneville had been chosen as a stop. The purpose of the trip was to endorse Senator Hattie Caraway, the first woman ever elected to the U.S. Senate, in her upcoming race for reelection. Dad was determined that his sons would actually gaze not just upon a president, which would have been awesome enough, but upon Franklin Roosevelt, into whose arms we would fly when we died —or so we had been taught. He was the South's Messiah. From the end of the Civil War until FDR became president, the South had been ignored at best and abused at worst, treated as a conquered nation. Roosevelt seemed anxious to welcome us back into the Union.

On the night of Roosevelt's first election, the men in Charleston had "shot anvils," which shook the foundation of every house in town. They used a well-anchored anvil, common in blacksmith shops, placed a bag of gunpowder on it, and then dropped a heavy metal object on it, causing a deafening explosion. It was frightening, but exciting, too.

Dad tried mightily during the miserable Depression years to bolster our self-esteem. One evening as we finished supper (not until my first year in college did I learn the evening meal was dinner), he pushed his chair back from the table and announced with obvious satisfaction, "I'm the luckiest man alive. I'm even better off than Franklin Roosevelt." The blasphemy was startling, but then he continued, "Because I have a finer family than he has." We almost popped the buttons off our shirts.

We left home two hours early for the twenty-three-mile trip to Booneville, because only one-third of the highway was paved and the other two-thirds was either gravel or crushed rock. Automobile trips were notoriously difficult, and one always had to anticipate a flat tire or blowout when traveling on such roads, especially the ones with crushed rock, built by the Works Progress Administration workers. The WPA was one of the many New

Deal programs under which men worked on public projects for a dollar a day plus commodities, such as cheese and beans, doled out at the courthouse on Saturdays. Well-to-do critics labeled it "We Piddle Around." It was a pittance, but it kept men and their families from starving.

My father's decision to leave home early paid off, because we had been on the rock road less than ten minutes before we suffered a flat tire. We had a spare, but it, too, was flat and the air came out as fast as we pumped it in with a hand pump. In those days tires had rubber inner tubes, and "fixin'" a flat meant finding the leak in the inner tube, patching it with a "hot patch," reinserting it into the tire, putting the tire back on the rim, pumping the tube up with a hand pump, and praying it would hold till you reached your destination. The normal method of finding a leak in an inner tube was to submerge the tube in a vat of water and rotate it till bubbles appeared. We didn't have water, so Dad pumped up the inner tube, placed one side of his face to it, and turned it till he felt air on his face. Then he spat in the general area till it bubbled. The hot patch held, and we arrived with time to spare.

Cars were scarce then, and far less than 50 percent of families had one, but the area around the Rock Island train station looked like a crowded parking lot. Just the sight of so many automobiles signaled that this was no ordinary event.

Booneville was a city of about twenty-five hundred people, and its primary source of employment was the Arkansas State Tuberculosis Sanitorium, located about one mile south of town on a low mountaintop. TB was an incurable disease, and many people avoided Booneville, though the local citizens had long since become indifferent to having hundreds of tuberculosis patients so close by. The sanitorium meant jobs.

Later, as a sixteen-year-old helping my father in his funeral home business, I once went with him to pick up a corpse at the sanitorium, and I remember being terrified that I would surely contract the disease just from handling the body.

At the train station, friends of my father's greeted him with, "Hi, Bill," or, "How are you, Bill?" and, occasionally, from someone he had grown up with, "Hi, Will." His name was William Rufus Bumpers, but he always signed his name W. R. Bumpers. Initials were more prominent and distinguished. My uncles were L.G. (Glen), G.L. (Leonard), J.J. (Joel), and S.T. (Sam). My grandfather was R.C. (Rufus Columbus).

We had been waiting a full hour when a train slowly approached in the distance and people farthest away from the track began to push forward for a closer view. The excitement was palpable. But the train hardly slowed as it continued westward. A man standing on the platform of the last car, looking for all the world like Roosevelt, didn't even wave as the train went by. He seemed to be reading a newspaper or document and ignored the crowd. I was crestfallen and felt terribly cheated. I couldn't imagine the president being so indifferent that he wouldn't even acknowledge us. He didn't even smile. But since the crowd stayed and hardly acknowledged the man, my spirits began to soar again as I concluded the man was not the president. I have never figured out whether the first train with an FDR look-alike on the back platform was intended to foil a possible assassination attempt or whether the similarity in looks was simply coincidental.

Within five to ten minutes the president's train came into view, and there was no mistaking the real thing. Even the engine was festooned with small American flags. The train slowed to a crawl before it reached the crowd, and it seemed an agonizing length of time from our first glimpse till the train finally pulled to a full stop. People pushed and shoved to get closer, but the shoving didn't create any hostility or harsh words. The platform on the last car was covered with red, white, and blue bunting. The Booneville High School band struck up "Happy Days Are Here Again," and I couldn't have had more goose bumps if the president had soared in from the cosmos. But soar he did not. Rather, he laboriously and painstakingly took the three or four steps from the door of the presidential car to the dais and microphone, holding on to the arm of his son James. I tugged at my father's shirtsleeve and whispered:

"Dad, what's wrong with him?"

"I'll tell you later," he said.

Senator Caraway had originally been appointed to succeed her husband, Thaddeus Caraway, who died in office in November 1931. She had promised the governor, who had appointed her, that she would not run in 1932, but she changed her mind, ran, and was elected—mostly thanks to Huey Long, who stumped the state for her for three days as a repayment for a number of votes she had cast at his behest.

Roosevelt's words that day were neither profound nor complicated, but I vividly remember his opening comments regarding Mt. Magazine, the highest point in Arkansas, which was in clear view about seven miles to the east from where we stood. With a wave of his arm toward the mountain, the president invoked the magnificent Mt. Magazine, which he described as the highest point between the Rockies and the Alleghenies. The crowd cheered wildly, as though Mt. Magazine were a product of their labors and ingenuity. In truth, Roosevelt was repeating a popular Arkansas myth. The mountain is 2,753 feet high. When I later discovered there were several mountains taller than Mt. Magazine between the Rockies and the Alleghenies, the impact was not dissimilar to learning there was no Santa Claus.

The president's speech was probably no longer than ten minutes, but I can think of no ten-minute period in my life more awesome, not because of his words, but simply because of his presence. He introduced Senator Caraway fulsomely and told of her unstinting assistance to him and the nation by supporting his New Deal programs. Actually, Senator Caraway spent much of her time at her desk reading Zane Grey novels. Her words were very forgettable.

As the train pulled slowly away, the president remained at the dais, waving to the cheering crowd until he was a distant, unrecognizable figure. Nobody saw him being assisted back into his private car. I was heartsick at the thought that I would never see him again and would probably never see any president again. But I was also childishly shattered that he didn't see me, know me, call my name, or even acknowledge my father, who had once been a member of the Arkansas State Legislature, which in my twelve-year-old mind was no small achievement.

I was absorbed in these and other thoughts as we left the paved streets of Booneville and hit the gravel-and-crushed-stone road for home. It was sobering and depressing to know that we were now on our way back to the reality of our drab existence. It was the same depressed feeling I always had when the Saturday afternoon matinee at the Gem Theater was over. As the end of the movie would obviously be nearing, I would begin to dread those final two words *the end*, knowing the dim theater lights would soon come on and I would have to leave the make-believe world of sequin-dressed women and men in tuxedos, attire that not one of us had ever seen in real life. As we would walk out of the theater, we could see glimpses of Francis Irby Gwaltney, "Fig" to us, in the projection booth, rewinding the last reel. He was fifteen. We were an affluent family compared to Fig's. His meals were often whatever he could sift from garbage cans. His father had died when he was a child, and his mother had become mentally ill following a stroke. Doc Fry, who owned Doc's Café and Pool Hall, had been appointed Fig's guardian, although nobody knew why.

Poverty is relative. Seated in folding chairs in a little cubbyhole beside the projection booth were usually three to five blacks. They had to climb a ladder to get to their segregated seats. Poor as Fig was, the blacks were poorer.

It was difficult to adjust our eyes to the glare of the bright Saturday afternoon sun upon leaving the theater and returning to the dusty streets, seeing pitiful storefronts, dilapidated automobiles, unpainted houses, and wagons parked in the alleys harnessed to docile teams of mules—grinding poverty no matter which direction one looked.

The mules and horses were not always so timid or meek. A dog could often spook them, provoking a dangerous "runaway" when the horses tore loose from the hitching post and ran amok down the alley and into the streets. I remember the stark terror I felt when I was running for our front porch as a runaway team tore through the alley behind Dad's store, turned left down the street where we lived, and ran into the sheet iron building across the street that housed a feed store. Until the building was demolished years later, a gaping hole in the sheet iron bore evidence of the wagon tongue where the team had run wildly into the building.

Gem Theater tickets read, "Adults—15 cents," "Children—10 cents." For ten cents we were provided two hours of absolute euphoria. Even the "coming attractions" were subjects of much discussion the ensuing week. It was the greatest bargain ever invented and easily worth the two lawn mowings it cost.

About ten miles into the trip home from Booneville, and after estimating the size of the crowd, discussing what people wore, whom we had seen from Charleston, and other trivia, my father began, "Now, boys, the reason the president had to hold on to his son getting to the speaker's platform is that he can't walk. He had polio when he was thirty-nine years old, and he wears steel braces on his legs that weigh twelve pounds."

I was deeply saddened to think that this man upon whom I had just gazed, who I had been taught was a veritable saint, couldn't even walk or stand without holding on to someone.

My father went on, "Now, you boys should let that be a lesson to you. If a man who can't even walk and carries twelve pounds of steel on his legs can be president, you boys have good minds and good bodies, and there isn't any reason you can't be president."

Chapter 2

851 Souls

There are twenty-seven Charlestons in the United States. The one in which I grew up during the depths of the Great Depression was a community of 851 people. It is situated in the rolling hill country of western Arkansas, south-southwest of the Ozark Mountains and twenty-three miles east of Fort Smith and the Arkansas River, which separates Arkansas and Oklahoma. From the time the area was first settled, people had tried to extract a living from the reluctant soil, growing cotton, corn, and vegetables with little success. They would later conclude that it was only suitable for pastureland and raising cattle, and by 1945, all three of Charleston's cotton gins had folded.

Charleston was little different culturally, economically, and socially from thousands of similar-size towns where hunger was a constant threat and often a reality, but it was worse in the South. There was no snob value in being poor. Everybody was poor. The Roaring Twenties barely purred in the South, so we had no cushion when the Depression hit. We had a two-block-long business district that was Main Street and also State Highway 22, which had been paved in 1929. Every other street in Charleston was six inches of dust in summer and an impassable quagmire on most days in winter. But mud was preferable to the clouds of dust raised by every passing car in the summer. It was suffocating on clear, still days when the dust never settled. Dusting the furniture and floors of our home was one of my Saturday morning chores, but within a few hours the furniture was covered with dust again. People died of typhoid fever because the water wells from which we drank were only a few steps from our outhouses, and we never made the connection. We took three typhoid shots, one week apart, every three years. The first shot put us to bed with a 102-degree fever for two or three days. God, how I hated it.

We had no water or sewer system, and the outdoor toilets had to have regular sprinklings of lime to control the odor. Not everybody was as religious about using lime as we were, but lime or no lime, in damp weather the entire town smelled like an open sewer. The favorite Halloween prank by roving bands of high schoolers was toppling outhouses. None escaped. Fig Gwaltney was the ringleader. Originally, outhouses were simply placed on top of the ground a few yards from the house. Later, WPA workers dug trenches over which the outhouses were placed. "One-holers" were about two feet long, two feet wide, and two feet deep. "Two holers" were four feet long, two feet wide, and three feet deep. Owners of two holers had braggin' rights.

On one or two Saturday nights each year, the Gem Theater had a midnight "owl" show. Eighteen-year-olds and over stood in line from 11:00 P.M. till midnight to make sure they got a seat. My fourteen- and fifteen-year-old friends and I were insanely jealous. Owl shows were not nearly as pornographic as lingerie ads in *The New York Times* today, but the town's preachers warned that perdition was the next stop for all who attended, as well as for the parents who allowed their children to attend. The coming attractions showed a beautiful woman with a seductive look slipping her bra strap off her shoulder. It was maddening to those of us just finishing puberty.

Everybody knew everybody else in Charleston, and few people ever moved in or out. When a new family moved in, there would be much conjecture about their religion. All the Protestant preachers descended on them. The parish priest never did, because if they were Catholic, they would find the church without assistance. Proselytizing was a competitive enterprise, and the church with the biggest attendance each Sunday lorded it over everyone else. The Baptists were consistent winners in both attendance and collections. We Methodists were occasionally exhilarated to learn a new family was Methodist, only to be disappointed when we learned they were Methodists in name only and rarely attended church. No Presbyterians ever moved in, and as Presbyterians died, so did the church. It is now Charleston's museum.

Our two-story home was built in 1925 at a cost of fifteen hundred dollars. It had a living room, bedroom, dining room, and kitchen on the first level and three bedrooms upstairs. Dad had the foyer converted to a bathroom when Charleston got a sewer system, so when people walked in the front door they usually got a full view of the bathroom. I was born in the front bedroom, which later became the living room.

The wooden icebox was kept in the dining room and cooled with a twenty-five-pound square chunk of ice delivered each day in summer and every other day in winter. Twenty-five pounds cost fifteen cents, and it kept the milk and butter from spoiling and provided ice for our iced tea in the summer.

We had a small Philco radio, which we listened to in the dark, because Mother couldn't bear the thought of the radio and the lights both being on at the same time. We listened to *Amos 'n' Andy* at 6:00 P.M. and *Lum & Abner* at 6:15 P.M. It never occurred to anyone that *Amos 'n' Andy* was degrading to blacks. But it was *Lum & Abner* to whom we related. Their Jot Em Down store was in Pine Ridge, Arkansas, and the colloquialisms and country talk were all too familiar.

Everyone was a rabid St. Louis Cardinals fan. St. Louis was the closest city to Charleston that had a baseball team, but, more important, KMOX radio in St. Louis, which carried the Cardinals games, was the only station we could get after dark.

The Crescent Drug Store painted a baseball scorecard on its windows during the World Series, with the American League team on the left window and the National League team on the right. The hits and runs were registered on the windows as the messenger, listening to the radio inside the drugstore, brought them out to the window scorer. The games were all played in the afternoon. The drugstore windows were also used on presidential election nights.

In 1932, we had two doctors, one drugstore, one bank, five churches, two hardware stores, three clothing stores, two funeral homes, three lawyers, one theater, four gas stations, seven grocery stores, two blacksmith shops, two car dealers, two lumberyards, one livestock-feed store, a post office, an abandoned hotel, and hundreds of dogs and cats, all of whom roamed at will. We had a town band consisting of about ten males ranging in age from fourteen to twenty-five. The standing joke was that Charleston was so small that after the town band was formed, there wasn't anybody left to watch the parade.

We also had a courthouse with a single jail cell in the basement, and the only occasional occupant was the town drunk, Euclid Gage. John Sommers, the city marshal, wore a cowboy hat, a western-style six-shooter, and a badge. He was a practicing coward, but Euclid was always too drunk to resist, so it didn't matter. The word would spread when Euclid had been jailed, and all the children would rush to the back of the courthouse to peer at him through the small barred window. I had to stand on tiptoes to see anything, and anything was Euclid either muttering at us drunkenly or sleeping on a filthy, bare cotton mattress on a steel bed. The cell was in the courthouse basement and lower than the window, so Euclid, like a zoo gorilla, would lie on the floor next to the back wall so we couldn't see him. When he sobered up, he was released. No time or punishment was imposed.

John Sommers was single and visited the Como Hotel, a whorehouse in Ft. Smith, every Thursday afternoon. When we were old enough to drive to Ft. Smith alone, we would cruise around the Como hoping to see John or someone else from

Charleston, or maybe even a prostitute. We all assumed that the occasional case of syphilis in Charleston had been "caught" at the Como. There was no cure for syphilis, but the mineral waters in Hot Springs were believed to have curative powers. When one of Charleston's "loose" women would suddenly disappear, people would whisper, "She's in Hot Springs."

Mother and Dad moved to Charleston in 1920 from a forty-acre mountaintop farm near Cecil, which consisted of two general stores, a Methodist church, and a Church of Christ, whose members were called Campbellites after its founder, Alexander Campbell. My grandfather Rufus Columbus Bumpers (Rufe), called "Pap" by his children, owned one of the stores, R. C. Bumpers & Sons. The Bumpers were all devout Methodists, and my grandfather knew about only one college, Hendrix, a small Methodist school in Conway, about one hundred miles away. So Dad was shipped off to Conway at age nineteen, the first Bumpers to ever set foot on a college campus. He played in the first football game he ever saw. He was a six-foot redhead, with high cheekbones and light skin, not very muscular, and with barely enough clothes to cover his body. He was painfully aware of his condition compared to that of everyone else at Hendrix, and it became such an embarrassment to him, he refused to return after one year. It was his first brush with class consciousness. He vowed to work hard and never be embarrassed by his status again.

In 1933, when Roosevelt closed all the banks in the United States, Uncle Sam ran down to the field where Granddad was plowing, shouting, "Pap! Roosevelt has closed all the banks. We're broke! We're broke!" Granddad reached in his pocket, found a dime, and threw it as far as he could, then turned to Uncle Sam and said, "Now, son, we're broke."

Like the one-eyed man being king in the land of the blind, Dad with his one year in college had more education than anyone else in the community, so he was hired to teach grades one through eight in a one-room schoolhouse with twenty-five to thirty students. He wrote the lines for the children's Christmas exhibition and loved this small brush with acting so much, he often lamented not being a Hollywood director.

Dad and Mother's courtship began shortly thereafter. Mother was from a one-store community, Anice, about six miles from Cecil. Her father owned the one store, which also housed the post office in the back. Lattie Jones, my mother and the fourth of six children, was made postmistress at age twenty. My maternal grandfather, Jones, was more affluent than my paternal grandfather, Bumpers, and Mother was sent to Charleston eight miles away to attend high school. Her father doted on her, bought her a piano, and took her to the St. Louis World's Fair in 1904, where she saw its exhibits on the Louisiana Purchase.

Mother was an intelligent, engaging conversationalist who wrote beautifully and perfectly and refused to be distracted until she finished the difficult Sunday crossword puzzle in the *Arkansas Gazette*. Often, when I came home from school for lunch, I smelled the potatoes burning the moment I opened the back door. The odor had not yet reached Mother, who was on all fours on the floor, working the crossword with her rear in the air and her head in *Webster's International Dictionary*. She didn't have a gregarious bone in her body and bordered on being antisocial. But people who knew her well adored her, as did her three children.

She was beautiful as a girl and young bride, but she didn't age well; by the time she was forty-five, she was wrinkled and totally gray. My father loved her deeply, but there was never any open reciprocation. Mother didn't have a romantic bone in her body. I never saw them kiss or embrace or even hold hands. On reflection, and especially after their deaths, I found their marriage a complete mystery. They were both devout and devoted to each other, but my father spoke often of scriptures he couldn't fathom. He could never reconcile the concept of a just and loving God with the suffering of the innocent. Mother never seemed to have a doubt, though she was more cerebral than Dad.

After Mother and Dad married, they moved into a small

farmhouse near Cecil, where Dad farmed forty acres and continued teaching school. He was twenty-four and Mother was
twenty-two. Raymond was their firstborn and arrived eight
months and three weeks after their marriage. Walter Deshan, a
uniformly disliked man in the community, remarked to a small
group including Dad that having a baby in less than nine months
after marriage was "cuttin' it close." According to Uncle Joel,
Dad's brother, Dad knocked him down and was beating him
senseless before other men in the group were able to pull him off.
The only other time Dad got riled enough to fight was years
later, after he became a hardware merchant. A customer accused
him of cheating him and hardly got the words out of his mouth
before Dad connected with a right cross to the jaw, rendering the
man unconscious.

I never saw my father lose his temper, though I did see him
upset a few times. He had a strong antipathy for violence, and
we were constantly taught that fighting was for the weak-minded
and never settled anything. He admonished us, though, that
there were overbearing bullies in the world and that we should
always be prepared to defend ourselves.

Tragedy soon struck the young couple. Raymond was one
month shy of four years old when, after having eaten rotten
watermelon from the garden, he developed an uncontrollable
case of dysentery. He died four days later because the doctor had
no idea what to do. Mother's grief was unrelieved until her death.

My sister, Margaret, was four months old when Raymond
died. Mother later confessed to me that she had resented her
after Raymond's death. Her life was unbearably lonely, and Raymond, bright and entertaining, had been old enough to be "company" to her. She said she had asked God, "Why couldn't it have
been Margaret?"

By the time the United States declared war on Germany in
World War I, Raymond had just died. Margaret's birth saved Dad
from service. Mother began pressing Dad to move from the
mountaintop to Charleston—that she wasn't going to have "ba-

bies only to watch them die" for lack of medical attention, though medical care in Charleston was little better than on the mountaintop. It took almost four years before Mother could convince Dad to move, but finally they left for Charleston with their meager belongings in a Springfield wagon pulled by a team of mules. Mother said Margaret, then four and manifesting a remarkable musical talent, stood behind the seat of the wagon and sang "Beulah Land," the great old gospel hymn, the entire distance:

> *O, Beulah Land, sweet Beulah Land*
> *As on thy highest mount I stand.*
> *I look away across the sea,*
> *Where mansions are prepared for me,*
> *And view the shining glory shore*
> *My heaven, my home forever more!*

When we had guests, Mother would play the piano and Margaret, at age four or five, would sing. She knew all the popular World War I songs. My aunt Floy told me that on one occasion, while Margaret was performing, one of the guests dropped her handkerchief. Margaret walked over to her, picked up the handkerchief, and handed it to her without ever missing a note. Margaret became accustomed to and loved applause at a very early age. She never got over it. Dad adored her and took great pride in both her beauty and her musical talent. She was always the brightest student in her class, but she grew more precocious with age and drove my mother to distraction.

Dad went to work for Mother's two brothers, Bill and Claude, in a grocery store on Charleston's Main Street. Four years later, in 1924, he went to work for the Charleston Hardware and Funeral Home, where he worked until he died. He and a partner bought the business in 1937.

Almost all small-town hardware stores had a funeral home, too, a carryover from the days when the casket was built in the store. There was another hardware store just two doors down the street, but the funeral home was an adjunct to the owner's home. The Charleston Hardware's funeral home was four doors down the street from the hardware store, and the odors of formaldehyde often covered a good portion of Main Street. I was fascinated with the big slab with the drainage hole in it. It was to drain blood during embalming, but neither Dad nor Herman Adams, his partner, were licensed embalmers, so they had to take bodies to Ft. Smith for embalming or sometimes have an embalmer come to Charleston. Embalming was twenty-five dollars extra for the family, and most people couldn't afford it. Later, the state made embalming mandatory.

Mother loved the funeral home part of Dad's business and would often "sit" at the funeral home to keep the deceased company when there was nobody else to do it. It was considered unseemly to leave the deceased without a companion. Caskets were often left open for viewing at the home of the deceased and usually during the funeral service. Many families felt it obligatory to wail at the top of their lungs and often fainted and had to be revived at the funeral, the cemetery, or both.

When the mother of the canning plant owner died, the family bought a three-hundred-dollar service, which included a solid cherry casket. It was the talk of the town. Dad didn't stock such high-priced merchandise, and they had to special order the casket from Ft. Smith. Most funerals were in the one-hundred-dollar range, and families had to pay for them in monthly payments. The payments were often difficult to collect. After all, the funeral was over, and the merchandise was in the ground. There was nothing to repossess.

I began driving the family funeral car when I was sixteen. Sometimes I could even get excused from school to do it.

In 1937, Dad and Herman built a new funeral home. The facility generated a lot of oohs and ahs. It even had a chapel, which was seldom used. To have a funeral service in the chapel rather than a church was like choosing purgatory.

When the new funeral home was completed, Dad and Herman bought a new Packard hearse. It cost thirty-three hundred dollars, and it converted easily to an ambulance. They kept it parked in the funeral home driveway so people could admire it. Our family car, a 1938 Chevrolet, doubled as a funeral car.

I soon learned to handle dead bodies and live families as well as an older, paid employee could. I learned to use comforting words of solace that I picked up from Dad, and no matter how grotesque some family requests were, we did our best to comply. One widow wanted to lie in the casket with her husband and hold him one last time. There just wasn't room, and we talked her out of it.

One summer, several children died on Arbuckle Island, which was a huge farm worked by sharecroppers living in shacks. Their deaths were mostly from dysentery. The poverty of the families was worse than anything I ever observed in Charleston. Sometimes there was only a graveside service, with Dad making a few remarks. One of my jobs was to fan the flies off the open casket and, after the funeral, return the family to their miserable existence. These funerals introduced me to the fact that some people come into this world without a dog's chance at anything worthwhile.

When I was in law school, a candidate for the Senate and later a famous senator spoke to the student body. He told us, "People must pull themselves up by their own bootstraps." I wanted to stand up and say, "Sir, some people don't have any boots, so they have no straps to pull up."

Dad was a consummate romantic and insisted till his death that he had never been happier than when he and Mother lived on the mountain and he had taught school. Mother couldn't have disagreed more about their early married life. She had been accustomed to a more comfortable life, and she detested the new hardships of the farm.

Carroll was born in 1921, shortly after the move to Charleston, and I arrived in 1925. The Great Depression, which began four years later, made feeding, clothing, and housing three children an endless and daunting challenge.

Mother and Dad regularly returned to Cecil to spend a night

or two with Granddad Bumpers or Dad's sister, Aunt Lillie. It was sixteen miles to Cecil, and ten of them were dirt or mud, depending on the weather. It was a difficult trip in the best of times and often impossible in winter. Dad would debate with himself about whether the ground had dried sufficiently since the last rain—or snow—to permit the trip. Our first car was a Model T Ford. When we became hopelessly bogged down in the muck and mire, we had to wait for Dad to walk to the nearest farmhouse and get a farmer to hitch up a horse, more usually a mule, to come and pull us out. Sometimes it would be well after dark, and it was scary as we sat immobile in the eerie quiet of the country waiting for Dad's return, with only the distant sound of a cowbell or a dog barking to let us know we were not totally isolated. Cars had no heat, and the Model T had only flaps for windows. We would bundle up in a shared blanket or quilt to ward off the chill of a winter night.

When Dad returned with help, the farmer would tie one end of a rope or chain to the front of the car and the other end to the harnessed mule. He would lay a strap to the mule, Dad would rev the motor, and the car would slowly ooze out of the deep rut in which it had been mired. I would be immensely relieved. Dad and the farmer would discuss the conditions ahead and our chances for getting stuck again. But we never got stuck more than once on a trip, and each of the three or four places that were likely to spell trouble were well known to Dad. On two or three occasions, we would reach a place that Dad would conclude was impassable, and we would turn around and go back home. I don't ever recall a farmer asking to be paid for pulling us out, but Dad would sometimes take a coin from his pocket and hand it to the grateful farmer.

There was a slightly shorter route to Cecil, the one Mother and Dad took in moving to Charleston, but it was all dirt and hilly, so we rarely chose it. While it was shorter, it also required our Model T Ford to go up a very steep hill, and whether or not the T had enough power to do it was always problematic. One time, on arriving at the foot of the hill, we paused, then Dad accelerated the T as fast as it would go prior to the ascent. But it wasn't enough. We got about three-fourths of the way up and no farther. The poor T labored mightily, but to no avail, so we backed down the hill. Dad then turned the T around and began backing up the hill. The car had more power in reverse than it had going forward, and we made it.

Our relatives had only kerosene lamps and fireplaces for light and heat. Only the well-to-do had Aladdin lamps, a more advanced kerosene lamp that put out more light. The food was greasy, mostly meat they cured themselves, but it was plentiful. So were the biscuits and gravy. Everybody raised sugarcane and made enough sorghum molasses to last through the winter. When Dad and all his siblings were still at home, his stepmother, whom they all called Aunt Jane—she was the sister of their deceased mother—would fill a gallon tin pitcher with molasses at the beginning of each meal, and it often had to be refilled.

Aunt Jane made all the preparations for Sunday dinner on Saturday so as not to labor on the Sabbath. Children slept on either a huge feather mattress made from flour sack material or a pallet consisting of two quilts on the floor.

My grandfather only knew the names of his grandchildren who lived in Cecil, except Margaret and a cousin, Bernice. He remembered them because they were both talented pianists and he loved having them play for him. The rest of us were only vaguely familiar to him. I well remember him looking at me one time with a puzzled expression and asking, "Ain't you Will's boy?" When Dad was growing up and company came to visit on Sunday afternoons—and that's the only time guests visited—Aunt Jane would line up the five boys and ask the guests which one they thought was the prettiest. He said after several of these beauty pageants, four of the five boys would always run under the house because they knew Uncle Leonard would win.

All the Bumpers were fiddlers, including Granddad. Uncle Sam, the second oldest son, won the Arkansas Old Time Fiddlers contest in 1936. There were occasional family reunions when the fiddling never stopped. Aunt Esther, Uncle Sam's wife, "seconded" on the piano, and I was more fascinated with her playing than with the fiddlers' fiddling.

Granddad Bumpers and Aunt Jane were married twenty-one years before she died on the day I was born. Two days later, Dad bought a bird-dog pup, a liver-and-white pointer. We named him Snap, and he was my constant companion from the time I began walking. Carroll and I often let a couple of older men in town hunt with him, until one night at dinner when Dad told us they whipped Snap if he flushed a bird or wouldn't retrieve. We never let them use him again.

Mother had always maintained that she had spaced her children four years apart because she knew she and Dad would never be able to educate more than one of us at a time. In truth, we were all accidents, and she detested each and every pregnancy, though it never diminished her love and devotion to us. I was heartbroken when at age sixteen I overheard my sister casually mention how upset Mother had been when she discovered she was pregnant with me. Based on my memories of sleeping in the same bedroom with Mother and Dad till I was ten years old, I know Mother detested sex, which might have been caused by her stark terror of getting pregnant.

Margaret's musical talent continued to improve, and by age fifteen she was an accomplished pianist and had her own radio show on Ft. Smith's only radio station, KFPW. The president of KFPW had attended a Commercial Club (later called the Chamber of Commerce) banquet in Charleston, heard Margaret play, and asked her to do a fifteen-minute radio show twice a week, on Mondays and Thursdays. She agreed and was later asked to play dinner music in the Goldman Hotel dining room following her show.

She attended the College of the Ozarks, a small Presbyterian school, for one semester and a portion of another. She had skipped the fourth grade, which was not uncommon for exceptionally bright students, so she was only sixteen when she entered. By skipping fourth grade, she missed learning the multiplication tables and to this day can't multiply. Dad was making seventy-five dollars a month at the time. The behavior code at the College of the Ozarks was very strict. The president of the college called Dad to come and get her before the second semester was over, and I have heard three different versions as to why: 1) she got in past curfew one night; 2) she shouted from her dorm window at the mailman; and 3) she said she was in church when she was not. Take your pick.

Ike Ragon lived in Clarksville, home of the College of the Ozarks, and had a dance band that played for Saturday night dances at the Wintergarden Ballroom in Ft. Smith, a very popular place. Ike recruited Margaret to sing in his band while she was a student, and she would ride to Ft. Smith with him, about fifty miles away. After playing for a dance, the band would go to Ft. Smith's most popular theater and play as people came in for the midnight movie. One night, Margaret looked out at the audience and saw Dad's business partner sitting in the front row. He could hardly wait to tell Dad. Singing for the dance band came to an abrupt halt.

When she came home from the College of the Ozarks, she began teaching "expression" for twenty-five cents per thirty-minute lesson. Expression was just that: teaching children to memorize poems and recite them with expressive gestures. She also taught piano for twenty-five cents a lesson in Greenwood, a nearby community.

Carroll and Margaret were both valedictorians of their high school classes. I was not. Carroll received a fifty-dollar academic scholarship to the University of Arkansas and started his freshman year there with a fifteen-dollar suit, two pairs of seven-dollar slacks, and a football sweater he had earned his senior year in high school. He had been a paper boy for four years, beginning when he was twelve, building a base of about sixty daily customers and one hundred on Sundays, plus fifteen "extras," which he left at the Esso station. By the Christmas season, he would have between fifteen and twenty dollars in the bank, after having bought most of his clothes.

Mother and Dad never spent money at Christmas on toys such as six-shooters, cowboy suits, tricycles, or mechanical or electric trains—all the things we desperately wanted. We got socks, handkerchiefs, and whatever they would have had to buy us anyway. Mother made our underwear from flour sacks. She bought flour in twenty-pound sacks as much for the material as the flour. Dad was extravagant in two ways at Christmas: He bought oranges, apples, bananas, and nuts, foods unknown to us the rest of the year, and he brought home firecrackers and a few Roman candles. Dad choreographed the Christmas Eve shooting of the firecrackers in the side yard with most neighbors in attendance, much to the exasperation of my mother, who regarded the display as a disgusting waste. We usually ended the frenzy around midnight.

Only one of my Christmas mornings was memorable. I desperately wanted a Benjamin pump BB gun, and there were none for sale anywhere in Charleston. They were much more powerful and more expensive than a regular lever-operated Daisy BB gun and had to be ordered from a catalog or purchased in Ft. Smith.

When I awoke on Christmas morning and found the usual clothing items under the tree, I was only mildly disappointed not to see the Benjamin, because I had never allowed myself to expect it and I knew my father couldn't afford the $7.50 price for such an extravagance. After all the gifts had been handed out, Carroll suddenly disappeared from the room and returned shortly with the Benjamin, which he had bought with his paper-route earnings. It was the first time I ever cried from sheer joy. It was a totally different feeling from any emotion I had ever had. I was overwhelmed by the knowledge that my brother had obviously worked so hard for so long just to make sure I had at least one truly great Christmas.

I never had a birthday party, nor did Carroll. Margaret maybe had two or three. They were too expensive, and my mother even resented, with a pained expression, my being invited to someone else's birthday party. She never told me I couldn't go, but the usual five cents required for a gift grieved her deeply. She equated a nickel with half a loaf of bread. On the first day of each month, she would call the grocer to find out how much the bill was for the preceding month, and the look on her face bore witness to whether it was over or under her fifteen-dollar ceiling.

In the 1920s, the Charleston Coal Company, wholly owned by the Pittsburgh Coal Company, began mining coal about three miles northeast of town. The seam of coal was fourteen inches thick, but it was close to the surface, running from just a few feet belowground to twenty feet, the maximum depth at which it could be economically recovered. Joe Lake came to town to manage the operation. He was a big, six-foot-three-inch, gregarious, red-faced guy from Pontiac, Illinois. He had a sixteen-millimeter camera, which testified to his affluence, and he filmed all the Christmas parades, beginning in 1931. They all show my father on the back of a large truck, shouting out lottery numbers to a crowd of about two thousand. They got one ticket for each dollar's worth of merchandise purchased from a Charleston merchant. First prize was fifteen dollars. Charleston had only 851 souls, but the parade attracted up to 3,000.

Santa rode in a jerry-built sleigh with concealed wheels that was pulled by a stout team of horses. His uniform was pitiful, and everyone knew Santa was really Charley Wakefield. Back of Santa's seat were boxes full of small sacks of candy. After the parade there was a mob scene, with as many adults as children pushing and shoving to get the most advantageous positions in the line at the courthouse, for fear Santa would run out of candy. Across the street from the courthouse in front of Moore's Hatchery, the blacks sat on a concrete abutment, watching with envy but not daring to intrude on an all-"white" Christmas.

Joe Lake built a brick home in 1932 that was reputed to have cost forty-five hundred dollars. People came from far and near to see it, and men also came from far and near to work on it because Joe paid four dollars a day in wages.

There were no reclamation laws, so the earth that was removed to get to the coal was simply put aside, creating a huge pile about twenty feet high, which we called "dumps." After the coal was removed, an open pit was left that promptly filled with water. There were dumps all over a four-square-mile area, with the pits on the outer edges of the last dump. The dumps were mostly shale, but there was enough dirt for blackberries and "poke" salad to grow in abundance on them and for wildlife to flourish. Mother and we three children would go to the dumps in the summer to gather blackberries, which she canned into jellies and preserves and used to make fresh cobblers. We would be covered with chigger bites despite Mother's dousing us with kerosene. The itch they caused was indescribable.

The "pits" were about the only place for us to swim. Most of them were full of clear blue but highly alkaline water, and though little vegetation grew, fish seemed to thrive. For nonswimmers or poor swimmers, the pits were dangerous and had no shallow havens. There was a cut in the side of the cliff that allowed us to walk down to the water. If a swimmer grew tired and wasn't near the cut, he had to find a rock on the steep cliff to cling to. From the top of the cliff to the water ranged from five to fifteen feet.

I was never a good swimmer, hated water, and felt safe in the pits only when Dad was along. The alkali left our eyes bloodshot and burning for hours. During my childhood, three children drowned in the pits.

Dad could never afford to give us money. Before I was old enough to mow lawns or work in the fields, I hardly ever had a penny to my name. Mrs. Floyd, an elderly widow who lived across the street, would occasionally give me two or three pennies to get a few grocery items for her at Joe Cone's store just a block away. Joe was a cranky guy—so tight that he squeaked—but when I asked for two cents' worth of "mixed candy," he would fill a small candy sack half-full. The candy pieces were about half an inch in size and had the texture of orange slices.

In the summertime, I would pretend to be playing in the yard, hoping Mrs. Floyd would peck on the window and summon me to make a grocery run. It was cruel, but sometimes I would give my best friend—my dog, Pluto—a piece of candy just to watch him go through so many gyrations trying to get it off his teeth. Sometimes I would save Mrs. Floyd's pennies until I had five cents, then go to the Conoco service station, where Snickers bars were kept in the Coke box on top of chipped ice. A cold Snickers bar was as close to heaven as I could get.

The summers were unbearably hot. We slept outside on cots, and the mosquitoes had a nightly feast. I had malaria twice before I was ten years old and, as a result, was rejected as a blood donor in the Marine Corps and, many years later, when my son was scheduled for surgery.

We had a cow that we kept in a lot behind the house, and she supplied enough milk and butter for the family and four cats. When I was eight years old, one of my chores was to take the cow to the pasture every morning before school and return her for milking that evening. The pasture was four acres of lush grass inside the city limits. Carroll had performed this task until he got his paper route. It was a six-block trip, and Carroll had trained her to let him ride her. She didn't seem to notice when the ridership changed. She knew her way to the pasture, so all I had to do was get on and let her amble at her own pace. I loved the old cow dearly and had no reason to think she felt less affection for me—until one morning. We were going through our ritual after arriving at the pasture, which was for me to dismount, cross a shallow ditch about four feet wide, and open the gate. It was summer and I was barefoot. There was about three feet of flat space between the edge of the ditch and the gate. Usually she would pause in front of the ditch until I opened the gate, whereupon she would jump the ditch to the flat space and stroll into the pasture. However, on this morning, after I dismounted and crossed the ditch to open the gate, she paused, according to custom, and then, after I unlatched the gate but before I could get out of her way, she lunged across the ditch. A small portion of her right front hoof landed on my right big toe, tearing my toenail right off. The pain was excruciating, and I bled profusely as I hobbled home. My toe has been disfigured ever since.

Behind our cow lot and garden was an alley seldom used except as a path, and behind the alley was Mr. and Mrs. Lane's rock wall–enclosed garden, and next to their garden was their home. John Oscar Lane Sr. and his wife, Lizzie, had four children. Lona was Margaret's age, and J.O. junior was Carroll's age. They were devout Baptists, but when the Holiness Church, later the Assembly of God, was started in Charleston, the Lanes became enthralled with it. The small flock rented a building on Main Street, built pews, and covered the floor with sawdust. They often went into paroxysms, rolled on the floor, and spoke in tongues. Their preachers and laymen alike preached on the northwest corner of Charleston's Main Street intersection on Saturday afternoons, just two doors from Doc's Café and Pool Hall, gasping for breath after each unending sentence, which ended with "and ah, and ah," and so on.

When I was a teenager, my date and I, along with other couples, would sneak up to the windows of the frame church they later built and watch the shouting, testimonies, speaking in tongues, and rolling on the floor. We considered ourselves brave, but I don't know what we thought would happen to us if we got caught.

John Oscar Lane Sr. was called "Ought," which was a fairly common nickname among men who had an O in their initials. This came from the fact that in those days, older people called zeros "aughts." At least three men in Charleston who had an initial *O* in their names were called "Ought." You could call J. O. Lane Sr. any name, but the one that fit him best was mean.

Ought Lane owned a big sheet-iron building a few yards behind his home that housed his blacksmith shop. In order to go from the back door of our home to the back door of Dad's store, we had to walk down the alley between Dad's warehouse and Ought Lane's blacksmith shop. Ought was the busiest blacksmith among three in Charleston. He was also a quack veterinarian. His formal education was probably less than eighth grade, but when he wasn't shoeing horses, he was reading books on veterinary medicine.

J.O. junior was not a bad child, but his father beat him mercilessly and regularly, usually in the doorless garage. He used either his belt or a thin board. J.O. junior's screams could be heard all over the neighborhood, interspersed with atonement and promises that he would never again do whatever he was accused of having done. Interfering with "parental discipline" was unthinkable then, so even though the neighbors abhorred Ought's barbarism, they dared not take up J.O.'s cause.

Pluto, my dog, had come to us as a stray, but, tragically, in his declining years, Pluto got hit by a car and broke both hips. He recuperated to some extent but could only drag himself. I rigged up a contraption similar to a skateboard. I disassembled one of my roller skates and nailed the rollers onto a board. I nailed two straps to it and then tied it around Pluto's back, hoping it would allow him some mobility. Of course it didn't work, but I still couldn't stand the idea of putting Pluto out of his misery, and Dad didn't insist.

One day, Pluto began to get lethargic, and only with strong coaxing would he lift his head from between his legs. After a day or two, I discovered that someone had castrated him. The incision had already become incurably infected. Shortly, Pluto was dead and I was devastated. My grief was unrelieved, and I had a desperate urge to castrate Mr. Lane, because I knew he had "practiced" his skills on a helpless dog whom he considered better dead than alive. I could have more easily forgiven him for euthanizing Pluto.

At about age sixteen, J.O. junior became the focus of an adult male's attention. He was a good-looking, well-dressed man, gainfully employed in a Ft. Smith packing plant and about ten years older than J.O. They developed a relationship, and J.O. soon learned there was money to be had in exchange for the relationship. There was always a lot of conjecture on what the adult would get J.O. for Christmas. J.O. had no real affection for him, often dated girls, and would sometimes ignore him for weeks at a time. The man, in turn, spent an inordinate amount of time fretting to all of J.O.'s friends, mostly Carroll and me, about how shabbily J.O. was treating him. We had little understanding of the relationship, but J.O. came and went as he pleased. The relationship ended when J.O. went to Oklahoma State (then Oklahoma A&M) to study veterinary medicine.

On Saturday afternoons, Main Street was a beehive. Doc's Café and Pool Hall was full. Knife fights among the Hewitts, the Waggoners, and the Blaylocks would often break out in the pool hall in back and progress through the café onto the street, where there would likely be a street preacher on the corner regaling sinners to "come home" to Jesus. The fights never involved guns but usually involved knives. There was always blood. We would stand around in the vicinity, waiting and hoping for the fight to break out, though when it did I was always terrified by the wild looks on the faces of grown men who were prepared to kill or be killed. Nobody ever was, but it was the thing of which nightmares were made. When Charleston finally voted to ban the sale of beer, the fights stopped.

Marks's Café, the other café where beer was sold, was upscale compared to Doc's Café and Pool Hall, and the food was edible. It also had tables and three booths, which were miniature houses. They even had a roof, seated four people, and had a door that latched from inside. The bottoms of the doors were about eighteen inches off the floor, so one could sit on a bar stool, look behind under the doors, and determine from the leg activity what was taking place. It was an exciting pastime.

There were three kinds of girls in Charleston: those who wouldn't be caught dead in a booth, those who would go into a booth only if the door remained open, and those who would sit in a booth with a boy with the door locked. Those in the last category might as well have publicly announced the loss of their virginity.

As much as I looked forward to summers, I hated working in the fields, and even before I was old enough to go to the fields, I hated "daily vacation Bible school." It was a church-sponsored affair for children four through eight years of age. We had to listen to Bible stories, memorize the Twenty-third Psalm, the Lord's Prayer, and, as Methodists, the Apostles' Creed. We learned the music scale by the shapes of notes, with each shape carrying its own sound. I sat impatiently through the classes, waiting for both hands on the clock to get to straight up, when I knew I was "outta there."

When Carroll, J. O. Lane, and Clayton Bonner were old enough to quit going, they taunted me mercilessly. I also had to attend the Baptist Bible school and the Presbyterian Church Booster Band, as well as the Methodist Bible school, the three of them taking three to six weeks. When I left home in the mornings with a sullen and pouty look on my face to go to the Presbyterian Church Booster Band, they would sing in childish words a song we were required to sing: "I belong to the Boota Band, the Boota Band, the Boota Band . . ." I, in turn, threw whatever I could lay my hands on at them.

On Sunday afternoons when we had company (guests), Dad would place Carroll in the middle of the living room and put him through spelling, history, and political drills. Dad served as the quizmaster.

"Carroll, what's the population of Chicago?"

Carroll would spout off the latest census count to the person. Next came New York, Cincinnati, Los Angeles. The questions would then turn to endless trivia on World War I, the Civil War, the Revolutionary War, names of cabinet members, Supreme Court justices, and on and on, all to the approving nods of the guests. Applause followed each correct answer, and none were incorrect. Carroll, after each answer, would assume a look of immense satisfaction and superiority.

Carroll was considered a genius by my father. He was also a gifted orator. He often entered oratorical contests, called "declamation contests." I remember him entering a countywide declamation contest at which he was to recite an oration by a legendary southern orator, Henry W. Grady, entitled "The New South."

Henry W. Grady was editor of the *Atlanta Journal-Constitution* but was far more famous for his oratorical skills. He tried through both editorials and stirring oratory to hasten the reconciliation of the North and the South following the Civil War. He delivered the widely heralded "New South" speech in New York City in 1879. It was a national bell ringer, and Dad thought Carroll could further immortalize it in a county declamation contest, an annual event in Ozark, the bigger county seat.

Carroll rehearsed every night for weeks, with Dad carefully orchestrating every nuance and inflection. He might as well have had a baton in his hand. Everybody in our household knew the speech by memory and could recite it as well as Carroll could. He won the contest hands down.

Chapter 3

California Here We Come

In the summer of 1937, my father, who had been elected president of the Arkansas Retail Hardware Association, was given three hundred dollars by the association to attend the national convention at the Biltmore Hotel in Los Angeles.

Even though my sister had been married less than a year, she decided to join us on this, the greatest adventure of our lives. She and her husband lived in Ft. Smith, twenty-three miles away, and when we went to her home to pick her up, they went into a passionate kissing and crying orgy that was so embarrassing to my eleven-year-old eyes that I turned away. One would have thought a cancer diagnosis had just been made.

Dad had asked the Conoco Oil Company to map the routes we should take in order to see all the best historic and scenic sites. The service was free. The trip would take almost two weeks, and I'm quite sure we got home with some of the three hundred dollars.

The 1936 Ford had been purchased for use as a family car in Dad's funeral business, but we also used it for our family. Dad had promised the *Charleston Express* (called the "Charleston Excuse" by the locals) a travelogue of our sojourn, and the whole town was abuzz with excitement about our trip. Many Arkansans had gone to California in the early 1930s in a desperate attempt to escape their poverty. Most Arkies and Okies had sought jobs on the truck farms in the San Joaquin Valley, where large acreages of vegetables and fruits were grown. The crops were labor-intensive. The conditions in the farm camps were miserable, as poignantly described in John Steinbeck's *Grapes of Wrath*.

Five people plus luggage crammed into a car that by today's standards would be classed as a compact was precisely what one would imagine—awful! Dad and Margaret alternated driving, and when Margaret was driving, Dad held his notebook on his lap, keeping a sharp eye out for anything—scenery, people, crops, or cattle—that he thought would be of interest to the folks back home.

My brother and I were forever relegated to the backseat, almost always with either my sister or Mother between us to prevent fights. There was another side to my brother other than the one that provided me with a great Christmas. Every little brother would recognize in a heartbeat the incredible ability of an older brother to dream up ways to taunt him.

About two or three days into the trip, Carroll suggested we play a spelling game, a game he had conjured up. He would spell a word by syllables, pausing after each syllable, and I was to guess the word. All nouns, proper or common, were permissible. I was doing well until, without telling me, he started cheating by pausing after one or two letters of a three- or four-letter syllable and placing the last letter of one syllable with the first letter of the next, scrambling them to make it much more difficult for me. Pandemonium was just around the corner over one of my heroes, baseball great Lou Gehrig. Carroll spelled it Ge-h-r-ig. I pronounced it twenty different ways, struggling mightily, but nothing I uttered sounded even remotely familiar. Despite my pleadings, he steadfastly refused to give me even a clue as to who it was, and I was getting no help from Mother, Dad, or Margaret, all of whom were ignoring us. I worked myself into an uncontrollable rage, but Carroll remained tight-lipped. Finally, to stop the bedlam, my sister told me it was Gehrig, as in Lou Gehrig. By then, I was ready to slit my wrists and his throat. At this point, Mother intervened and stopped the game.

The quietude was eerie and short-lived. The silence lasted about ten minutes when Carroll began singing an oldie that he knew drove me insane the way he sang it. The title was "I'm an Old Cow Hand from the Rio Grande," but he sang it, "I'm an old cow handee from the Rio Grandee . . ." I began screaming, and Mother, seated in front, turned around and scolded him, and he withdrew from the battlefield for a minute or two. When he was sure I was watching and while looking straight ahead, he began lip-synching, "I'm an old cow handee . . ." I let out a screeching caterwaul: "He's doing it again, Mother, he's doing it again!" This continued until Dad pulled over on the shoulder of the road and instructed Mother to get in the backseat and stop the madness once and for all.

We saw the petrified forest in Arizona, the Grand Canyon, and Boulder Dam, and we stayed in a "tourist court" at the foot of the San Francisco Peaks in Flagstaff, Arizona, for the sum of three dollars. Then we drove on to California and the green orange groves, which were continuous from San Bernardino to Los Angeles. I could hardly wait to tell friends that popcorn was ten cents a bag in the Los Angeles theaters, almost an hourly wage back home. And, as one Arkansan said on returning from California regarding pedestrian crosswalks, "You gotta give way to them Protestants out there." "Out there" was always California.

On the last night of the hardware convention, there was a huge ball in the Biltmore ballroom. It was breathtaking to us. Women were in long dresses and men in tuxedos. We had seen tuxedos only in the movies. My father wore his seersucker suit and my mother her best pink cotton eyelet dress. My brother and I wore the best we had—long pants and white shirts. No coat, no tie. For the first time in my life, I was embarrassed about my clothes. Entertainment was provided by children about twelve years old from a dance studio. They wore top hats and tuxedos and tap-danced with canes. I was not only distracted from concerns about my clothes, or lack thereof, I was also consumed with sadness, because I was the same age as the dancers, and I knew I would never have an opportunity to attend dancing classes in Charleston, Arkansas. I assumed that each of the dancers was destined for Hollywood stardom.

The following morning, Dad, apparently having sensed his sons' embarrassment the preceding evening, assured us that he understood how we felt. He told us, "What's inside you, what's in your heart, is much more important than the clothing on your body." It was a standard, almost daily, sermonette by parents all over America. I had heard it in various contexts, but Dad's saying it gave it more meaning.

The day after the hardware convention ball, we learned that Arkansas's beloved senior senator, Joe T. Robinson, had died. Senator Robinson was a certified hero to my father, and his death cast a pall over what until then had been a trouble-free trip.

The following day, my mother received a call telling her that her brother, my uncle Elbert, who had been ill before we left, had died of typhoid fever. She wept quietly for much of the remainder of the trip.

We had one night remaining in Los Angeles after the big ball, and we used it to visit the temple of Aimee Semple McPherson, a nationally known female evangelist. She had built the Angelus Temple as a monument to herself in 1923. It seated five thousand, and it was full most evenings. She called her religion the International Church of the Foursquare Gospel. She was beautiful, a healer, a mediocre singer, and probably no more talented than many of today's televangelists, but a female evangelist was unique then and rare today.

She began her career as an evangelist during the flu epidemic of 1918. She had been preaching for eighteen years, but by then she had added healing to her spiritual agenda. Her first, most publicized case was the healing of a goiter in a woman's neck. She moved to California and hit town wearing a leather jacket and bearskin coat. Many photographs showed her in a white, silky robe with her arms outstretched, which gave the appearance of Jesus ascending into heaven.

The lights were dimmed when she came on stage and spread her arms, providing a sense of surrealism. It was hypnotic. Many Hollywood celebrities were fans, and even the cynical H. L. Mencken admired her. Sinclair Lewis's book *Elmer Gantry* was loosely based on Aimee's life.

In May 1926, she disappeared while swimming in the Pacific. Some clothes were found, but so were some footprints walking toward shore. Foul play was suspected, but thirty-two days later she appeared in a small Mexican village with a fairly implausible story of having been kidnapped by a couple who wanted her to heal their son. She was allegedly seen during her absence in a love nest with a married man. The whole affair created such a stir, she was charged with fraud but was acquitted.

She was married several times and, in 1944, was found in a hotel room unconscious from an overdose of sleeping pills. She died shortly thereafter at the age of fifty-four. The funeral was said to be the largest ever in California.

Aimee was absent the evening we attended, but her stand-in succeeded admirably in relieving the congregation of a substantial sum of money anyway. A man, presumably a preacher, started off by asking the congregation to show a "sea of green." Most male attendees whipped out a bill of some denomination and waved it. Then he asked all those with a twenty-dollar bill, a princely sum at the time, if they were "willing to share it with your Lord and Savior, Jesus Christ." Several held up twenty-dollar bills, but the preacher insisted they raise them higher. Some stood on tiptoes so the Lord could better see the denomination. The procedure was repeated for tens, fives, and ones. A lot of music and "testimony" accompanied the ritualistic fundraising. Finally, people from outside California were asked to come up on the stage and announce into the microphone from whence they hailed. Dad handed the honor to Carroll and me. It was an exhilarating moment for us, and even though Carroll did the announcing, I felt important. It was the first huge crowd I had ever appeared before, and I liked it.

The following morning, before leaving for San Francisco, we took the obligatory tour of the "Homes of the Stars." We paid a driver five dollars to drive our car and show us where all the beautiful people romped in the evenings. The names Gable, Garbo, Lombard, Harlow, Errol Flynn (whom we had seen on the wharf at Santa Monica), and more all rolled easily off the lips of the driver. He could have simply used a name every time we passed a beautiful home and we would have been none the wiser. We were mesmerized. My heart had pounded like a trip-hammer earlier as I placed my hands in the concrete indentation of Clark Gable's hands at Grauman's Chinese Theatre.

The trip home was via San Francisco. We crossed the Golden Gate Bridge, which had just been completed. Then we saw Yosemite, Reno—where Carroll and I were unceremoniously asked to leave a casino—Yellowstone, the Great Salt Lake (in which we swam), and the Royal Gorge.

Carroll and I drew crowds for several days after we returned. Having been to places seen only in pictures before, we embellished everything and made it all personal and exciting. We were just short of being on a first-name basis with Clark Gable and Carole Lombard. We had thirteen stickers of famous sites and national parks on our car, a status symbol nobody in Charleston ever matched. It took the *Charleston Express* eight issues to print Dad's descriptions of our two-week journey.

‖ *Chapter 4* ‖

Learning Politics at the Dinner Table

Most children in Charleston had to work during the summer months from the time they were eight or nine years old. We went barefoot all summer, stepped on nails, and got tetanus shots. We mowed lawns with push mowers. Mrs. O'Bar's lawn across the street took all morning; she never called me until the grass was high and it took all my strength to mow her lawn. She paid me the princely sum of five cents, but only after I went back over the spots she insisted I had missed.

We also worked on the farms, picking cotton. Carroll could pick 150 pounds in one day. Fifty was my maximum. The sharp cotton bolls punctured our fingers and set up festering sores and infections. For our labor, we were paid a penny a pound. We picked peas and picked up potatoes after they were "turned up" with a turning plow, and, before child labor laws were enacted, we worked at the canning plant, Charleston's only industry. The plant employed fifty people during the summer months it operated. At the age of twelve, I made fifteen cents an hour feeding cans into a conveyor apparatus from the upper level of the metal building from whence they went to be filled with whatever vegetable was being canned. Adults earned up to twenty-five cents an hour and worked twelve- to sixteen-hour days. The plant canned four vegetables primarily: green beans, mustard greens, black-eyed peas, and spinach. The temperature hovered around 110 degrees on the upper level, so periodically we had to go down for a drink of water and a salt tablet. In the evening, the day's production was loaded onto a long flatbed truck, covered with a tarpaulin, and taken to St. Louis. Owner Joe Burt was once overheard saying he wouldn't open the plant for less than a hundred-dollars-a-day profit—an astronomical sum of money. His remark became a major topic of conversation in town. Joe was an avowed Republican, one of about twenty to thirty in Charleston, and invested all of his money in tax-free municipal bonds. He detested governments generally, and the federal government in particular, but more than anything, he hated FDR. I never saw him in anything but overalls, except at his son's funeral. He spent money only to make money but would spend any amount to defend himself against what he considered an unjust claim. After I returned to Charleston to practice law, I defended Joe against a twenty-two-dollar claim by the Missouri-Pacific Railroad for a freight bill, called demurrage. Demurrage was a fee levied by the railroad for failure to unload freight within the time allotted after it arrived. Mo-Pac alleged that a carload shipment to Joe was not unloaded within the time allotted. It took all day to try the case, and we prevailed in a jury trial. My fee was one hundred dollars.

One of the Roosevelt New Deal programs, designed to keep people from starving, was the Civilian Conservation Corps (CCC). FDR's goal was to preserve our national forests while employing young men from desperately poor families for thirty dollars a month, twenty-five of which they were required to send back home to needy parents. There were CCC projects all over the Ozark and Ouachita National Forests in Arkansas, but the work of the young men was not limited solely to forestry. Our high school band played at the dedication of a beautiful new lodge and amphitheater on top of Mt. Magazine, which had been built mostly with CCC labor.

Of all the summer work we did, picking up potatoes was the hardest. It was backbreaking, and the basket was quickly heavy and difficult to drag or lift. For eleven- and twelve-year-olds, it was cruel work, but we were paid by the pound, which lightened the basket a little. Our labors also involved sacking and loading the potatoes for shipment by rail. Charleston had a small Missouri-Pacific Railroad depot and loading dock, where we grunted and sweated grading and filling one-hundred-pound bags and then lugging them into boxcars on dollies. By day's end, we were so bone weary and sore, we could hardly walk home. I tried to grin and bear it, but by the end of the first week I could do neither. I was mildly embarrassed that I had to quit, but my embarrassment was ameliorated by the knowledge that I was trying to do something that was utterly impossible. The full potato sacks weighed more than I did.

Wendell Smith, my best buddy, and I were inseparable. We started in first grade together and graduated together. We both played trumpet in the band, double-dated, and entered the University of Arkansas together. He joined the navy about the same time I went into the marines.

Wendell was an only child, and his parents doted on him. His mother was a member of the Eastern Star, and his father was a Mason. They had dances, and the women wore long dresses. My parents had no interest in such things. I was jealous because it all seemed so glamorous. My mother and father belonged to Charleston's First Methodist Church. Finis. They had no interest in glamour. Dad had once joined the Masons, attended one meeting, found the ritual to be elementary and inane, and never went back. He also thought many of the members used the Masons as a substitute for church.

When Wendell and I were seven years old, Ray Bonner, one of the older boys in our neighborhood, told us that if we went down the middle of Logan Street, where I lived, singing "f-u-c-k" in a singsong voice, people would be awed by how quickly we were learning to spell. We were spellbound by the prospect and the next day after school we walked arm-in-arm down Logan Street singing the newly learned word. My father was also spellbound when the neighbors told him about it. However, with no show of anger or concern, he casually asked me that evening where we got the idea. "From Ray Bonner," I said. Dad simply told me not to do it anymore. He didn't chastise me or tell me why I shouldn't do it.

At age six, Wendell and I tried, unsuccessfully, to nurse a crippled sparrow back to health. We succeeded for two days before the poor bird died. We had fallen in love with it and were brokenhearted when it died. We conducted an elaborate funeral service, with flowers and much weeping as we interred the sparrow in a deep hole we dug in the side of the ditch in front of Wendell's house. As our tears dried and the hole was covered, we could still hardly stand to leave the gravesite, and we visited it regularly for about a week after the funeral.

Carroll, at the age of sixteen, gave up his paper route and bequeathed it to me. No more fieldwork. I bought a used bicycle with no fenders for five dollars. I had saved half that much working in the fields, and I paid the balance out in weekly installments. For reasons unknown, my parents expected Carroll to buy most of his clothes with his earnings while there was no such expectation of me.

Saturday was collection day, and I always sought out the customers who paid without a hassle first. Of all the others, some would beg off for another week, some were hard to find, and some hid or refused to answer the knock on the door to keep from having to make an excuse for trying to stiff a twelve-year-old kid for fifteen cents. My father insisted that I not allow anyone to get more than two weeks behind, but I was a softie. I felt sorry for them and thought it was unfair to cut somebody off until I knew their intentions were not honorable. My father warned me about certain customers whom he knew from personal experience to be deadbeats, but as is often the case, the deadbeats were usually the most disarming and interesting.

Dad made me a generous offer. I had to pay for my papers by Monday of each week, so I would buy a postal money order and mail it to the paper company. Dad told me I could write a check on him to pay the paper company each week and save the fifteen-cent cost of a money order. In turn, I was to deposit the amount of the check into his bank account. This worked fine at first, but soon I was letting many people slide by without paying, and that, along with my rather profligate tastes for Eskimo Pies, candy, Cokes, and other indulgences, often left me with the "shorts." I soon found myself in a king-size scam, stiffing my father by depositing a little less each week than the amount of the check I had written. At first, I shorted his account by only twenty-five cents or so, but as time went by, it was as much as fifty to sixty cents. I had been taught at home and in Sunday school that "steal one apple and the next thing you know you're robbing banks." I was a textbook criminal in the making. The longer my transgressions went unnoticed, the bolder I became, though I was living in abject fear of what I knew would be the inevitable day of reckoning. Four months after my first theft, that day arrived.

I was in the living room listening to the radio, in the dark, of course. Suddenly, the ceiling light (we had no lamps) came on and my father stood towering over me, bank statement in hand. He reached over me and turned the radio off. He didn't ask questions, he just started chronicling the week-to-week shortages, which came to more than sixteen dollars, a month's groceries by Mother's standards. I wanted to slit my wrists. He was "sorely disappointed." He was "disappointed"—I was dying. Tears began streaming down my cheeks, but I said nothing. No confession, no "I'm sorry," no damned nothing. I worshiped my dad and could hardly endure this moment, disappointing him—especially on a matter of honesty. At the end of this gut-wrenching affair, I was offered a chance for redemption: I was to add fifty cents a week to my checks until I had made full restitution. I was expecting the gas chamber, so this was anticlimactic. The punishment I suffered was in being caught, which was ten times worse than merely having to pay back the loan. I had always planned to do that. I just hadn't gotten around to it.

Dad believed the "hay was in the barn" by the time a child

was fifteen years old, that a child's character was molded by then and wouldn't change perceptibly thereafter. I was thirteen at the time, so I figured I had two years to get my act together or face life as a derelict at best or a criminal at worst.

Charleston was one of about six communities in western Arkansas with a sizable German population, all Catholics who had come to the area around the turn of the century during one of Germany's periodic potato famines. Arkansas's Catholic population is under 5 percent, but in this small area of western Arkansas it is much greater. Originally, these immigrants referred to themselves as Deutsche (German), and the locals translated that to "Dutch," so they were usually referred to as Dutchmen, and until I was seventeen or eighteen years old, I thought they were from Holland. The Germans were good citizens, good farmers, honest, and devout.

There was an eight-grade Catholic school behind the church. The church itself was old world architecture made of chiseled and shaped native rock, with a magnificent steeple and a huge bell that could be heard for two miles on a still day. It rang at noon and 6:00 p.m. each day and people would set their clocks. On the day of a funeral it tolled one ring for each year of a deceased Catholic's life. When the bell started tolling, we would stop whatever we were doing and count, knowing the deceased but not his age. Then we would comment, "I didn't realize he was so old," or, "He wasn't as old as I thought." The steeple could be seen for three miles east of town: It was a landmark and a comforting sight to veterans returning from the war or families returning from lengthy trips.

Despite the large Catholic population, Charleston was predominantly Protestant and was always rife with rumors started by Protestant adults and spread by their children about the Catholics or their priest. Catholicism was a mystical religion to us, and we felt the use of Latin in the worship service was designed to communicate secret messages and conceal them from the rest of us. One of the most enduring rumors was that the basement of the Catholic church (I don't think it had a basement) was filled with guns, to be used in an uprising the minute a Catholic was elected president and the pope gave the order.

The Catholic church and school were on the east end of town, and the public schools were on the west end. Catholic children were allowed to ride the public school buses, but many of them had to walk through town after school to catch them at the west end of Main Street. They walked on the north side of Main Street, and the public school children walked on the south side. As we walked on opposite sides of the street, Protestant children sometimes yelled at the Catholic children and called them "pot lickers," but nobody knew what that was supposed to mean. I never joined in the name-calling. While I knew it was mean and spiteful, more important, I knew my dad would strongly disapprove. The Catholic children were well disciplined and never looked at us or acknowledged us. I admired their discipline and restraint and felt sorry for them because they were hopelessly outnumbered. It was the same with blacks. They had to ignore epithets hurled at them and look away or walk away or risk a confrontation. Even a scowl or resentful look could be dangerous.

When Al Smith, the New York governor and a Catholic, was the Democratic nominee for president in 1928, rumors of the pope becoming the de facto president abounded. Dad had to force Mother to vote for Al Smith. Her distrust was not limited to his Catholicism. He was also a known whiskey drinker who openly advocated repeal of the Eighteenth Amendment—Prohibition. Al Smith came south to Arkansas for a running mate. He chose Joe T. Robinson, Arkansas's senior senator, popularly known as Joe T., who was also the majority leader in the Senate. Joe T.'s task was to carry the South where Smith was weak. Joe T. carried six southern states, but Smith didn't even carry New York.

My mother hated whiskey for reasons other than her piety. Dad's brother Joel was a hopeless alcoholic, and often we had to keep him at our house until he sobered up. Mother sometimes rebelled, but Dad always prevailed. I didn't mind, because Uncle Joel was the most engaging of all of Dad's brothers.

Mother demonstrated her sanctimony in other ways. Clyde Hiatt, the banker, emceed the Commercial Club banquet one year and told the story of the mother going to stay with her daughter after the birth of the daughter's first child. The mother, while changing the baby's diapers, called to her daughter, "Honey, is this a little boy or a little girl?"

The daughter, aghast, said, "Mother, is your eyesight that bad?"

The mother said, "No, honey. It's not my eyesight, it's my memory."

Mother was appalled and swore she would never attend another banquet where Clyde Hiatt was on the program.

One of my paper customers, Francis (Frank) Xavier Classen, was a first-generation Deutsche Catholic, who owned a feed, seed, and produce company. His building, which was constructed of sheet iron, was across the street from Mr. Cagle's blacksmith shop and across an alley from the bank. He also dealt in furs of any kind—opossum, skunk, squirrel, raccoon, and an occasional mink. He bought eggs, cream, chickens, and anything else on which he thought he could make a profit. He spoke English well but with a slight German accent, mostly on words starting with a *T* as in "dese" (these), "dose" (those), and "dere" (there). When Mother had a chicken or two or eggs to sell, I was instructed to take them to John Gibson's store. John was a good Methodist. I was never told to take them to Mr. Classen.

I liked Mr. Classen a lot and was flattered that he obviously enjoyed talking to me. He was short, bald, and, even by today's standards, an unabashed liberal. When I returned home after law school, we joked about the two of us being Charleston's entire liberal bloc. Even though I liked him and was flattered that he liked talking to me, I delayed going to his feed store on Saturdays to collect for the paper, because he would never pay me until I sat and talked politics with him, usually for an hour or more. We agreed that FDR was a savior, that "coloreds" were just as good as anybody else, and that you could tell a lot about a man's character by going quail hunting with him or by serving on a jury with him. A man who claims virtually every quail that falls tells you all you need to know about him, and a juror's rationale for a guilty or not guilty verdict is often equally revealing. When I later began trying jury cases, I realized how perceptive he had been.

Mr. Classen was one of a handful of people in Charleston who felt compassion for blacks. But everyone, including that handful, seemed oblivious to the fact that our schools were segregated.

In one of our Saturday discussions, I told Mr. Classen I planned to be a lawyer. "Where?" he asked. I told him I didn't know. He then told me about a lawyer in Danville, Arkansas, a community about the size of Charleston, who developed such a reputation that people from a wide section of the state sought his services. He assured me I could do the same if I chose to return.

In 1932, as the Great Depression took hold, my father, against my mother's wishes, decided to make a run for the Arkansas State House of Representatives. A little money for gasoline was all that was required. At the time, Franklin County had two representatives and two county seats, Ozark and Charleston. The Arkansas River ran through the middle of the county, with Ozark on the north side and Charleston on the south, but there were twice as many voters on the north side. Since Arkansas didn't have run-offs, the two top vote getters were the winners.

The campaign kept Dad away some nights, because he was too far up in the mountains to make it home. He would stay with whoever invited him as an overnight guest. When he left in the morning, his host would give him biscuits with sausage patties and maybe a fresh cantaloupe or watermelon from the garden for his lunch. There were only two paved highways in the county, and he had to choose areas in which to campaign based on the conditions of the roads. Some were impassable when it rained. But that was not often during Arkansas summers.

There were two candidates from the Charleston side of the river and six from the Ozark side. The vote was split evenly among the six from the north side, while Dad and John Bollinger, both from Charleston, got all the votes on the south side, giving them a plurality, though the vote was very close. It was the last year Franklin County would have two representatives.

Dad loved being in the legislature, and the twelve hundred dollars he received for his two-year term afforded us new living and dining room furniture. He roomed in a house that was filled with "country" legislators like him. A hotel was out of the question. For one weekend, we also had a new Dodge, courtesy of a Little Rock car dealer who allowed Dad to drive it home, hoping to make a sale. It was the most beautiful car I had ever seen, and Carroll and I spent the weekend with friends just sitting in it and admiring its interior. But Dad made the only decision he could make, and that was to return it. Nevertheless, for forty-eight hours we were the envy of the town.

Carroll spent two days in Little Rock with Dad during the legislative session, and his description of the capitol building and the elevators in the Marion Hotel made him the center of attention in the neighborhood. I had heard about elevators but had seen them only in movies.

I was jealous of Carroll getting to spend time in Little Rock with Dad, and also jealous of Dad's attention to Carroll. Just to get his attention, I would often go to the store in the late afternoon just so I could walk the one and a half blocks home with him after work. The corner in front of Doc's Café and Pool Hall was what my mother called "spit" corner. There were usually four or five old geezers sitting on the protruding brick in front of the plate-glass windows, chewing tobacco, spitting, whittling on a piece of wood with no design or purpose except to keep from being totally idle, and telling tall, highly embellished tales. Esau Heathcock, the most humorous and original of the geezers, said to my father as we walked by one evening, "Bill, I took up for you today."

Dad dutifully asked how.

"Somebody said you'd quit stealing, and I said it was a god-damned lie."

Dad laughed heartily with the rest of them, seemingly unoffended that I had heard the story. Mother never attempted to conceal her disgust as she was occasionally forced to walk by the geezers and through their spittle on the sidewalk.

Dad was badly smitten with politics and yearned above all else to serve in Congress. There was a representative in the legislature with Dad named David D. Terry, a wealthy man, or at least married to a wealthy woman, who had been elected to the U.S. House of Representatives in 1934. He was from Little Rock, and though we were 125 miles west of Little Rock, we were in the same congressional district.

Dad decided he could defeat Dave Terry and was receiving some spotty encouragement to run. Mother was apoplectic. She was not only unalterably opposed, she was determined to convince Margaret, Carroll, and me that Dad would get trounced and that we would wind up in the poorhouse and die hungry and uneducated. We heard over and over again that Dave Terry's wife "owned that big Blass Department Store building in Little Rock," which she equated with certain defeat for Dad. I was too young to know what went into Dad's decision not to run, but I would guess that Mother's implacable opposition and the stark terror he saw in our eyes were dominant.

Dad never lost his enthusiasm for the political chase. He never wavered in the honest conviction that there was nothing as exhilarating as a political victory and nothing as rewarding or as honorable as being a dedicated, honest politician who actually made things better and more just. He vaccinated me with that philosophy.

From age eight or nine, we were strongly encouraged to attend all political speeches on the courthouse lawn, especially those by candidates for governor, the U.S. Senate, and the U.S. House of Representatives. Unless a candidate had a good friend or supporter in town, Dad was almost always called on to introduce the candidate. I can remember him, over the course of one summer, closing his introductions of as many as four gubernatorial candidates with, "And now it is my honor to present to you the next governor of Arkansas. . . ."

As a result of his stint in the legislature, Dad knew many of the candidates and was pleased to accommodate most of them. Yet because he was in business and anxious not to alienate anyone, he was selective and never allowed a candidate to put a placard in his store windows.

At dinner, following a candidate's speech on the courthouse lawn, he would quiz Carroll and me about what we thought of the speech and the candidate and what he had said that appealed to us. My impressions were usually based on superficial things, such as a simple, emotional story the candidate told, his oratorical skills, his looks, his voice, his attire, and maybe his humor. Dad would gently suggest that I should be more thoughtful and not judge people on appearances as much as on ideas and values. He never talked down to me because of my age, and he taught me that voting and politics were deadly serious matters. Many of my favorites finished last. I couldn't resist tearjerking stories and handsome faces.

By today's standards, Dad would not be a liberal on race, but by the mores of the time, he was rare. He extended credit to blacks at the store, which was frowned on by other merchants.

A young black man in Charleston once approached Dr. Bollinger, the wealthiest man in town, who owned a lot of land, much of it near the black community east of town. He wanted to borrow a small amount of money. Dr. Bollinger's farms used black labor in the summer, and he sometimes loaned money to them. He told the young black man, "You go get James Ferguson to cosign your note and I'll make you the loan." James Ferguson was, by the standards of the day, a relatively well-to-do elderly black man and very highly regarded by both blacks and whites. When the young black man told Mr. Ferguson the story, he said,

"You go get Dr. Bollinger to cosign your note, and I'll loan you the money."

·　　　·　　　·

There was a wonderful man in Charleston whom everyone knew as Sis. Sis managed a dry goods store called Seaman's, one of about six stores in the Seaman's chain. He was a devout Baptist, a civic leader, and beloved by all. All the spinsters in town vied for his attention because he was attentive, entertaining, and a great dancer who loved to party. Almost everyone assumed he was gay, but nobody cared. He was effeminate, but some of the spinsters professed to know firsthand that he was not gay at all.

In those days, homosexuality was not only a cause for firing, but a violation of the Arkansas criminal code that carried a prison sentence. Sis's name was Wayne, but nobody called him Wayne, and it really never occurred to anyone why he was called Sis. I was an adult before it dawned on me that Sis was a nickname. Even though homosexuality was strongly condemned, I don't know of a single incident in which anybody was abusive toward Sis. The words *gay* and *lesbian* were not in anybody's vocabulary.

Even though our schools were adequate and teachers often superior, there were only a few extracurricular activities: football, basketball and track, 4-H Clubs, Future Farmers of America, and Future Homemakers of America. No band, no chorus, no drama club. But in the fall of 1941, a band director was hired from the nearby town of Hartman, much smaller than Charleston. He moved to Charleston with his wife and two students from Hartman—one, his wife's brother, a fine clarinet player; and another, a high school junior who was a first-rate trumpet player who could "triple tongue," a very difficult achievement.

Within a year, we had a thirty-five-piece band that was making remarkable progress. Not only were we becoming musicians, we often went to the director's home in the evenings and listened to his record library of great symphonies and operas, some of which were a part of our repertoire, such as "Finlandia" and

"Jesu, Joy of Man's Desiring." It was my first brush with classical music. We began to win at competitive music festivals, and our soloists and ensembles began winning at both state and regional contests. The band director was temperamental and at times screamed and stomped at the podium, demanding perfection. At first he frightened us, but his tirades also caused us to strive for perfection.

There had always been whispers about the director's sexuality, and in time the whispers grew into troubling, condemning comments. The rumors were rife and took on a life of their own. In a small town, one such rumor was enough to tarnish someone for life. This rumor, totally without foundation, grew until the school board felt it had to act, so the director was summarily dismissed in the middle of the semester. That was the end of Charleston's band until long after the war. People never recognized the contradiction in insisting the band director be fired at the first suggestion that he might be gay while Sis enjoyed an enviable reputation. But Sis had always been part of our small community; the band director was a stranger.

The firing of the band director led to a unique opportunity for me. As student conductor at the age of sixteen, it fell to my lot to hold the band together. I had no disciplinary authority, so it was a losing battle. However, I conducted the Spring Concert and took the band to the Bi-State Band Festival in Ft. Smith, where we finished second in our division.

·　　　·　　　·

When I was fifteen, I gave up my paper route and started working at the Kroger store after school and on Saturdays during the summer months. I kept the shelves stocked, the floors clean, and the foul smell out of the fresh meat box. I even developed some skills as a butcher, though it took no skill to grind up lunch meat butts, add cornflakes and red dye and a small portion of red meat—usually meat we couldn't sell—and call it hamburger. Some people lavishly praised the conglomeration. If there was a

Food and Drug Administration then, or a Food Safety and Inspection Service, they never investigated the Kroger store in Charleston.

I had one other duty at the Kroger store. A married woman of some affluence started visiting in the mornings when we had no customers and spent an inordinate amount of time buying nothing. She and the store manager, who was a notorious flirt, seemed to get along well, and they prattled idly for long periods. Slowly but surely, their relationship became more than an innocent flirtation, and finally the affair was consummated on the sacks of cow feed in the storeroom. Thereafter, two or three mornings each week, it became my tacitly understood duty that I was to tend the store while she and the manager were on the cow feed sacks and make sure nobody trespassed. We seldom had a customer in the morning, and I lied lamely if someone asked for the manager, saying he had gone to the post office. The affair slowly petered out.

Another regular customer was an obese, devout German Catholic named Jacob. He had a scraggly beard, wore filthy overalls, and emitted an unbearable body odor. He had five children and a little stringy-haired wife with a perpetual snaggletoothed grin. She was equally filthy and odoriferous, but also sweet, surprisingly intelligent, and likable (if she didn't get too close). Their home was small, and the yard was littered with junk and trash. Jacob apparently never held a job, and I never knew how he sustained his family. Welfare was virtually unheard of.

They would spend an hour or two shopping and reading labels but hardly ever bought anything except dog food, though they had no dog. It finally dawned on me that they were raising their family on dog food. Jacob was an intelligent man with an uncontrollable stutter. His children were well mannered and hardworking. I don't know what happened to any of them.

One of my assignments at the Kroger store was to clean the meat box on Saturday night. This was many years before meats were packaged. I usually started the process around 9:00 P.M., and it took about an hour. All meat had to be removed and the meat box thoroughly washed with soapy water and then rinsed with clean water. It was a chore I detested. Just removing the various parts of beef and pork carcasses, plus fresh chicken, was a huge task. But the box had to be emptied before cleaning.

The H. E. "Babe" Flanagan family had moved to Ft. Smith from their upland farm, north of Charleston, in 1936. The plight of the family had been terrible, but things were beginning to look slightly better. Babe had three daughters and Betty was the middle one. Even though we had attended the same grade school, she was a grade ahead of me and we hadn't known each other.

The family moved back to Charleston in 1941, and Betty and I started dating. She would come to the store around 8:30 P.M. and hang around until I finished with the meat box, after which we would drive to the cemetery and park. It was the favorite spot for smooching for all the high schoolers. We recognized every car. We knew the girls who would "do it" and those who wouldn't. I smelled like a goat barn from cleaning the meat box, and Betty's devotion got tested every Saturday night.

Chapter 5

Miss Doll—Revivals—Keith Robinson

In the 1930s, there were only two professions open to women, teaching and nursing. Children were the beneficiaries of sexism at its worst. Even though Charleston was a wretchedly poor community, I have never felt cheated by my elementary and secondary education. The faculty was the cream of the female crop, and we were the scions of the brightest, most dedicated, and talented women. The one who had the greatest influence on me was Miss Doll Means, an exemplary, diminutive teacher of English and American literature. Miss Doll was a demon on diagramming sentences and believed it was the only means by which grammar could be taught in a correct, meaningful, and memorable way. She inspired me, built my self-esteem and confidence, and had it not been for her and my father, my life would have been quite different.

When I entered the University of Arkansas as a freshman in the summer of 1943, I was assigned to an English section taught by the dean of the College of Arts and Sciences, Dr. John Clark Jordan. He still taught this one course, freshman English, because he loved teaching and couldn't stand the idea of giving it up completely. In the first meeting of the class, he wrote a sentence on the blackboard and asked if anyone could diagram it. Out of twenty-five students, a boy from Little Rock Central High School and I were the only two to hold up our hands. We went to the blackboard and diagrammed the sentence identically and correctly. Dr. Jordan then asked each of us our name and where we were from. When I told him my name, he immediately asked, "Are you Carroll Bumpers' brother?"

"Yes," I said.

"Then you studied grammar under Miss Doll, right?"

I felt like a celebrity.

Miss Doll also taught English literature, and one day we were studying the great eighth-century English poem *Beowulf*, the author of which has never been determined. Miss Doll would choose a student to read a paragraph, after which we would discuss its meaning. When it came my turn to read, she didn't stop me after I had read a paragraph, so I continued. Finally, I stopped and looked up. She had an elfin smile on her face, pencil to her lips, which was a habit, and said to the class, "Doesn't he read well?" She paused. "And doesn't he have a beautiful voice?" Another pause. "And wouldn't it be a tragedy if he didn't take advantage of those talents?"

My first thought was that she might be ridiculing me, but I knew she would never do that to a student. No other teacher could have said the same things and had anything remotely close to the impact Miss Doll's words had on me. She did more for my self-esteem in a few seconds than anyone before or since. While she was magnificent at building one's self-esteem, she was equally effective at chastising the lazy, the laggard, and those who were trying to "get by." She demanded the best of everyone.

She was a spinster, about sixty years old at the time, and had suffered a terrible neck injury in her youth when her elder sister accidentally dropped her on her head. She had to turn her entire body to turn her head.

In 1946, when I returned home after the war, and after visiting with Mother and Dad and Betty, I hastened to Miss Doll's home. It was a ritual for many returning veterans. Our visit was exhilarating, but while it had been only three years since I had seen her, she seemed much older, though her teasing manner was intact. She had been granted a grade one teacher's license at the age of twenty-two in 1912 but didn't receive her college degree until 1943, my senior year in high school. It was also the following year that, due to a shortage of men, she was made superintendent of schools, though she never received as much as a hundred dollars a month. She was a woman and not entitled to the hundred and twenty-five dollars per month her male predecessors had been paid.

Miss Doll died two days after her ninetieth birthday. I kept her picture prominently displayed in my Senate office for twenty-four years. Few people inquired as to who she was, and the ones who did, asked, "Is that your mother?"

"Yes, in many ways," I always answered. The mother of my self-esteem, my ability to communicate in writing and speaking, and my appreciation of the English language.

In 1977, Charleston's dilapidated two-story "firetrap" grade school, which I had attended, was razed and replaced with a new classroom building and auditorium. The auditorium was named the Doll Means Auditorium. I delivered the dedicatory address.

Unhappily, all teachers were not Miss Doll. When I was in the fourth grade, the makers of Ipana Tooth Paste sent a representative to our school. He gave each of us a small tube of toothpaste, a toothbrush, and a lecture on dental care. The closest dentist was in Ft. Smith, and nobody in the class had ever sat in a dentist's chair. Shortly afterward, Mrs. Cooper decided our class should elect a "King of Health." I was handily elected, to her consternation and dismay. She didn't know what to do about this poor, filthy urchin being elected King of Health. The soles of my shoes were loose and flapped when I walked, and the bib on my overalls wouldn't stay up because the wringer on our Maytag washer bent the snaps that held the galluses on the bib, rendering them useless. One side of the bib was always dangling. It was more than Mrs. Cooper could bear for me to be King of Health, so with autocratic authority, she summarily took the title from me and gave it to the immaculately scrubbed Welton Jetton, an only child who wore a clean white shirt and tie each day. No explanation, no apology. It hurt, because I knew why I had been replaced. And while I never forgave her, I later wondered why Mother and Dad hadn't been more sensitive to my cleanliness and at least to keeping my overalls and shoes in wearable condition.

The average annual pay for classroom teachers in 1931 was $730. By 1934, the average dropped to $489, although they didn't actually receive that much. Teachers were paid with warrants rather than cash. They could cash the warrants at the local bank at steep discounts or peddle them to three or four relatively well-to-do men in town who bought them for some percentage of their face value—usually 60 to 70 percent. The school district would honor the warrants at face value at some future time, usually two years, but teachers couldn't afford to wait two years. They had to eat, so they took what they could get.

Despite their impoverished condition, Charlestonians, like most people similarly situated, never lost their sense of humor. They often relieved their misery with self-deprecating humor, such as the story of a young eighteen-year-old telling his boss, who owned one of the cotton gins, that he was getting married. When the boss asked whom he was marrying, he was told Quita Belle Jones. The boss said, "James, I can't believe you're going to marry Quita Belle Jones. She's slept with every man in Charleston."

To which James replied, "Why, Mr. Floyd, Charleston ain't no big town."

We joked that Charleston was so small that both city limit signs were on the same post, and hitchhikers would go either way. Even as late as 1973, during the energy crisis, we spoke of Charleston's good fortune, because "its whole power system was a Sears DieHard." One old nester said he lived so far back, the sun set between his house and the mailbox.

Dad tended our vegetable garden religiously. His success with the garden determined, to some extent, how well we were fed the following winter. It usually produced abundant supplies of fresh vegetables all summer and an excess that my mother canned for future use. Mother's determination to keep us adequately fed at the least possible cost was made much easier during the summer growing season. In addition, fruit peddlers knocked on the front door daily. Incomparable Elberta peaches were twenty-five cents a "peck," a fourth of a bushel, and apples were fifty cents a bushel.

One summer, a new schoolteacher, both beautiful and well endowed, rented a room on the second floor of Mrs. Bonner's house, which was directly across the side street from our garden. Dad often worked the garden till dusk after coming home from the store. The schoolteacher, whether purposely or not, quite often undressed with the lights on and the shade up. Mother said we had the best garden that summer we'd ever had.

As beautiful and welcome as spring was, we also dreaded it because we lived in "Tornado Alley." When the humidity was high and the barometric pressure was low, squall lines broke off miles ahead of approaching cold fronts, creating a constant stream of lightning that was terrifying to watch. Mother would become frantic, throwing us into the bathtub or under the bed as the thunderstorm or possible tornado approached. Sometimes, in the middle of the night, she would awaken us and we would run in our nightclothes to Mrs. Bonner's house next door because Mother thought it was sturdier. She would pace the floor, praying frantically, "Oh Lord. Oh Lord. Please spare us." Dad seldom got out of bed, slept soundly through the storms, and never went to the Bonner house with us. One storm tilted our entire two-story house about ten degrees. Dad paid Othel Swift eight hundred dollars to straighten it, and we watched in awe as he used a complicated system of hydraulic jacks, cables, and hoists, and after several weeks, straighten it he did.

The bane of every child's summer vacation, other than Bible school, was the church revival. It was a time when we all wished we were Catholics, who never seemed to feel the need to be revived. The Methodists and Baptists were always in competition to see who could draw the biggest crowds and save the most souls, but the competition intensified during revival time.

Revivals were an age-old southern Protestant tradition designed to save the drunks and unfaithful husbands who had succeeded in resisting the importuning of the preachers during the preceding year and steadfastly refused to "walk the aisle" and "be saved." They enjoyed "sweet Willie" (cheap wine) and life on earth too much to accept the promise of a celestial one later. "A bird in hand . . ." But it was simply unacceptable to the locals that a man would mindlessly, or by design, opt for perdition when the promise of the Lord was so crystal clear on how he could just as easily enter the gates of heaven, live forever among friends in a land of milk and honey, and never feel a temperature above seventy degrees Fahrenheit.

The evangelist might be a traveling charlatan with fake credentials, white suit, pink shirt, loud tie, and slicked-down black hair or a preacher from a neighboring community who had cut a deal with the local preacher that he would invite him to his church to hold a revival the following year. There was money, and quite a lot of it, involved in these deals. But local preachers were never as successful in separating the congregants from their money as the traveling evangelist who, before having been saved, had seen the world, had been an alcoholic, chaser of women, racetrack tout, or whatever. His wardrobe was invariably garish but impressive to the locals.

If the evangelist was a first-class fire-eater who could make adults shudder and children cower with his description of hell, the crowds would be huge. It was pure entertainment at a time when most people lived drab lives. The revival provided people with an opportunity to perform their Christian duty and be entertained at the same time. They had nothing better to do, anyway. Even radio was in its infancy, and clear reception was rare after dark.

The altar call to the sinner at the conclusion of each service began with the piano or organ, or both, playing mournfully while the congregation sang softly:

> *Just as I am, without one plea,*
> *But that Thy blood was shed for me,*
> *And that Thou bidd'st me come to Thee,*
> *O, Lamb of God, I come! I come!*

The evangelist would chant a mighty mantra about how people in hell divinely wished they had another chance to seize "the opportunity being offered this evening to those of you who still have time to be saved, time to confess Jesus Christ as your Lord and Savior." At times, the evangelist seemed to be challenging himself on how graphically he could describe hell. It was nightmare material to me, and I wanted desperately to ask Dad not to make us go, but even that small request might be so offensive to God that it would land me in hell.

On the evenings when the evangelist got no takers, he would often call on the congregation to bow their heads and close their eyes, then invite timid sinners to hold up their hands and only he and they would know. Children always peeped, but I only ever saw one sinner, a local drunk, hold up his hand. The person everyone wanted to save more than any other was Old Buck. The evangelists always called on Old Buck, the alcoholic mechanic, every day at his garage, knowing that if they could get him to agree to walk the aisle the last night of the revival, they could spread the word that Buck was going to be saved, and people would be hanging from the rafters and the revival hailed as a *howling* success. But Old Buck continued to elude their grasp. Some evangelists would go into the audience and confront and cajole a known sinner.

On the last night of the revival, a "love offering" would be taken for Brother Evangelist, for his powerful sermons, and, in general, for keeping people out of Doc's Café and Pool Hall for a week or two until the euphoria wore off. The love offering could go on for thirty minutes if the congregation didn't hit the collection plate hard enough on the first pass, and they never did. The local preacher handled this chore, since it would be unseemly for the visitor to plead for money for himself. As the chanting, pleading, cajoling, and badgering grew louder, some, with little to eat in their pantries, were intimidated into giving every dime they had on them to feed the insatiable greed of the visitor, who dreamed of a down payment on a new car, a new suit, or getting caught up on his grocery bill. Then the collection plates would be passed again and again, and the embarrassment was palpable if you were flat broke and sitting next to someone who gave and you couldn't. The local preacher was actually ambivalent because he knew that the bigger the love offering, the smaller his collections would be in the weeks to come.

Dad told me that as a young man, he and his best friend, John Graham, once attended a brush arbor meeting in Cecil, where they both grew up. It was a typical outdoor brush arbor meeting, taking place behind or beside a church, where a few poles were cut in the woods, placed in three-foot-deep holes, and strung across the tops with chicken wire. Then, small limbs with a lot of leaves were placed on top of the chicken wire. Benches were brought from the church and chairs brought from home. This outdoor meeting was simply to avoid the heat of being indoors on a stifling hot summer evening. The place was lighted by kerosene lamps.

One evening, the evangelist invited anyone possessed of demons to come forward and have them exorcised. When a miscreant came forward and knelt, the evangelist would pray and pray and occasionally would look up to the congregation and announce, "There goes one." He would point at the demon's path, and the people, like a crowd at a tennis match, would follow his pointing with their eyes and heads, ostensibly watching the demons take flight.

On one poor demonized soul, the evangelist strained mightily, but no demons came forth. Finally he said, "I cannot remove demons when there are some who sit nearby that don't believe in removing demons. Unless these nonbelievers take their leave, no demons will come forth." Dad and his friend John got up and left.

One of the more entertaining things about revivals was watching people spring from their seats in a state of rapture and run up and down the aisles, waving their arms in the air, shouting praise to Jesus, and speaking in unknown tongues. Mrs. Shumate, a devout Baptist, would often soar out of control, and children waited excitedly if she was in the audience because she could never contain her fervor, nor did she ever try. She seldom attended a Methodist revival, but when she did, we found her shouting and speaking in tongues, a marvelous thing to witness. "Want all you'ns to pray fer me till Lord says s'nuf." We giggled at "it's enough" sounding like "snuff."

There were three other summer events that we looked forward to with great anticipation: medicine shows, the Davis-Brunk Comedians, and carnivals. The medicine men were immensely entertaining with their chants and claims for themselves and their products. They were always graduates of the University of Hong Kong, Shanghai, Singapore, Bangkok, or some other exotic Asian city. Their medical products were all carefully aligned on the stage in impressive displays of bright green, blue, and red bottles of liquids. There were no known ailments, from corns and ingrown toenails to heart failure and cancer, that the medicine man's elixirs wouldn't cure. He, and usually his wife, played musical instruments, sang, danced, and royally entertained the audience in brightly colored costumes. She was always dressed in brightly colored, seductive garb. The shows were on an uncovered stage, and the whole affair took place in a vacant lot. The only tent was a small one just behind the stage, and it was used for costume changes. The audience stood in the open.

One night, the "doctor," in displaying the marvel of his soaps, lathered his hands fulsomely and rubbed them together until the soap totally disappeared. Then his assistant poured a little water on his hands as he began to wring them again and describe in a fast-paced monotone the contents and all their healing elements. As he spoke, the soap foam began to emerge, the point being that when the soap reappeared it brought with it dirt, grime, and germs from under the skin. After I got home, I tried the same thing with our soap, and lo, our soap disappeared and reemerged, too, and ours was considerably cheaper.

The carnivals were small and not very interesting. Charleston was too small for the big carnivals, and even the small ones lingered only a couple of nights. The nudity, or near nudity, of one or two over-the-hill women was saved for the second night, because it spelled the end of their stay anyway. The preachers, who carefully monitored such goings-on, saw to that. We younger males were more interested in seeing our local hero, Ken Woods, wrestle the carnival wrestler. Ken didn't have to win. The five-dollar prize was his if he could go some period of time without being pinned, which he usually did. Ken was a slim, wiry, muscular man with more courage than brains, but he was our hero for one evening. He was a water-well cleaner and always sang, "Praise Je'ah!" (Jesus) for each piece of junk he pulled out of the well.

The Davis-Brunk Comedians were a traveling troupe of actors who, for six consecutive nights, made us laugh, cry, applaud the heroes, and hiss the villains. The tent held about three hundred people, counting the "chicken roost" (bleachers) in the rear. Tickets were twenty-five cents for the folding-chair seats and fifteen cents for the chicken roost. Dad provided the furniture for the stage sets, in return for which we got free tickets.

We were deeply saddened when we awoke on Sunday morning to find the tent gone and only the once green grass, now dead, giving evidence of where the stage, the chicken roost, and the chair seats had been. The excitement was gone, and we were dejected as we were forced to return to the tedium of our lives.

The trampled grass area looked very small compared to how big the tent had seemed.

Carroll was perhaps sixteen and I was twelve when we became fascinated with the game of tennis, though I don't know how or why, because Charleston had no tennis court. Our tennis originally consisted of hitting tennis balls at a designated point just above net height, on the garage door or any other building where we could get away with it. We were becoming rabid about the game, and finally my father allowed us to scrape the grass off the side yard and build a dirt court. It took up the whole lawn, plus some land that belonged to the hardware store. We went to the woods on the outskirts of town, cut poles about fifteen feet long, and built backdrops using chicken wire Dad knowingly allowed us to filch from the store. Along with our neighbors, we came up with four dollars to purchase a real tennis net. Then we stole lime from the store to mark off the court, and we were in business. My father said he would allow the court to remain until he heard profanity or things got too loud and unruly. There was not a single soul in Charleston to give us any help learning the finer points of the game, so we simply learned "country" tennis.

I became engrossed in World War II long before the United States got involved. One of Dad's bosses when he first went to work at the hardware store was Joe Yunker, one of the German immigrants in Charleston. He was an elderly man, kind and wise, who translated Hitler's speeches for us when we picked them up on the shortwave radio at the store. According to Mr. Yunker's translation, Hitler sounded incoherent. I was in my early teens, but Hitler's rantings seemed ominous, and even though he was thousands of miles away, I was childishly apprehensive, and my fear was heightened by the crowds roaring their approval. Deutschland! Deutschland! Deutschland!

Luther Smith, the barber and mayor, once said to three or four loafers as they stood around the red-and-white barber pole in front of the barbershop, "I know ole Hitler's a bad actor, but it's hard to blame him for what he's doin' to them Jews." Not only was there not a single Jew in Charleston, few people in Charleston had ever seen one or, more important, had the remotest knowledge as to what Hitler was doing to them. What they subsequently did know, because the *Fort Smith Times Record* had screaming headlines every day during the late summer and fall of 1940, was that Hitler was sending two thousand bombers over England every day in broad daylight, and that despite the indomitable spirit of the British people, England was slowly being brought to her knees. Most people felt that the ocean was an insuperable barrier, but I began conjuring up dreadful and dire scenarios of how Hitler might invade the United States.

Charleston had two doctors, Dr. Bollinger, who had gone to medical school in Little Rock for maybe a year, and Dr. Neissl, another of Charleston's Deutsche émigrés who had come to Charleston via Arizona, where he had first settled after coming to America. He was a brilliant man who, though German, had graduated from medical school at the University of Prague. He was about seventy years old in 1941 and the only person in town who used a monocle. He did his own lab work, was an apothecary extraordinaire, made house calls day and night, and didn't own a car. Few people went to his office, which was in his home. He hid his whiskey from his wife on the shelves behind his medical books.

When Dr. Neissl walked down the street where we lived, Mother would watch until she saw where he stopped. It was a normal curiosity to know who was ill. She would then call Mrs. Showeiler, the telephone operator, who listened in on most conversations, to find out who was ill in the household where he had stopped. Everybody was either a Bollinger person or a Neissl person. Our family passionately supported Dr. Neissl, but we were a minority. One woman who had moved to the area from Chicago said, "If I get sick, don't call Dr. Bollinger. Just let me die naturally."

Mother hated flies above all else, and they were plentiful. But when one got in the house, she went berserk until it was dead.

She once stood on the arm of a rocking chair, flyswatter in hand, in order to slay a fly on the ceiling. As she swung the swatter, the chair rocked, and she lost her balance, crashed to the floor, and broke her left arm. For reasons I never understood—Dr. Neissl was probably ill or out of town—Dad took Mother to Dr. Bollinger to get her arm set. He set it wrong, and she had very little use of it the rest of her life. It was a confirmation that Dad had chosen wisely many years before when he chose Dr. Neissl to be our family doctor.

I had pneumonia twice before I was six, and it was "touch and go" both times as to whether I would live. I was a very frail child, and there was always speculation in the community each fall whether I would live through another winter. Dr. Neissl was due, and received, full credit from our family for my recovery each time.

While Dr. Neissl was brilliant medically, he was a consummate admirer of Hitler. Dad regularly admonished him to curb his outspoken opinions, but until the United States declared war on Germany, he remained an open and avowed Hitlerite. Subsequently, he became a silent Hitlerite. Once the United States was at war with Germany, people began to abandon Dr. Neissl in droves, but he never turned his back on Hitler and died a few years after the war, a broke and broken man.

Dr. Bollinger had a thirteen-bed hospital where pregnant women squatted over a slop jar and pushed to have babies. The baby would be caught before actually falling headfirst into the pot. My dad and I took women home from the hospital in the ambulance after a week's stay, lifting them carefully onto a stretcher so the mothers didn't exert themselves. They were then instructed to stay in bed for another week or two at home. It was medical treatment at its worst. Most women, and all of Dr. Neissl's patients, had their babies at home.

Dr. Bollinger once told me that his final tests in medical school were orals. He said one question the dean asked him was, "What causes arthritis?" He said he thought, he grimaced, he agonized, and pleaded with the dean, "Don't tell me, now. I know. Just give me a minute and I'll think of it." Finally he gave up and said, "Well, I knew and I just forgot."

The dean said, "For God's sake, Bollinger, think! We've been trying to figure out the cause of arthritis for centuries, and here you knew and forgot."

·   ·   ·

Keith Robinson swept the streets of Charleston. Rather, he swept the two blocks that constituted Main Street. He was about fifty years old in 1941, tall, stooped, lean, and mentally borderline. He had lost his teeth but couldn't afford dentures. High school boys taunted him, and Keith's protests only encouraged them. It was cruel. Keith owned maybe two pairs of denim overalls and a trainman's cap. As a paper boy, I had known where everybody in town lived, but one day I realized that I had no idea where Keith lived! My curiosity led to a few inquiries, and I found his "house" behind the Conoco service station. It was about seven feet wide, seven feet long, and six feet high, framed with wooden two-by-fours, all four sides covered with cardboard and the roof covered with sheet iron. Every time there was a hard rain, Keith would have to go looking for a new refrigerator carton to replace the siding on his hovel. It was not tall enough for him to stand and barely long enough for him to lay down his six-foot-three-inch frame. He had a cot to sleep on and a coal stove on which to cook and keep warm. Those two items constituted his worldly possessions. In 1940, the city paid him forty dollars a month, and most of that went to Doc's Café and Pool Hall, where Keith usually ate. Doc also allowed Keith to sleep in the pool hall on nights when the weather, especially strong winds and thunderstorms, threatened. When his older brother died, he was left without a single relative or friend. The three big churches in Charleston, Catholic, Methodist, and Baptist, were all within 250 yards of Keith's "home," but nobody noticed his plight. They were too busy competing for members, counting collections, and planning building programs.

No matter what wee hour of the morning it was, Keith would be on the street faithfully sweeping away in a cloud of dust and muttering to himself about the cars that were left on the street overnight and what a nuisance they were. An occasional heavy rain would bring joy to his heart, giving him a two-day respite as it washed away the dirt and grime. He got paid the same whether he or the rain got rid of the dirt.

Keith knew where the scarce walnut trees were in the wooded areas around Charleston. In the fall of the year, he was able to supplement his scant income by gathering walnuts and picking out the meat. He sold all he could gather to a few housewives who pitied him and many of whom threw the walnuts in the trash once they saw his filthy hands.

When Keith grew too feeble to sweep, he simply disappeared. Years later, I searched the cemeteries to find his grave, without success. On hindsight, I'm incredulous and ashamed that while I was sympathetic, I did nothing to make his life more bearable. I once sold him a clock on credit for $3.50, because he needed an alarm. One day, after he had owed me for the clock for over a year, I saw him walking down an alley and asked him when he was going to pay me. It was cruel and unforgivable. He turned away from me and toward nobody in particular and said, "That boy ain't nearly as smart as his daddy was." He couldn't have been more right.

·   ·   ·

In my senior year in high school, I landed the male lead in the senior class play. My role required me to kiss the female star, Francis Underwood, in the final scene, but in rehearsal, both because her boyfriend usually attended and because it would have raised eyebrows among the attending adults, I was not permitted to kiss her. I plotted to "lay it on her" in both public performances, and I relished the thought. The play was *Small Town Romeo*, and it was probably the worst play ever written, made worse by high school amateurs. Rehearsals gave us an excuse to get out of the house at night. In the final scene at the Friday matinee, I gave Francis a long, romantic kiss, which we were both enjoying until we were suddenly pulled apart by her boyfriend, who had bounded up the side stairs to the stage the minute the curtain fell. For a short time their relationship barely survived, but one year later they were married.

The Arkansas State High School band contest was always held in Hot Springs. I was a high school junior when I made my first trip to Arkansas's premier tourist city, with its famous bathhouses, racetrack, alligator farm, and big hotels. It was my first time to stay in a hotel, and I was mightily impressed, though by today's standard it was a dump. You couldn't get much for five dollars a night (for two) even then. My roommate and I took everything that wasn't nailed down: towels, fountain pens (cheap quill pens on the end of wood), and the soap.

When I got home, I proudly displayed my ill-gotten gains to my parents. Dad was not amused. I'm sure he understood it was a childish prank, but after a short sermon on honesty, he insisted I return the loot. The principle was more important than the value, he said. So I packed up the items, which were worthless anyway, and mailed them back along with a note to the hotel manager, apologizing.

The preachers made sure we were not allowed to have a prom in high school, because it would have included dancing, so we had a junior-senior banquet, with seniors hosted by juniors. It was still an exciting event and generated a lot of speculation about who would invite whom. Since we could not invite anyone from another class, the pickings were slim. There were about thirty-three seniors and a like number of juniors. Paul McIlroy Jr. and I, both athletes, not as cute as we thought, decided we would invite Edith Daniels, the ugliest girl in both classes and from a deeply impoverished family, as our date. It would create a lot of sick humor, break all the other girls' hearts, and focus attention on us as we winked and nodded at our cleverness. Edith would excitedly accept, of course. But when I explained all this to my father between giggles, he found it not at all amusing. On the contrary, he found it disgusting. He proceeded to give me a lecture I have never forgotten about the cruelty of it. The idea of drawing attention to oneself at the expense of a poor creature under such circumstances was contemptible. I was ordered to extricate myself from this tawdry affair immediately, which I did the following day. Paul junior faltered, too, and we wound up without dates at the banquet.

.   .   .

As the Depression deepened, America became a nation on the move as people reached for a better life or just tried to survive. Charlestonians were no exception, migrating mostly to California. The exodus increased during World War II, when whites moved to the West Coast and blacks to Kansas City and Detroit to work in defense industries. Many who left were later returned for their burials.

In 1940, as America was beginning to escalate its preparations for war, the Defense Department decided to build an army camp fifteen miles west of Charleston on Highway 22, the state highway that ran from Charleston to Ft. Smith. Businessmen were excited about the economic activity they felt it would generate, but the people who were losing their homes and land were brokenhearted. My father was brokenhearted, too, because it meant losing his "best trade territory." Many of the displaced families took the compensation received for their homes and farmlands and, instead of rebuilding or relocating in the area, chose other parts of the country—again, mostly California.

During construction of the camp, my mother rented two of our upstairs bedrooms to three men from Beeville, Texas, who came to work as carpenters. The rent was five dollars per month for each, and the additional fifteen dollars gave Mother a new lease on life. They stayed almost a year and never created a problem, except for our having only one bathroom.

.   .   .

The Babe Flanagan family was known to my father and perhaps to a few other townspeople, but not to us children. Babe was a cattle farmer, and like most farmers during the Depression, was in the process of losing what little property he had. Babe had an eighth-grade education, but he had an incredible native intellect. He and Ola Callans Flanagan had four children, Callans, Margaret (Maggie), Betty, and Ruth, in that order. They avoided starvation by growing enough food in the summer to carry them through the winter. Babe was a genius at trading anything for something else and coming out a little ahead. Two enviable qualities coalesced to save him and his family—determination and a creative mind. He conceived the idea of butchering a hog, grinding the whole carcass into sausage, and then hurrying off to Paris, a nearby community, with wife and children in tow, where they all went door-to-door peddling it. He netted five dollars on his first trip. This was more than all but a very few people were making per day. He then decided to move up a notch by butchering a steer, which he cut into steaks, roasts, and hamburger and sold door-to-door in Ft. Smith, a much bigger market. This proved to be even more profitable. In what spare time he could carve out, he began hanging around Joe Bonner's livestock auction barn in Ft. Smith, buying a cow when he had the money and selling her before sundown for two to five dollars more than he paid for her.

Ola had become desperate and despondent trying to feed and clothe four children while Babe was in Ft. Smith, and she finally issued a non-negotiable demand that he move the family there. She said she was not going to live long raising four children alone. He acceded, and in 1936 he rented a two-story furnished house just a few blocks from Joe Bonner's barn, and the six Flanagans moved into the mostly furnished three-bedroom house with their pitiable possessions. Cost: thirty-eight dollars per month, more than some people were making per month.

Another amazing and fortuitous coincidence occurred shortly thereafter that would totally change the future of the Flanagan family. Babe had heard that Jersey cows, common in the South, were in demand in Iowa because their milk was rich in butterfat. He talked Joe Bonner, the auction barn owner, into financing a railroad car–load of sixty Jersey cows for shipment and sale in Waverly, Iowa. They agreed to share the profits. Babe rode in the cattle car to ensure the welfare of the cattle. The sale exceeded all expectations. The minute it was concluded, Babe headed straight for the local bank and got cash for every check he had received. The Depression had taught him not to hold a check any longer than necessary. He had never seen so much cash before. He then called Maggie, his sixteen-year-old daughter, and told her to drive to Kansas City and pick him up, which she did alone. Later, during summer months, Maggie and Betty, each in their mid-teens, would travel either with him in a car or in the cattle truck he rented. They would work the auction ring by prodding the cows and often grabbing a cow's udder and squirting milk as high as the roof to prove her milk-producing potential. Success begat success, and thereafter, he was off to Iowa as frequently as he could buy a load of cattle.

Babe soon began to make enough money to start buying land near his old farm. He also bought a truck big enough to transport fifty cows and hired a driver. He would usually follow the truck to Iowa in his car. Betty not only traveled with her father, but when she was fourteen years old she often traveled to Iowa and back with the driver of the cattle truck. She sometimes slept in the sale barns to see that the cattle were properly fed and watered pending the next day's sale. Soon, Babe hired his own auctioneer, Colonel Piper, a real flimflam artist, who taught him how to bid on his own cattle when they weren't fetching a high enough price. Piper would indicate bids from nonexistent bidders, often causing a bidder to bid against himself. Babe would sometimes wind up with four or five cows he had bought by their shenanigans, but he always managed to sell them privately at a profit before sundown.

Colonel Piper was a classic phony southern gentleman who feigned culture and a knowledge of philosophy. He sported a white mustache, long white hair, and six diamond rings around and just below the knot of his tie, which was also covered with samples of everything he had eaten in the past month. He never bathed and always smelled to high heaven. He often stayed in the Flanagan home, until Ola once again delivered an ultimatum. The odor was too much.

Babe tried to meet as much of Iowa's demand for high-butterfat-producing Jersey cows as possible. One afternoon in 1943 in Waverly, Iowa, he made five thousand dollars on fifty cows—an average profit of one hundred dollars per cow. It was an all-time record. While keeping the highways hot between Arkansas and Iowa, he was buying all the land that became available near the farm he had abandoned, usually paying thirty to thirty-five dollars per acre.

There was also a growing demand for Holstein cows in Arkansas because Arkansas dairymen were interested in heavy milk producers. So the truck became loaded with Jerseys going north and Holsteins returning south, and Babe making scads of money going and coming.

He was indefatigable. Like all cattle traders and mule skinners, he would take the shirt off your back and turn around and sell it back to you. He never indulged in formalities. He was profane, outspoken, and observant. He once said, "You can take ninety-three percent of all the people—no, make that ninety-seven percent—put them on your thumbnail and flip them, and it doesn't make a goddamn where they land. It's the other three percent that make the mare go." While that was a gross exaggeration, I fully understood his point. He considered himself in the 3 percent category.

His land holdings were becoming large enough that they needed more attention, so in 1941 Babe moved his family back, not to the farm, but to Charleston. He bought the old home formerly owned by Dr. Neissl. The three Flanagan girls knew all the new dances that were alien to us and they also had access to their father's big Buick. They were crushed at having to return to such a rural "bumpkin" setting, but we were smitten with their big-city ways. People would often remark that they could live on what the Flanagans spent on Cokes. This was the same family that was barely surviving a few years previously.

Betty was in blue jeans, cowboy shirt, boots, and hat the first time I saw her. She was with her brother, Callans, and they had obviously been working cattle and were going into a local café. Cattle ranchers around Charleston wore similar duds, trying to emulate Gene Autry, Tom Mix, and Hollywood cowboys, but not many women did. No woman ever looked quite as authentic, I thought, or as glamorous as Betty did that morning. She was trim and sloe-eyed and had a beautiful 110-pound figure. We didn't speak or acknowledge each other, though I knew who she was. She was sixteen and I was fifteen. I had the sinking feeling that her lifestyle in Ft. Smith—wearing fancy clothes (though not quite designer outfits), going to movies at the incomparably beautiful Joie Theater, and having access to a new Buick—put her beyond my reach. Even so, I knew I was going to try.

Carroll began dating Maggie, who had the best personality and was the flirtiest of the three girls. After first seeing Betty, I would see her occasionally as I bicycled by her house on my paper route, and I finally screwed up enough nerve to stop and try to get acquainted. This became a ritual, and though our conversations were casual and brief, I soon began to get anxious about whether or not she would be outside as I rode down the street approaching her house. She shared none of my angst or anticipation. She later told me she hadn't even liked me. I finally suggested that we go out with Carroll and Maggie some night. To my great surprise, she agreed, and thus the romance began. Several dates later, we clumsily engaged in our first kiss. She was still crazy about a boy in Ft. Smith who, along with some of her other former friends, came to Charleston frequently. It not only made me jealous, but I felt she was going out with me because "they" weren't around. But their visits became less frequent, and I soon began to feel I was winning the battle.

Soon, the boys eighteen and older began to leave for military duty. The war changed everything but Babe's cattle operation.

His business was considered essential to the war effort, so obtaining high-priority gas ration coupons was no problem.

In 1941, the Sixth Armored Division came to occupy what had just been completed and named Camp Chaffee. They came by truck, tank, jeep, and half-track from Ft. Knox, Kentucky. Betty's family home was the last house on the east end of town, and we all stood and waved at the soldiers one entire Sunday afternoon as they neared the end of what had been an arduous journey. Betty and her two sisters, Ruth and Maggie, were attractive teenagers, and it didn't take me long to realize it was not me to whom the soldiers were waving back. Fourteen thousand came, and at one time during the war, Chaffee's population was eighteen thousand. They later conducted maneuvers on and destroyed Charleston's thinly blacktopped streets, for which the city was never compensated. It would have seemed unpatriotic to complain.

Chaffee soon employed several hundred civilians, providing a shot of prosperity that would never have been thought possible by the locals. The Depression was almost over, though the national unemployment rate, 25 percent in 1933, was still 12 percent when we entered the war.

Maggie wound up in love with a good-looking Deutsche lad with gold bars on his shoulders. Archie Schaffer was from Allentown, Pennsylvania, and they were married shortly before he was sent to Europe, where he fought in several major battles. He left the army a major, came back to Charleston, and went into the real estate and insurance business. Within a little over three years, they had four sons. Archie became a pariah when he supported the opening of a liquor store in Charleston. In the election, the "wets" received two votes.

Chapter 6

The War Intervened

O n Sunday, December 7, 1941, Mother, Dad, and I went to
Ft. Smith to see an afternoon movie. Ironically, it was
Sergeant York, starring Gary Cooper. It was only mildly entertaining because Gary Cooper's contrived southern accent was so
awful that it was distracting.

After the movie, we went to Margaret's house, and as we
drove into the yard, my cousin Edith, a dental assistant and living
in Ft. Smith, bounded out the front door onto the porch, shouting, "The Japanese have bombed Pearl Harbor!" Of course, nobody except Dad had ever heard of Pearl Harbor, but everybody
was excited and anxious. None of us immediately grasped the
gravity of the situation, just as most Americans didn't, but it all
sounded ominous. I had visions of Ft. Smith being the next target
of the Japanese.

I was a junior in high school, and the following day, all the
high school students were herded into the study hall to hear
President Roosevelt address Congress and ask for a declaration
of war on Japan, Germany, and Italy.

The United States, throughout the remainder of 1941 and
most of 1942, suffered one terrible defeat after another in both

the Pacific theater and Africa, but America got its first big morale boost with the stunning U.S. naval victory at the Battle of Midway in June 1942. The United States made a strategic decision that the war in Europe must be won first, so the Pacific became a costly island-hopping operation. By early 1943 people began to allow themselves to think, for the first time, that the tide of battle was turning. Even so, there was a huge cost in human lives yet to be paid, and I was beginning to think mine would be one of them.

From the day Germany invaded Poland in 1939, I ingested all the front-page news in the papers as I folded them each afternoon. I became intensely focused on European and South Pacific geography, much more so than if I had had only an academic interest. I knew the names of all the Russian rivers, mountain ranges, cities, lakes—and many of the Russian and German generals. I studied the battle lines and carefully calculated how many miles the Russians had pushed the Germans back, or vice versa, since the preceding afternoon. I knew the sizes of the armies arrayed against one another and the names of the commanders on most fronts. As I studied the lines of battle, which seemed to change only glacially, I became obsessed with how the United States might become involved. After Pearl Harbor I knew all I had to do was reach eighteen.

I graduated from high school in the spring of 1943 and headed for the University of Arkansas to enroll in summer school. I wanted to get as much education as possible before being drafted. Carroll was already in basic training at Ft. Sill, Oklahoma.

Dad wanted me to take a lot of Latin because he thought it was essential to a knowledge of the law. It wasn't. He wanted Carroll and me to be lawyers for two reasons: First, he considered it the best training for a political career; and second, he believed that having a profession would always allow us to make a living without depending on an employer who could hire or fire on a whim. He said, "All you have to do is hang out your shingle and you're in business. No inventory necessary except a library and knowledge of the law."

I signed up for three hours of English and twelve hours of Latin. How does one take twelve hours of Latin? By meeting classes at 8:00 A.M. and 3:00 P.M. each day, five days a week, and going insane. There were only five students in the class, including a high school Latin teacher. I became so completely immersed in Caesar, Cicero, and Ovid that I translated Latin in my sleep, which was always better than when I was awake. I lived and breathed Latin every waking moment. I was a walking zombie by the end of the semester.

I registered for the fall semester, after having turned eighteen in August, knowing I would almost surely be drafted before I could complete it. I had hardly gotten my seat warm before I received notice to report to the induction center in Little Rock for a physical examination. I passed with flying colors. I was asked what branch of service I preferred.

"Air force."

"Sorry, all full up today," replied the army sergeant.

I said, "How about the navy?"

"Sorry, navy's full, too."

"Coast Guard?"

Wham! The stamp in his hand hit my personnel sheet, and when he lifted it, I was in the United States Marine Corps. I hadn't given the Marine Corps a moment's thought. I knew nothing about the marines except that they were fighting bloody battles in godforsaken places in the Pacific, Guadalcanal, New Guinea, Tarawa, and a host of other places nobody had ever heard of. I didn't bother returning to campus. I went home to make the most of my last few days of freedom. Betty, along with her sisters, Ruth and Maggie, had enrolled that fall at Iowa State, and Babe let Betty come home for two or three days before I left.

It was a chilly November 3 morning when the alarm clock rang at 2:00 A.M. My mother, father, and I got dressed, and I packed a small bag with enough clothes to keep me covered for the three-day train trip from Little Rock to San Diego. We walked the short block to the drugstore on Main Street, which had an arrangement with the bus company to sell tickets for a commission. We stood in the entryway of the drugstore, shivering and waiting for the bus. We made small talk to help ease our nervousness. I promised to write often, exacted a similar promise from them, and assured them I would be okay. There was no traffic, not one car, or one person to be seen, east or west, only silence in the dim glow of the streetlights. Even Keith Robinson, the faithful city street sweeper, who usually worked from midnight till dawn, was nowhere in sight. Finally, the reflection of what we knew were the bus lights could be seen over School House Hill to the west. Within seconds the lights of the bus crashed brightly as it topped the hill just a quarter of a mile away. Nobody spoke.

The reality of the moment was more unsettling than I could have ever anticipated. I was determined to be brave for my mother's sake. But as the bus came closer and began slowing as it approached where we stood waiting, she began to cry openly, "My baby, my baby . . ." Then Dad began to cry, something I had never seen in my life, and my apprehension suddenly turned to something akin to stark terror. I'm sure Dad and Mother felt they would almost surely lose one, if not both, of their sons. Only parents can fathom the unrelieved grief of such a scenario.

The bus driver indulged us our last hugs, kisses, and goodbyes. As I stepped aboard, and the driver slowly pulled the door handle toward himself, Dad said, "Son, be a good boy." I took the window seat near the middle of the bus in order to wave goodbye as long as possible. Then we slowly pulled away, and every single home and building suddenly had a new and added significance as I thought of never seeing them again. I remembered when this house was built, that one was remodeled, throwing papers on all the porches, the Methodist church, the Catholic church, Bollinger's grocery, and then the spot where Betty and I sat in the car in front of her old home, and, finally, Nixon Cemetery.

The 125-mile trip seemed interminable, but in reality it took about three hours. At different stops along the way, we picked up three or four other boys, also headed for induction. We would cover that same 125 miles within a few hours when we headed back west toward San Diego by train.

The stay in Little Rock was a few short hours, and then we were on our way. We began rolling westward through the Arkansas hills, and I grew sickeningly nostalgic as we sped through the town of Booneville, only twenty miles from Charleston and where I had stood at that very train station five years earlier, waiting to see the president of the United States.

Several boys—soon to be men—on the train were from northwest Arkansas, which even then was a big poultry-growing region. They were mostly uneducated, having finished the eighth or ninth grade, and were mostly "chicken catchers," whose job it was to get out to the chicken farms before daybreak, catch chickens in the long, narrow chicken houses by using a stiff metal wire with a crook on the end to hook chickens by one leg, put them into coops, and then load them onto trucks for delivery to the processing plants.

One of the chicken catchers was a twenty-year-old named Bill Elderton. He was six feet three inches tall, had an ingratiating smile, and was Hollywood handsome. But for his station in life, his company would have been much sought after for his looks, native intellect, and wry sense of humor. He was a gentle person, slow to anger, and unfailingly polite. His grammar was that of an Ozark Mountains eighth grader. He had been married only a short time and his wife was pregnant, so his all-consuming fear was of being killed without ever seeing his child. Bill and I had gravitated to each other in the Little Rock train station and continued the budding friendship through boot camp.

I had relatives in Shamrock, in the Texas Panhandle, and we had spent many summer vacations there visiting my mother's sister, Hassie, who had also married a Bumpers, Archie, a cousin of Dad's. They had moved to Shamrock during the early years of their marriage and settled on a small farm three dirt-road miles west of town, with only the road separating their front lawn from the Rock Island Railroad tracks. As a child, I had spent up to an hour at a time waiting for the train so I could wave at the engineer, who dutifully waved back. Now, at 2:00 A.M., as our train sped westward through Shamrock, I made my way to the open space between my assigned car and the one behind it to await the train's passage by my aunt and uncle's house. There was a full moon and the house, the mailbox, the windmill, and the picket fence were clearly outlined by the moonlight. Cherished memories flooded over me: The first time I ever steered an automobile was on that dirt road as my father held me in his lap, and where I watched my uncle slaughter a steer, the carcass to be peddled door-to-door. In a few short seconds, it had all come into view and was gone.

We arrived in San Diego at dusk three days later and were immediately taken by bus to the marine base with its beautiful Spanish architecture. The San Diego Marine Base was familiar to most Americans because it had been featured in virtually every movie about the Marine Corps. While it was beautiful, it was not to be where we would stay while in boot camp. Behind this beautiful setting lay another kind of architecture, wooden floors over eight inches of sand and covered by a tent big enough for four cots and four marines.

It was 10 P.M. when we left the mess hall. Platoons of marines were marching to the chant of DIs. We were taken to a comfortable barracks, then lectured and lectured some more about the corps, how proud we should be, but what a bunch of "shitbirds" we were, and how we'd be damned lucky to win the war with a bunch of trash like us, and how we would probably be killed because we were "too goddamned dumb to live." Finally we were allowed to bed down at 2:00 A.M., only to be awakened by reveille at 4:30 A.M. It was a harbinger of what was to be a very brutal ten weeks. Our drill instructor was a Georgia sadist named Sergeant Kelly. He had no first name. There are not enough adjectives in the English language to describe the viciousness of this ignorant, congenitally evil man.

The only time I ever saw Sergeant Kelly unnerved was one

morning when we fell out for roll call. When one man failed to answer, Kelly shouted an inquiry of the whole platoon as to the missing man's whereabouts. At first, there was total silence. Finally, someone responded, "He's at the hospital." Kelly, knowing he had brutalized the man the night before until he was semiconscious and that it was surely the reason for the man's hospitalization, immediately paled and obviously became frightened about just how bad off the hospitalized marine might be.

It turned out that the man had become almost comatose during strenuous calisthenics and beatings administered by Kelly and had been carried to the hospital by other buddies in the platoon. But Kelly's fears were unfounded. The man survived but was never returned to our platoon. I don't know what happened to him. What I do know is that while such things were not common, they weren't rare, either. I later heard that Kelly had received a mild reprimand from a captain. We had about a week's respite, but the slap on the wrist was a license for Kelly to continue his barbarism. Of all the drill instructors in platoons with which we had any interaction, none were in Kelly's league.

Three weeks after arriving at boot camp, I got a letter from Dad saying he had received a letter from the president of the University of Arkansas congratulating him on my academic record. I had made all A's in Latin and a B in English. Dad wrote that he had never been prouder of me, though I suspect he had never been so shocked, either. While none of us ever doubted Dad's love for us, he was never demonstrative or gushy about it. For him to say he was proud of me meant he was absolutely enraptured.

During boot camp, we spent two weeks at the Camp Matthews rifle range just north of San Diego. The standard issue was an M-1 rifle, which held eight shells in a clip. We learned to fire from prone, sitting, kneeling, and standing positions, from distances of two hundred, three hundred, and five hundred yards. The days at the range provided a respite, because Kelly had to turn us over to the rifle range instructor by day. Most were decent, dedicated men. We dreaded going back to the barracks at night, where Kelly had spent the day conjuring up new forms of torture for us when we returned. We had to "fall out" in our underwear at 2:00 A.M., do calisthenics, duck-walk, and perform other torturous physical acts. If Kelly went into town, we knew we were in for an especially rough night, because he always returned drunk.

During the last two days at the rifle range, each marine fired "for record." Scores were determined by where you hit the paper targets. The targets were raised and lowered by men in trenches at the varying distances. A bull's-eye was worth ten points. Anything outside the bull's-eye was less, how much less being determined by the distance from the bull's-eye. Completely missing the target was called "Maggie's drawers," the drawers being waved by the men in the trenches. A score of 340 was perfect. Not being a smoker helped my breathing, which in turn allowed me to squeeze the trigger more steadily. My score was 326, not only the highest score among the platoons firing for record at the same time, but the highest on the entire range for the preceding year. It was cause for considerable talk on the range and jubilation in our platoon. The Marine Corps even sent a press release back to the *Charleston Express*.

That evening, Kelly sent word by an emissary for me to report forthwith to his quarters in the front of the barracks. Normally, Kelly would have stood in the aisle (my bunk was a full barracks length away) and bellowed out, "Bumpers, front and center, on the double!" Sending an emissary was obviously a concession, but for reasons I knew not. When I got to his quarters, which was simply an open space, not a private room, he had three or four DIs from other platoons with him. I, as required, stood ramrod straight.

"Private Bumpers reporting, sir."

"Bumpers, tell these shitbirds what you fired today."

"Three hundred twenty-six, sir."

Whereupon Kelly walked around the room, taking money

from each of the other DIs. Obviously a bet had been made on which platoon would have the marine with the highest individual score. The money having been collected, he turned and presented me with a five-cent tub of ice cream and said, "Dismissed." I gave the ice cream to my friend Bill Elderton. I would have choked on it.

Before we left the rifle range to return to the marine base in San Diego, I wound up having words with a guy who had developed a dislike of me from the first day I was selected as a squad leader. I had no yen whatever to take him on, because he was bigger, more muscular, and, apparently, anxious to do major damage to me. Finally, we reached a point of no return, and he started toward me. Bill Elderton stepped between us.

"This ain't none of your business, Elderton," he said.

"I'm making it some," Bill said as his face grew redder and he clenched his fist.

The guy had hardly drawn back his arm before Bill landed a haymaker. The bully hit the deck and whimpered about being taken advantage of, but he didn't choose to continue the altercation. The bully never got a chance at revenge because one week later we were all headed in different directions.

At the end of boot camp, there was a huge parade on the drill field of the marine base. The buildings were spotless, and so was the drill field. As much as we had suffered and hated every minute of boot camp, suddenly there was a feeling of intense pride that we had made it as we strutted along in formation with all the other platoons in our group. There we were, Platoon 1070, sixty men marching past the reviewing stand to the strains of the "Marines' Hymn," shoulders swinging side to side in perfect unison. As a squad leader, I was the lead marine in one of the three twenty-man lines. After all the bitching we had done for ten weeks, enduring a barbaric psychopath, I couldn't believe the way I felt. I was even pleased to be promoted to private first class, which carried a twelve-dollar-a-month pay increase.

Before we were dismissed to board cattle trucks to wherever

we had been assigned, in my case Miramar Marine Corps Air Depot, we had to be reviewed while in standing formation by a short, stocky colonel who was obviously of German descent.

"Bumpers!" shouted Kelly. "Step forward."

I was already at the head of the platoon, so I took a couple of steps forward. The colonel came over to where I stood, and I saluted. Until graduation, we were considered too lowly to be permitted to salute an officer or even wear the coveted Marine Corps emblem on our caps.

"Bumpers, I understand you fired tree hundred twenty-six," he said. "Correct?"

"Yes, sir."

"Goot shooding. Dere won't be many Jap snipers in de trees when you get true wid dem, I bet."

Since I was to be a marine airman, I wasn't likely to be pulling sniper duty.

That was the end of boot camp. Before boarding the cattle truck that would take me to Miramar, Bill Elderton and I vowed to stay in touch. I wished him luck and said I hoped the baby would be a healthy boy who would never have to go through what we had.

The trip from San Diego to Miramar Marine Corps Air Depot, north of San Diego, took about an hour. Miramar was a holding pen for those who had just finished boot camp until they could be assigned to a marine air base for whatever future training the Marine Corps decided on. When we straggled into the barracks, we were greeted with what could only be described as a roar.

"You shitbirds thought you were going into the Marine Air Corps, huh? You got a surprise coming. You're in the Raiders." My heart sank.

"Belke's Raiders," he bellowed. "I'm Belke."

He was a massive man, six feet four inches tall, with a black mustache, who grunted between phrases and sentences. It was to be a six-week extension of boot camp. It was worse in many ways because we had nothing to do except wait for what new horrors Belke could think up.

Belke was louder and not quite as barbaric as Kelly, but he tried. The 2:00 A.M. fallouts, the duck-walking, the calisthenics, all were de rigueur.

A few days after arriving at Miramar, a much anticipated ten-day furlough began by taking a bus from Miramar to the San Diego train station. It was the first time I had been on my own in ten weeks, and I kept looking over my shoulder to see if they were gaining on me. It must have been the way an inmate feels on being released from prison.

The trip was three days each way, which left only four days at home. It was January 1944, and Betty's father had allowed her to come home from Iowa State just to be with me for that very short period. I was hard as a rock, my hair was about an inch long, and I found myself consciously walking stiffly to impress people with the fact that being a marine was no small thing. Two days after I got home, I began developing a moroseness about having to return. My mother's genes convinced me that when I left this time, I would never see Betty or Charleston again. Even so, the return trip to San Diego was not as traumatic as the first departure. I was a little more mature and seasoned, and my parents knew I had to get some kind of specialized training, which would require a few months during which I would not be in any danger.

After surviving six weeks of Belke, I was assigned to the Jacksonville Naval Air Station in Florida to become a radio operator preparatory to becoming a rear gunner in a dive-bomber. The trip took four days on the train cooped up in a cattle car—no showers, no shaving, no nothing.

Learning the dit-dot Morse code was easy for me. It all seemed so foolish—learning how to use a telegrapher's key in order to be a rear gunner. In truth, it was unimportant, but we had to be kept busy doing something.

I had heard that there was a dance at the First Episcopal Church every Saturday night, and though the girls were young, mostly high school age, and closely chaperoned, at least you could hold a girl for a couple of minutes for a dance. I made a beeline toward becoming an Episcopalian. I met Joyce Williams, the most sought-after and by far the best dancer. The electricity was instant and palpable. Soon, she didn't want to dance with anyone else, nor did I. Her mother was a chaperone, so nothing was going to happen, but getting to the church recreation hall every Saturday night became a week-long obsession. I wrote Betty to tell her I had won a waltz contest. She wrote back and said I was probably the only person who had ever won a waltz contest alone. I knew when I wrote that I was sending a message.

Training had been intense. Even after I became proficient in the Morse code, I still considered it an anachronism. We also learned semaphore, which was a method of ship-to-ship communication by flags. It was all utterly worthless. A navy chief petty officer was our instructor. He tapped the messages and we transcribed them. Sometimes the messages were funny, and as I wrote I wondered where he was headed. One was, "A sailor and a marine went into the latrine to use the urinal. When they finished, the sailor washed his hands and the marine did not. The sailor asked, 'Didn't your father teach you to wash your hands after you urinated?' 'No,' the marine replied. 'He taught me not to piss on my hands.'"

When my six-month stint in Jacksonville ended, I was transferred to Cherry Point Marine Air Base in North Carolina. Joyce and I had a teary parting, and for the first time we kissed and momentarily held each other in front of her mom. We were both brokenhearted. We promised to write often, and we did—for a while.

When I left Jacksonville, I knew all I would ever know about a telegrapher's key and very little about dive-bombers. Most important, when I finished radio gunnery school, I was promoted to corporal at a pay grade of forty-two dollars per month, a ten-dollar increase.

We arrived at Cherry Point around midnight the following

night and were assigned to prefab shacks that slept eight men each, with a stove in the middle. We were exhausted when we got in our bunks at about 2:00 A.M. At 6:00 A.M., we were awakened by a sergeant yelling for everyone to go to the hospital, that a hurricane was brewing. The hospital was a brick building that was assumed to be, and was indeed, a much safer place than the shacks. By 10:00 A.M., the winds were up to 70 mph, but that was the worst of it. A few shacks were toppled, but luckily ours was not. That was my first and last experience with hurricanes.

Shortly after arriving at Cherry Point in December 1944, I was granted a fourteen-day furlough, which ended just before Christmas. All the news was concerning the epic Battle of the Bulge, but on a back page of the Ft. Smith paper, a heading caught my eye. It read: WIDOW OF MARINE TO RECEIVE PURPLE HEART POSTHUMOUSLY. My friend Bill Elderton had been killed in the first wave of the First Marine Division's invasion of Peleliu, a small island in the Pacific and site of one of the bloodiest battles of the entire Pacific campaign, a terrible mistake from the outset.

I knew there was an excellent chance that Bill's worst fears of never seeing his child had come to pass. I wrote a letter to his widow expressing my deep sympathy, and of the thousands I've written since, that was one of the most difficult.

Since entering the Marine Corps, I had been corresponding with my lifelong best friend, Wendell Smith, who was now in the navy, and while I was keeping my promise to be a faithful correspondent with Joyce, I had also met a beautiful girl in Beaufort, North Carolina, and we had been seeing each other every weekend. One day I wrote two letters, one to Wendell and one to Joyce. Joyce usually answered promptly, but not this time. I got to thinking that I must have gotten the two letters mixed up, maybe put them in the wrong envelope. The letter to Wendell was mostly about my new love life and what a great dancer she was. About a week later, I got a letter from Wendell that began, "My dearest darling, I knew we were friends, but I had no idea you cared for me so deeply." I never heard from Joyce again.

At Cherry Point, I was transferred into an air traffic control unit. It was a radio system, a backup for the radar traffic control system. Again, it seemed out-of-date and even an unsafe method of guiding pilots, particularly a disoriented one. It was based on the strength of a radio signal from a pilot. If for any reason the radar system went out, or the pilot lost radar contact, he could contact us by radio and we would use the strength of his voice to determine where he was.

The whole thing was based on personal judgment. The operator could easily direct the plane away from the base instead of toward it. That actually happened, or was reputed to have happened, at about 2:00 A.M. one morning. A pilot was directed out over the Atlantic instead of toward the base in very bad weather, and the pilot and plane were lost.

I finally became eligible for a three-day pass, and I wanted to do only one thing—go to Washington, D.C. I wrote Dad and asked if he could spare fifty dollars for the trip, and, of course, he could. He was as anxious for me to see Washington as I was.

The day before I was to leave for Washington, President Roosevelt died in Warm Springs, Georgia, and the nation went into deep mourning. I seriously considered canceling the trip but decided it was much too historic an event to miss. I had bought my train ticket in advance with my own money. Feeling that fifty dollars might not be enough, I got into a game of blackjack on the train and promptly lost thirty dollars. Even though I planned to stay at the YMCA, I knew twenty dollars wasn't enough to sustain me. Fortunately, I had bought a round-trip ticket, but I had visions of having to tell Dad all about FDR's funeral, when all I had actually done was get off an arriving train and get on an outbound train headed back to North Carolina. My luck couldn't get worse, so I decided to risk all but five dollars. Within thirty minutes I had my fifty dollars, plus five dollars more. I thanked God for letting me win and left the game. I have never gambled since, except for a few small bets at the horse track.

Roosevelt's body arrived at Union Station after the trip from

Georgia, from whence it was carried to the White House. I was trying to see everything possible, and the following day, I stood in Lafayette Park across from the White House and watched the limousines disgorge their passengers and, about two hours later, pick them up. I had no binoculars, so I could only guess at the identities of some of the prominent men and women. I especially remember seeing Tom Dewey, whom Roosevelt had just defeated. In writing Dad, I embellished the whole story rather lavishly, but it was indeed a most memorable time.

I was smitten with everything about Washington.

Before leaving for Washington, I had scoured the barracks for telephone numbers of girls. One marine generously shared a number with me and wished me well. I called her immediately upon arriving, and after a five-minute conversation, she agreed to meet me at a restaurant the evening after FDR's funeral. The restaurant was the Casino Royale, though there was no gambling. It was on the second floor of a building and, by my limited experience, fairly nice.

We met at 7:00 P.M., and I was shocked that she was cute, personable, and didn't giggle much. My more immediate concern was my limited resources, which stood at about thirty dollars, five of which I owed to the YMCA.

When she asked me if I had "a preference in wine," I knew my entrée was going to be meager. I had never tasted wine, so I insisted she choose it. I didn't know the name of a single wine anyway. She asked if Mogen David was okay, and I assured her it was fine, though I had never heard of it.

The total bill, including the wine, was twenty-two dollars with no tip. After dinner, we walked to her bus stop. She lived in Silver Spring, too far for me, and I didn't have money for a hotel room. So I gave her a brotherly kiss and said good night. I walked to Union Station the next morning, bought a doughnut on the way, and hopped a train back to Cherry Point.

I was always strapped for money, so I advertised on the barracks bulletin board that I would iron shirts for fifteen cents each.

I didn't own an iron, but I had enough inquiries from would-be customers that I bought one the following weekend and thus began my first entrepreneurial undertaking. I was soon ironing up to fifteen shirts in an evening. It was hard work.

Someone told me that a marine in an adjoining barracks was making grilled cheese sandwiches and selling them for twenty-five cents. For ten cents, the PX sold cheese sandwiches that consisted of two slices of bread with one slice of cheese between them. All one had to do was put a thin coat of butter on the outside of the bread, slap it on a small griddle with a top on it, heat for about two minutes, and sell it for twenty-five cents. It was much faster than ironing, and after buying a used griddle, I was in business. I would canvass the barracks to determine how many marines were staying in and make a guess as to how many sandwiches I could sell. It was never less than ten and never more than forty, but a three-dollar profit on one evening was a land-office business. I sold sandwiches till we left Cherry Point and then sold my griddle for almost as much as I had paid for it, ten dollars.

When the war in Europe ended, I wrote Mother and Dad, "Today is V-E Day and a great day it is. I am very thankful for our victory and thankful Carroll's safe." Three months later, I was ordered to San Diego, where I would receive an overseas assignment. Everyone was heading for the West Coast to receive further orders. The massive movement of men and matériel to the forward areas of the Pacific, in preparation for the invasion of Japan, was just that, massive. After almost four years of experience, there was more planning, more efficiency, and fewer snafus. Despite the incredible might of the Allies, everyone felt the final battles would be the bloodiest in history, with every Japanese soldier and sailor fighting to the death for the homeland. There were estimates that the United States could lose a million men.

When we arrived in San Diego, we went directly to North Island, a U.S. Navy base from which most marines sailed. We were there for about five days when, on August 6, the first A-bomb was dropped on Hiroshima.

The San Diego paper was a Hearst paper, given to big headlines every day, but this headline was extraordinarily large. I couldn't begin to fathom the awesomeness of what had happened, and had no idea what an atomic bomb was, but I knew by the description of the damage that it might have the potential for ending the war much sooner than anyone would have thought possible. There was also talk that the story was not only embellished, but possibly a hoax.

We sailed at dusk the next evening, headed for an unknown destination. I stood on the deck of the small aircraft carrier near midship, and soon the only sound was the sloshing of the ocean against the ship. I moved to the ship's stern and looked back toward San Diego for almost two hours, watching the city slowly disappear. First the buildings, then the lights, and finally the reflection of the lights against the sky, until there was nothing but utter blackness in every direction. I suddenly felt a serenity I had never experienced before. My mother's Irish blood had never allowed me to fully enjoy the moment, but right then I was totally at peace with myself. I have heard it said that this serenity of feeling often visits the condemned man who finally realizes there is nothing more to fear, that time has run out; similarly, people with terminal illnesses, once they finally accept their fate, frequently experience a kind of inner tranquility.

At 2:00 A.M. on the morning of August 9, a B-29 named *Bock's Car* took off from Tinian in the Mariana Islands to drop the second atomic bomb on the city of Kokura. The plane was named for its usual commander, Frederick Bock, but on this mission it was commanded by Charles W. Sweeney. His orders were to drop the bomb only on a visual target, and when he got to Kokura, a heavy industrial haze rendered the city invisible, so Major Sweeney flew on to Nagasaki, where, at 11:02 A.M., the bomb was released. We had been at sea for two days, and our spirits soared with the dropping of a second bomb.

On August 12, 1945, I celebrated my twentieth birthday playing basketball on the elevator that carried planes from the hangar deck to the flight deck. But it was hard to concentrate on basketball following the Nagasaki bomb. It was becoming apparent that Japan had no alternative but to surrender. Nevertheless, accounts of Japan's final days were that the decision was highly controversial among many in the top military-political circles in Japan, notably with the warlord Tojo, the Japanese leader Americans hated most, who was later tried, convicted, and hanged.

I never knew our destination, but with the war ending, we pulled into Hawaii, and that's where I spent the next eleven months, doing mostly military police (MP) duty at the Eva Marine Air Base. A mesh wire fence separated Eva from Barbers Point Naval Air Station.

I had been promoted to corporal when I finished radio gunnery school in Jacksonville and sergeant at Cherry Point by playing end on a ragtag football team; then, with the war's end and so many noncommissioned officers being discharged, I was promoted to staff sergeant. This put me second in command of the entire MP detachment at the base and raised my pay to ninety-six dollars a month, a pretty handsome sum in those days, considering that room, board, clothing, and health care were free.

Our main function as MPs was to keep liquor from being brought onto the base, and we had to be ingenious to cope with the creativity of thirsty marines. Among other techniques, they taped pints of whiskey to their legs and in their crotches (they knew we tapped them on the legs below the knees with our nightsticks). We never reported anyone, but when we did discover a marine trying to conceal a bottle of booze, we simply took it and struck it against a big coral stone about forty feet down the fenceline. One night I was out checking the gates and asked about a man who was supposed to be on duty at the main gate but was not.

"Where is he?" I asked.

The Corporal said, "He's down licking the rock."

One day, I saw a notice on the PX bulletin board inviting anyone interested in Shakespeare to come to a numbered building on the following evening. Four other marines and I showed up, plus the teacher, who was a Harvard professor and Shakespearean scholar. He had decided to undertake this project because he was bored stiff. So a few bored people got excited about Shakespeare.

After a few introductory remarks, he recited Hamlet's speech to the players into the tape recorder. It was beautiful. Then he passed the tape recorder around and had each of us recite the same passage. I had never heard my voice on tape before, and it was shockingly pure, redneck southern. I found it difficult to believe I was so hopelessly "country" and totally lacking in emotion or inflection. My long-dreamed-of political career went "a-glimmerin'." I vowed to immediately start trying to improve my speaking skills, though I knew it would sound pretentious to friends back home. Over a period of four sessions, under the tutelage of the professor, I made progress. Time was limited, but I worked hard at improving my pronunciation. I learned to "saw the air," but not too much.

I was discharged in July 1946 at Great Lakes Naval Base just outside Chicago. I took the train to St. Louis and arrived with about five minutes to catch the train to Ft. Smith. I had my duffel bag, which was packed to the top, and had to run across a distance of twenty-six tracks filled with trains to get to the Ft. Smith train. When I got there, the train was a hundred yards down the track, slowly picking up speed. I was in excellent physical condition and desperate to get home. I took off as fast as I could run with a full duffel bag over my back. I was slowly catching up. A soldier was standing on the platform of the last car, urging me on. Finally, as I reached the rear of the train, and the train and I were going at about the same speed, I was able to hand the bag to the soldier, which helped me run a little faster. Then we locked hands, and when my feet were off the ground, I turned loose of one hand and grabbed one of the steel bars of the back railing. With the steady help and encouragement of the soldier and my determination, I finally climbed aboard. I had survived! I was going home!

Chapter 7

Law and Tragedy

Carroll was discharged from the army in May 1946 and immediately applied for admission to Harvard Law School. Dad could never have afforded Harvard, but Congress had passed the GI Bill, which, along with Social Security, were the greatest domestic initiatives of the century. It paid tuition and provided all books plus the princely sum of fifty dollars a month for living expenses for single veterans and seventy-five dollars per month for married veterans.

Harvard wrote Carroll that the fall class was full, but they would accept him for the fall class of 1947 if he used the ensuing year to get a master's degree. So we both returned to the University of Arkansas, he to get a master's degree and I to continue my undergraduate studies. The university was ill prepared for the huge increase in enrollment. Housing was critically short, and barracks-type housing was going up all over the campus. Temporary barracks built to house troops during the war were purchased from the government and moved on long flatbed trucks to college campuses to house the same troops, now students.

The university's enrollment had suddenly surged from fifteen hundred in 1943 to almost five thousand. Carroll, three other friends, and I rented a basement apartment, which required hip boots when it rained. The furnishings were only slightly better than we had enjoyed the preceding three years. The landlord had even thoughtfully provided double bunk beds and a stopped-up toilet to make us all feel at home. Rent was fifteen dollars per month, which left us thirty-five dollars for our meals, clothing, and having a good time. One of our four roommates, Neil Eugene Harlan—Gene to his parents and "Snake" to us—came from Bay Village, Arkansas, where he was one of six students in his high school graduating class. Bay Village was so small, the state maps didn't list its population. He had been Carroll's roommate before the war, and was there to complete his last year of undergraduate work. He would later follow Carroll to Harvard, but to the business school, where he would receive both a master's and a doctorate in business. He subsequently taught at the Harvard Business School until President Kennedy tapped him to be assistant secretary of the air force.

We had been a prolific letter-writing family during the war and began corresponding again after returning to school. Dad was a faithful correspondent, and Mother would insert her short messages on small grade school tablet paper.

Fayetteville was seventy-five miles northwest of Charleston, but Carroll and I chose to remain on campus most weekends. His work on his master's degree was demanding, and I was trying to achieve a grade-point average that would enhance my chances of getting into a prestigious law school. Betty had returned from Iowa State the summer of 1946, but then enrolled in the Chicago Academy of Fine Arts that fall. Our romance was hectic, and we spent a lot of time waving at each other from trains going in opposite directions.

The Christmas holidays were filled with embellished tales by ex-GIs, mixed with a lot of partying and dancing to Glenn Miller, Tommy Dorsey, and other swing-era orchestra recordings. Jitterbugging was the rage, and Betty and I had our own routines, as did most steadies.

Arkansas won the Southwest Conference football title in 1946 and played LSU in the Cotton Bowl in Dallas on New Year's Day 1947. My friend Dean Curlee and I drove to Dallas for the game and some serious partying. The weather intervened: It snowed, sleeted, and rained on New Year's Eve night. Downtown Dallas was deserted, and the next day, in a stadium filled with a lot more ice and snow than people, Arkansas and LSU played to a 0–0 tie. One of the dumbest things I ever did in my life was to sit out in that weather to watch that game.

The remainder of the school year was uneventful, and the following September, Carroll took off for Harvard. I returned to Fayetteville, and Betty took a fourth grade teaching job at the Charleston Elementary School for $125 a month.

Beer drinking was the rage on the campus, and I naively tried to develop a taste for it, which I had never been able to do in the Marine Corps. It was still a futile effort. In the spring of 1947, after an all-night beer-drinking binge, I took a six weeks' exam in an economics course and flunked it miserably. I knew a C would be the top grade I could manage in the course, so I dropped it.

I had also tried to develop a smoking habit when I was in the Marine Corps. Cigarettes were heavily rationed, and I was often the only nonsmoker in the barracks, so I was heavily courted for my ration coupons, worth one pack a day. Cigarettes were five cents a pack, and my reticence at giving up my coupons stemmed not so much from a desire to learn to smoke as from curiosity: I wanted to find out what magic lurked within the thin white paper that seemed to drive men crazy. It was difficult, because I didn't tolerate tobacco well at all; but finally I became addicted, even though I never truly enjoyed smoking. I especially hated the first cigarette in the morning and enjoyed the others that day precious little more. Betty had taken up the habit long before I did and thoroughly enjoyed it. In 1942, when I saw the movie *Now, Voyager* and watched Paul Henreid put two cigarettes between his lips, fire them both up while never diverting his scandalously seductive eyes from Bette Davis, slowly take one, and hand it to her, I knew life would never be as sensual or exciting for me until I mastered both the lighting and the look.

Many years later, at the age of thirty-five, I had managed to get my habit up to two packs a day and knew without medical advice or research that they were killing me, so I switched from cigarettes to cigars, Ben Franklins. Ben Franklins were paper wrapped and five cents each, and even though they were laughable to real cigar lovers, they gave me no cigarette hangover, and I could smoke prior to a meal without losing my appetite. I didn't inhale, but doctors snorted when I said that. I was assured that plenty of smoke was getting into my lungs.

Carroll's departure for Harvard in the fall of 1947 left a gigantic void in my life. He had been a great source of help to me in my history and political science courses. We corresponded regularly and mapped out plans for the Christmas vacation.

Dean Curlee also left in the fall of 1947 to attend law school at Northwestern and immediately began extolling its virtues and urging me to join him. I applied to three of what I considered the top ten law schools and by spring had been accepted at all three. I chose Northwestern because it was in an urban setting, and I had learned in the Marine Corps that urban life was something about which I knew nothing. I wanted to fill that gap, knowing I could never be president unless I had some understanding of and on-the-ground experience with big-city life and politics.

Carroll had no steady girlfriend, so when we were home for the Christmas holidays and summer weekends, he went out with Betty and me, along with a cousin, Bequita Bumpers. We went to a New Year's Eve party in Ft. Smith in 1947, and when we got home at 2:00 A.M., Carroll drove the car into the garage, rife with the smell of potatoes that Dad stored in the garage on a bed of straw to keep them from rotting. As an avid quail hunter, Dad always owned liver-and-white pointer bird dogs. The door to the dog pen was just beside the garage door. The quail season was in full swing, and Dad had been hunting two or three times a week.

When we closed the garage door, we heard Linda, a female

pointer, growling and snapping at her litter of six-week-old pups, a most unusual thing for a mother. She was extremely agitated, and for no readily apparent reason. Carroll opened the gate, went into the pen, scolded her, and cuffed her on her head a couple of times. Linda snapped at him and nipped him just enough to break the skin on his hand. It was a bizarre experience. Linda, a normally beautiful, friendly dog, skulked into a corner and snarled, only perhaps a little softer than before. The next morning we told Dad about her conduct, and he immediately went out to check on her. By this time, she was beside herself and beginning to foam around her mouth. Dog owners didn't routinely immunize their pets against rabies, and Linda had not been immunized. It seemed almost certain that she had rabies, and within forty-eight hours she was dead.

Carroll had to return to school earlier than I did and was gone when Linda died, so Dad and I loaded her into the trunk of the car and headed for Little Rock to the Arkansas State Health Department to get a definitive diagnosis. The state health department director personally took a hatchet, just like the ones Boy Scouts used, and split open the dog's head just as one would split a log. He took a tissue sample from her brain, left the room, and returned shortly to announce that Linda had indeed died of rabies.

There was little to debate about what should happen next. The doctors who were consulted all agreed that since the dog had broken the skin on Carroll's hand, his chances of having been infected were great and, therefore, rabies shots were imperative. The complicating factor was that Carroll had been bitten by a rabid dog when he was six years old and had taken the shots. Taking the required series of fourteen shots a second time carried some risk. Taking them a third time was sometimes fatal.

Carroll immediately found a doctor in Boston to administer the shots, but the doctor had a difficult time finding the vaccine. There probably hadn't been a need for it in Boston in years. Once the vaccine was found, the debate centered around whether the fourteen shots would be administered in the stomach, which had always been considered essential. The Boston doctor was convinced that there was no plausible medical reason for what seemed like a barbaric procedure and proceeded to give Carroll the shots in his arms, thighs, buttocks, and wherever he could find a spot he hadn't used. The side effects were horrendous. Carroll couldn't sleep, couldn't concentrate, and was horribly nauseated much of the time. He also started wearing suspenders because he couldn't stand the pain of a belt.

I arrived in Chicago five days before classes began. The next day, I met four or five students, one of whom suggested we go out to Wrigley Field the following evening to hear Henry Wallace, a former secretary of agriculture, vice president under FDR from 1941 to 1945, and now a candidate for president, on his newly created Progressive Party ticket. I was flirting with the idea of voting for Wallace, not because I knew anything about him, but because I couldn't abide either Harry Truman or Tom Dewey. It is a political anomaly that people will vote for someone about whom they know nothing rather than for someone about whom they know a lot, the assumption being "He can't be as bad as the others." I thought Tom Dewey was too superficial, unctuous, and overconfident, and along with millions of Americans, was repulsed by his Hitlerian mustache. I still can't believe he kept his mustache when the memory of Hitler was so fresh in the minds of every American. Truman plastered his hair down with Vaseline Hair Tonic, wore small, round, metal rim glasses, had a nasal twang voice, and chopped the air incongruously when he spoke, apparently trying to be dramatic enough to distract his listeners from his terrible voice and speaking style. I had also been offended by an incident in which, reacting to a music critic who had criticized his daughter Margaret's singing, he wrote the man an angry response and called him an SOB.

Three of us arrived at Wrigley Field on a pleasant September evening. I was anxious to attend because I thought I might see Norman Mailer, with whom I had spent an evening at the Uni-

versity of Arkansas when he had visited our mutual friend Fig
Gwaltney. Norman was a strong Wallace supporter, according to
The New York Times, but if he attended the rally, I didn't see him.

The Wallace rally made watching grass grow seem exciting.
After about two hours, Paul Robeson appeared. Robeson, the
great Negro basso who had become famous for his magnificent
rendition of "Old Man River" in the movie *Showboat*, had by then
virtually embraced communism. He sang a couple of songs, neither of which was "Old Man River," and then closed with "The
Internationale," anthem of the Soviet Union and international
communism. I was beginning to get nervous, because Commie
baiting was already in vogue and Robeson had a national reputation for being far left in the political spectrum. I had visions of
someone inadvertently getting a picture of me and later using it
to accuse me of being a Communist sympathizer should I ever
seek public office.

At about 10:00 P.M., to drumrolls and klieg lights rotating
against the sky, all spotlights suddenly centered on the ivy-
covered brick walls of Wrigley's center field. A door opened in
the wall, and a yellow Cadillac convertible rolled through and
began heading slowly around the infield, thence to where an elevated platform (a flatbed truck) had been placed at the pitcher's
mound, all to a standing ovation of about ten to fifteen thousand
people. Wallace dismounted the Cadillac and ascended the steps
of the platform. Considering the populist issues Wallace was
championing, the Cadillac seemed a bit incongruous. After a lavish introduction by some highly forgettable person, Wallace
began to speak from a script in a monotone voice. Wallace's syntax was unemotional, and his voice was unappealing, yet he spoke
and spoke. People began to leave, at first just one or two, then
finally a Leon Uris–size exodus, which seemed not to bother
Wallace. He seldom looked up from his prepared text. He obviously had a good mind but limited political skills. Even so, many
of his ideas were later adopted.

Wallace never received a single electoral vote and ran behind

Strom Thurmond, the states' rights candidate, in the popular vote. However, he would later be recognized as one of America's great visionaries in agriculture. When he suggested that there should be no such thing as overproduction of food as long as there are hungry people in the world, one critic responded, "Wallace wants to give every Hottentot a bottle of milk." President Truman would later defend Wallace in one of his lengthy interviews following his presidency, when he said, "Wallace was right. Every Hottentot *should* receive a bottle of milk."

About three weeks prior to the election, which all the pundits and pollsters had long since ceded to Dewey, the Chicago Democrats staged a "rally" featuring the president's cabinet. Tickets were being given away at the law school, which was a good indication of how hot Truman was running in Chicago. Three or four other political junkies and I attended on a Sunday afternoon at the Chicago Stock Yards. It was a disaster. Only two little-known cabinet members showed up, which almost exceeded the size of the crowd. If I had ever entertained any lingering doubts about the outcome of the election, they were quickly dispelled. However, two weeks later, Truman came to Chicago, and the local political apparatus pulled out all the stops. There were huge crowds everywhere Truman went, and everywhere he went he blasted the "no-good, do-nothing Eightieth Congress." Even the Republican bugle, the *Chicago Tribune*, called the enthusiasm surprising and said the momentum in Illinois was beginning to move toward Truman.

On election night, most of the Democratic students were more concerned about Adlai Stevenson's race for governor than the presidency. Stevenson's eloquence and urbane mannerism stood in stark contrast with Truman's raucous and rural ways. Early in the evening, it became apparent that while the presidential election would be closer than predicted, nobody was predicting the upset that was about to shock Americans as no political event ever had.

At about midnight, after listening to Stevenson's victory

statement, a group of us who had been following the evening's results on radio decided to walk the three or four blocks from the dormitory down to Michigan Avenue, where there would surely be some later news than we were getting. The avenue was crawling with people, and the newsboys and kiosk newsstand operators were all hawking the now famous edition of the *Chicago Tribune* with its banner headline screaming DEWEY WINS. I bought one copy because I thought the *Trib* had probably done a state-by-state analysis and knew something contrary to the information we had been getting on the radio. Of course, I have lamented all my life not being farsighted enough to have gambled and bought a hundred copies. I even threw my one copy away.

Norman Thomas, a quadrennial candidate for president on the Socialist Party ticket, was running again in 1948. He was a silver-haired, strong-voiced champion of the poor, and he championed economic decency (detractors called it "sharing the wealth") and more ethical business practices. While he was an avowed Socialist, to the unsophisticated he might as well have been a Communist. His name was well known in American politics. I had been shocked when I was an undergraduate to learn that one of my economics professors was an active Socialist and devotee of Thomas. Thomas's economic principles were wild for the time but would place him just left of center today. It was shocking to hear him espouse the proposition that one or two large grocery stores could give consumers a much better bargain than a host of small mom-and-pop operations because of the economies of scale. He maintained big retailers could buy in truckload or carload quantities directly from the factories at deep discounts and pass on the savings to their customers. Putting mom and pop out of business was a radical idea, but Sam Walton later founded Wal-Mart on that very principle. Sam, of course, considered his ideas to be free enterprise at its best. The professor also didn't care how high the price of any commodity might go (he always used a hundred-dollar box of matches as an example) as long as workers were paid enough that the commodity was in line with wages.

Norman Thomas received one vote in Franklin County, Arkansas, in 1948. Dad was chairman of the Franklin County Democratic Committee, and as such, he and his Republican counterpart (there probably weren't over a hundred people in Franklin County who would admit to being Republicans) had oversight roles in the counting of absentee ballots, two of which Carroll and I had cast. Carroll and I were home for the holidays following the election, and one evening during dinner, Dad told us that a vote for Norman Thomas had popped up in the absentee box. It was the only vote Thomas got in the entire county. Dad had heard Carroll and me both express our antipathy for Truman and some admiration for Norman Thomas, and, of course, he knew we would never vote for a Republican. Neither Carroll nor I had told Dad how we voted, and as he told the story, we exhibited a total lack of interest.

It was not a complicated case of deductive reasoning by which Dad concluded that one of his sons had cast that lone vote for Norman Thomas, the Socialist, though he could never force himself to accuse us. He told us about the *oohs* and *ahs* of the people doing the counting when the Norman Thomas vote was called out. Neither Carroll nor I said a word, continuing to feign total indifference. I had held my nose and voted for Truman, so I knew, but Dad did not, which of us had cast the lonely vote.

Chicago offered two exciting things for me that I had never anticipated: going to the Chicago Sunday Evening Club at Concert Hall and spending Sunday afternoons at the Lincoln Park Zoo with Bushman, the nationally famous silverback gorilla.

The Chicago Sunday Evening Club featured some of the greatest thinkers in America, and my favorite by far was Reinhold Niebuhr, theology professor at the Union Theological Seminary in New York. He was a powerful speaker, had a brilliant mind, and was the most respected theologian in the country. His theology was called neoorthodoxy, which is relating theology to modern times. His gestures when he spoke were those of a symphony conductor. I felt superior to everybody else after hearing Niebuhr and freely plagiarized his ideas.

Bushman and I were very close friends. We would spend hours staring at each other on Sunday afternoons. Unlike many animals, notably dogs, who can't make eye contact for long periods without moving, Bushman would stare for minutes at a time without breaking eye contact or moving a muscle. He would occasionally get up, amble over to an immense tractor tire, and turn it wrong side out. After a minute or two, he would resume a sitting position, and we would stare a while longer. I desperately wanted to know what he was thinking.

Bushman came to Chicago from Cameroon in the late 1920s. He died at the age of twenty-three in 1951, weighing five hundred pounds. He was terrified of snakes, and once when he escaped from his cage, the zookeepers used a snake to coax—or scare—him back into it. He now stands seven feet tall on a pedestal in the Field Museum in Chicago, and I never go to Chicago without going by to have a silent, nostalgic conversation with him about our unforgettable Sunday afternoons.

·   ·   ·

I have had two haunting ESP-type experiences in my life, even though I don't believe in ESP. The first was when I was on guard duty at the main gate of Miramar. A fellow marine and I were carrying on an idle conversation at approximately 6:00 A.M., and I suddenly changed the subject to ask him what he thought would happen if a bomber flew into the side of the Empire State Building. Would the impact irreparably damage the building, or would the plane just fall to the street below?

I remember his response. "What the hell made you think of that?"

"I don't know. It just popped into my mind."

A couple of hours later, a car approached the gate driven by a master sergeant. He had his radio on, and while I was checking his ID, an announcer interrupted the program to report that a B-25 air force bomber had crashed into the Empire State Building. Thirteen people had died, including the crew of three on the plane.

The second experience occurred on Sunday evening, March 22, 1949. Art Harris, my roommate, and I had been studying. It was about 5:00 P.M. when cars below our eleventh-floor dormitory room began making the all-too-familiar sound of tires on a rainy street. Our room was on the east end of the dorm and we had a magnificent view of Lake Michigan. It was that change of sounds that caused me to stop studying and go to the window overlooking the lake. There were no people below, only cars on Lake Shore Drive. A light rain was falling, visibility was poor, and I could barely see the Navy Pier across the way. I pondered the depressing dreariness of the scene for a while and then turned to Art and asked, "Have you ever experienced the death of a loved one, someone in your family?"

"Well, my aunt died a couple of years ago," he answered.

"No, I'm talking about someone in your immediate family, a brother, sister, or parent."

He shook his head and then asked, "Have you?"

"No," I said, "but it just occurred to me what a horrible thing it would be to lose someone so dear to you."

Dusk can be a lonely time, especially on a rainy Sunday evening. Neither of us said anything more, and we both returned to our books. Two hours later, someone came to the door of our room, which was open, and told me I had a long-distance call. There were two telephone booths in the hallway next to the elevator. Prentiss Ware, my sister's brother-in-law and a dentist in Ft. Smith, was on the line. He was a very soft-spoken man, so his words seemed fairly normal at first.

"Your mother and dad have been in a car wreck. I don't really know their condition, but they're in the hospital and I think you had better come home."

I knew he wouldn't suggest that I "come home" from Chicago to Arkansas unless the situation was dire.

I began asking all kinds of questions. "Where did it happen? How did it happen?"

He said, "Harmon and Bess were with them, and Harmon was killed instantly."

I went limp. Harmon and Bess Flanagan, Betty's aunt and uncle and Mother and Dad's next-door neighbors, had been with them on a trip to Vian, Oklahoma, about thirty miles west of Ft. Smith, where Dad and his brother Glen had bought a two-hundred-acre farm in the Arkansas River bottoms just a few months before. They were returning home after looking over the spinach crop, where harvesting was to begin soon.

It was dusk and the highway was narrow, with no shoulders. Dad was driving a Chevrolet, the first new car to come to Charleston after the war and for which he had paid eight hundred dollars. They had just gone through the small community of Roland, Oklahoma, a few miles west of Ft. Smith, and were heading up an incline that had a slight curve at the crest. An oncoming car with a roaring drunk man at the wheel came over the crest of the hill on Dad's side of the road. Apparently, Dad veered to the left since the oncoming car occupied his lane, and the drunk did what drunks almost invariably do. He simultaneously pulled back to his right. The two cars collided head-on.

I told Prentiss I would catch the earliest flight I could get on the next day. I was so addled, it didn't occur to me to call friends in Ft. Smith to get additional information. I didn't even call Betty, assuming she wouldn't yet know about it. Betty, after teaching one year, had returned to the university the preceding fall, and as it turned out, she and her cousin Bequita, also a student, had been home for the weekend. Home to Quita was Vian, Oklahoma, where Mother and Dad had been visiting, and home for Betty was Charleston. Quita had visited with Mother and Dad that afternoon and considered driving with them back to Ft. Smith, where she and Betty were going to meet and drive to Fayetteville with a friend. At the last minute, Miller Huggins, Bequita's boyfriend, decided to take Bequita back to Fayetteville. Betty arrived in Fayetteville first, and when she walked into the apartment, the phone was ringing. It was her mother, calling to give her the tragic news. When Quita arrived, they immediately got back into the car with Miller and drove to Ft. Smith. Betty found that Mother was in St. Edward Hospital, so she immediately went there and spent the night with her. Two women from Charleston, members of Dad's Sunday school class, stayed with him.

Air travel was still primitive by today's standards, but I booked a flight for 10:00 A.M. the next morning. The flight was harrowing. Planes had no weather radar, which created a hazardous situation: Many crashes could have been avoided had the pilots known they were heading into vicious storms. I knew the situation was dangerous because it was March 21, close to the height of tornado season. It was a terrifying experience, and I vomited in a bag furnished by the airlines for such contingencies.

Uncle Glen met me at the airport and was the first to tell me that Dad and Mother were both in critical condition and that Bess was in serious condition. Harmon, who had been sitting in the right front seat with Dad, was thrown through the windshield and killed instantly. Mother was in the backseat behind Dad, and Bess was seated beside her.

We rushed to Sparks Hospital, and when I saw my father, the man I had always assumed to be indestructible, lying in a semiconscious state, I was devastated in a way I never dreamed possible. Witnessing his murder could not have been more shocking. I was terrified as I looked at his comatose, broken body and realized how my life had been so dependent on him. I felt life would be utterly impossible without him. I tried hard, unsuccessfully, not to cry. Dad roused slightly, saw me standing over him, and asked, "How's Mother?"

"She's fine. She's worried about you."

He closed his eyes and showed no further interest or awareness.

We drove a couple of miles across town to St. Edward Hospital and repeated the scene, though Mother was in even worse condition. She was a collection of broken bones, obviously dying. The world in which I had been nurtured was ending, and neither I nor the medical profession could do anything to stop it. I was twenty-three years old and suddenly realized I was still a child, totally incapable of fully understanding, let alone dealing with, the reality of what was happening. I hated not being able to stem the flow of tears, but more than anything, I hated my immaturity.

The following day, Mother died at about the time Carroll arrived from Boston, less than forty-eight hours following the wreck. All the previous soothing words of friends—"It's going to be okay," "They're in the hands of fine doctors," "This is in God's hands," and other palliatives—had raised my hopes only slightly, and now that she was dead, I, for inexplicable reasons, resented what had been well intentioned but trite. All the soothing religious assurances were suddenly offensive. I didn't want her in "the hands of God."

Mother's funeral was held in the little Methodist church where she had taught a women's Sunday school class, where she had sat in the same pew every Sunday, and where tears had streamed down her cheeks on an Easter Sunday when I, along with seven other nine-year-olds, "got saved" and were sprinkled by the minister as we knelt at the altar in the front of the church. I had no idea what it was all about.

The minister at Mother's funeral intoned a series of banalities, and while he didn't know my mother well, he said one thing that was all that needed to be said: "Those who knew her best loved her most." Very few people, perhaps six or seven, knew her well.

Mother was dour and antisocial. She harbored an irrational dislike of Baptists and distrusted Catholics. She was both Welsh and Irish, and she never allowed herself a single moment of sheer unrestrained happiness, no matter how perfect the moment might be. She could always conjure up a tragedy in the offing. She could spot a tornado farther off than anyone.

Dad loved having a formal picture of our family made every two or three years. It was a major event for all of us to dress in our best, drive to Ft. Smith, and have Mrs. Mitchell take a finely posed portrait. Mother detested it, resisted it, and on one occasion, as we were dressing prior to departure for Ft. Smith, fell across the bed, feigning horrible nausea and sticking her finger in her throat in an effort to throw up. Dad understood the ruse perfectly. We completely ignored her and continued getting dressed for the trip. She finally got up, gave up, and finished getting dressed, and off we went, with Mother wearing the most pained expression she could muster.

Mother had very few friends, her closest being Miss Mayme Robinson, an "old maid" who was a deputy county clerk with an office in the courthouse. My father deplored their friendship and insisted Miss Mayme's goal in life was to convince Mother of how much happier she would have been had she remained unwed. Worse still, he suspected Mother of agreeing.

Despite Mother's piety, she loved it when Carroll and I came home from school on weekends and told her off-color stories, as long as they weren't too profane or vulgar. It was a contradiction in her personality, because she couldn't abide such stories if told by others. Yet she couldn't abide pretense. When the "summer revival season" began and the churches began advertising their approaching revivals with a picture of a well-coiffed evangelist in the Charleston paper, she would mutter, "They all think they're so pretty." Such finely posed photographs were a form of sacrilege to her.

When the Depression began, Mother had eleven hundred dollars she had saved by selling eggs, chickens, and butter, plus some money her father had given her. Her money was on deposit in the Bank of Charleston, and banks, including the Bank of Charleston, were closed and liquidated by the thousands. Mother lost every nickel of her eleven hundred dollars, and she never got over it. The only interest I ever saw her demonstrate in politics was when the man who had been appointed "receiver" to liquidate the bank ran for the Arkansas Supreme Court. She actively campaigned against him. He lost badly, but more because of an insipid-looking mustache than his poor stewardship as receiver of the bank.

With Mother's death, I somehow felt sure that Dad, who was never fully conscious and only semiconscious some of the time, would also die. I have been tormented all my life for not spending every minute with him, but I simply could not bear the emotional trauma of seeing him in that condition.

The orthopedic surgeon put a screw in Dad's sternum and attached a cord up to and across two pulleys, on the end of which he put a weight, believing it would lift Dad's crushed chest and allow his lungs to inflate. The contraption looked like an invention of the Middle Ages. It was terribly worrisome to Dad when he occasionally roused, and I am convinced it did more harm than good.

We spent sixteen to twenty hours each day at the hospital. A constant stream of friends came by daily, many offering to donate blood should it be needed. On Saturday evening, the sixth day after the wreck, the doctor said he thought Dad was some better. I could detect no physical improvement. He was still comatose most of the time, but I indulged myself the hope that he might make it. Betty's brother, Callans, had agreed to stay with him, along with a special nurse we had hired.

About 10:00 P.M., I went to Betty's sister's home utterly exhausted and fell into a deep sleep. At 1:30 A.M. the phone rang and I grabbed it before the first ring ended.

"Mr. Bumpers?"

"Yes," I answered.

"Your father has just passed away," the voice said.

Dad was easily the most admired and respected man in our small community. He was the pillar on whom so many leaned. He was chairman of the board of stewards at the Methodist church, had been president of the school board, president of the Commercial Club, and the man to whom most people turned in sickness and in death. People wanted him to deliver their eulogies, even though they carried their burial insurance with the competing funeral home. It galled him, but he always agreed to do it anyway.

The funeral was on Monday afternoon. The church was full

and a throng of people stood outside. Dad was sixty-one and Mother was fifty-nine, though Dad seemed much the younger. The preacher's words were not memorable and his delivery was unctuous. He was the district superintendent of the Methodist church for the western part of the state. We had no personal relationship with him.

The floral tributes were beautiful. The number of flower arrangements were scrupulously counted as a way of determining the stature of the deceased, and there was a record number for Dad.

All the business houses in Charleston closed the afternoon of the funeral. The funeral procession began at our home one block north of Main Street, from whence we proceeded south on Logan to Main. As we turned left onto Main toward the church, I saw Uncle Matt Jones pick up two long boxes in the entryway of the drugstore, obviously flowers for Dad's funeral. The drugstore also served as the bus station, and the bus from Ft. Smith had dropped them off.

I had always detested Uncle Matt, and so did Aunt Dora, his wife and Mother's sister. The hypocrisy of his carrying flowers to the church, obviously for a little attention, nauseated me. He disliked Dad intensely.

Uncle Matt had wanted desperately to be somebody, had once run for county tax assessor and gotten swamped. That was a few years before Dad was elected to the state legislature, and that's when Uncle Matt's jealousy had become all-consuming. He subsequently, for absolutely no reason, quit speaking to Dad. Driving a school bus would always be the pinnacle of his adult life.

None of this interfered with Mother and Aunt Dora's relationship. Aunt Dora endured her marriage, though she could hardly abide living under the same roof with Uncle Matt. She was one of my favorites and often took me fishing in Doctor's Fork Creek. She was a woman of great native intellect, funny and creative in keeping my brother and me entertained. She was a snuff dipper and could spit as far and as accurately as any man.

One day, Uncle Matt came into Dad's store and, without

speaking, motioned Dad to follow him to the back. Dad obliged, and Uncle Matt whispered, "Bill, I want to talk to you, but not here."

He then motioned Dad to follow him and proceeded through the store, out the front door, catercorner across the street to the drugstore, and down the side street to the trash heap in the rear, where the drugstore trash smoldered twenty-four hours a day, 365 days a year. He stopped, turned to Dad, and said, "Bill, I'm ready to bury the hatchet."

Dad said, "Matt, that's fine. You and Dora and Lattie and I have had some wonderful times together and we can again."

When Uncle Matt went home that night, he told Aunt Dora, "Well, I told Bill today that I was ready to bury the hatchet."

Aunt Dora replied, "I'm sure Bill hasn't a clue as to what you're burying the hatchet about."

That remark irritated him, and he never spoke to my father again. Aunt Dora never visited his grave after he died, a period of many years before her own death. I once asked her why. She said, "I couldn't stand him when he was alive. Why would I go visit him when he's dead?"

Carroll and I went to Uncle Glen and Aunt Floy's home in Vian after the funeral, and I slept fourteen hours without waking—a record till this day for me. The next morning we went to the farm, and roughly fifty people were harvesting the spinach crop my father had gone to see on that fateful Sunday nine days earlier.

The following day I wrote Dean Harold Havighurst, the law school dean at Northwestern, and told him I was emotionally shattered and would not be coming back to finish the semester. I sought permission to return for summer school. I received a very thoughtful and kind note in response, assuring me that Northwestern would welcome my return.

Harvard did not have a double semester program. The only tests given were on an annual basis, and if Carroll dropped out, he would lose the entire academic year. So he decided it was

worth a try, but it was a mistake. He found it impossible to concentrate and decided that even if he stayed, his grades would be
terrible. He was an academic competitor and couldn't abide the
thought. After three weeks he came home, and we spent the next
few months selling everything from silverware to the kitchen
table.

The drunk driver was charged with "negligent homicide,"
tried, and convicted in Sallisaw, Sequoyah County, Oklahoma.
He was sentenced to five years in the Oklahoma State Prison and
was released after serving three. Fifteen years later, a delegation
from the local Assembly of God church came to tell me that the
man who had killed Mother and Dad had "been saved" while in
prison and was now a preacher. He was holding a revival at the
local church in Charleston, and they would be most honored if I
would attend and "hear the reverend give his testimony"—that
is, describe how he found Jesus as a result of the wreck and his
subsequent incarceration. I declined.

Neither Mother nor Dad drank. My guess is that Dad might
have tasted alcohol as a youngster, but not after he married. One
of the real ironies of Mother's and Dad's deaths at the hands of a
drunk was that the Methodist church set aside one Sunday each
year for members to sign a pledge card saying they would abstain
from the use of all alcoholic beverages for the ensuing year. It was
called Temperance Sunday. After both Mother and Dad died and
I got my first chance to go to our home in Charleston, the first
thing I saw on the bedroom dresser were temperance pledge
cards, which Mother and Dad had signed the preceding Sunday,
just a few hours before the wreck.

We probated Dad's will, and the inventory of his estate
showed him to be worth approximately sixty thousand dollars.
Most of his small estate had come from a woodworking operation he and his partner had started in the warehouse behind the
store, making pallets for the army during the war. My share of his
estate that was immediately salable was about ten thousand dollars. That excluded the farm and what was popularly known as

the "locker plant," in which Dad had a 50 percent interest. It was simply a place to store frozen foods, mostly meat, in metal compartments. Locker plants are an anachronism today, but at the time they were about the only place where frozen foods could be stored. Freezer space in refrigerators was pitifully small, with room only for ice cube trays. Home freezers were unaffordable. The charge for a space at the locker plant ranged from twelve-fifty to fifteen dollars a year. Margaret wanted to sell her share, so Carroll and I paid her five thousand dollars for her one-third interest. We thought it would be a good investment to hang on to, but it turned out to be a loser, and we were lucky a year later to recover most of our investment when we finally found a buyer.

In June, I returned to Chicago and law school, after Betty and I had decided to get married in September. I had to discipline myself as never before in order to concentrate on my studies.

Betty was making plans for our wedding and attending wedding parties. We had agreed on September 4 as the wedding date, about two weeks following the end of summer school. Before I left Chicago to return home, I rented a one-bedroom apartment on Chicago's north side for fifty-five dollars a month. The elevated trains ran about fifteen feet from the one bedroom, and noisewise it might as well have run through the middle of it. The only respite night or day was when it snowed, which muffled the noise. There was a Murphy bed in the wall of the living room, and it quickly became our preferred bedroom because it was marginally quieter and the coal dust from Chicago's furnaces that seeped under the windows didn't seem to choke us quite as badly.

The night before the wedding, Genevieve Raney, a cousin of Betty's, had a prewedding party at her home in Booneville. As wedding party participants and a few relatives arrived, the mood was jubilant and the wine was flowing. But by 8:00 P.M., Carroll hadn't arrived. He had to drive fifty miles to pick up his girlfriend (now wife), Catherine, but he'd had ample time to make the trip, and I was becoming mildly anxious.

After Mother's and Dad's deaths, I had developed a phobia

about phone calls when everyone wasn't in place. At about 8:30 P.M. the call came. Carroll had been involved in a wreck. A man and child in the other car had been killed, and he was at the Franklin County Sheriff's Office in Ozark. He didn't know what to expect but would still try to get to the party before 10:00 or 11:00 P.M. It had been four and a half months since Mother and Dad's accident.

When he arrived about 10:30 P.M., he described the tragedy as almost identical to the one in which Mother and Dad had been killed. A hopelessly incompetent driver had come over the crest of a hill on the wrong side of the highway. He said, "The last thought I had before we hit was, Now I know how Dad must have felt." The other car was driven not by a drunk, but by the wife of a drunk, who had no driver's license, who had driven only a few times in her life, and who had been placed behind the wheel by the sheriff of Logan County with instructions to take her drunk husband home or get out of town with him. Otherwise the husband was going to jail. She headed for the home of friends in our home county of Franklin. The sheriff's action was incredibly irresponsible.

When the woman came around a slight curve on the crest of the hill she was on the wrong side of the road, and when she saw Carroll she swerved back to her right at the last second, barely scraped the left front of Carroll's car, lost control, and reeled down the highway about one hundred yards before turning over. Carroll's skid marks showed that he was perfectly aligned in his lane. There were eight people in the other car, the father, mother, and six children. The father and a four-year-old daughter were killed.

Like our parents, Carroll had never had a drink of anything alcoholic, not even a beer, in his entire life. Yet the judicial system failed him utterly for the most contemptible reasons. The following morning, a state trooper, whom we knew, came by the house and told us that Carroll would be held for a hearing to determine whether or not there were sufficient grounds on which to charge him with negligent homicide. We were stunned and incredulous. The physical evidence of how the wreck happened and the admitted ineptitude of the other driver were all irrefutable. The sheriff of Logan County had already told the prosecuting attorney the whole story. The woman, sobbing hysterically, told the first man on the scene of the wreck that it was all her fault, and he testified to that statement at the trial.

The prosecuting attorney who issued the citation was a former housemate of Carroll's at the University of Arkansas and a family friend. A preliminary hearing was held in Ozark, the county seat of our county. After one hour of testimony, the judge found no evidence to warrant a further hearing or grand jury investigation on Carroll's possible negligence. While Carroll had been exonerated, he was a physical and mental wreck from lack of sleep and anxiety. But, predictably, and almost immediately after the hearing, Carroll and Margaret, whose car Carroll had been driving, were served with a civil complaint by the wife of the deceased husband and mother of the deceased child, alleging negligence and claiming one hundred thousand dollars in damages. The complaint would have been laughable except that anyone who has ever either been caught up in our criminal justice system or received a summons in a civil action knows that anything can happen. The case was settled shortly for eighty-five hundred dollars by Margaret's insurance carrier. The carrier felt that it could not risk a case with a widow and five orphaned children in front of a jury.

Carroll's life was jinxed. Consider two series of rabies shots, the trauma of his wreck, and then the threat of a criminal charge. Later, his firstborn, a brilliant son, was a victim of grand mal epilepsy and committed suicide at the age of twenty. Carroll subsequently suffered a stroke and underwent eight hours of brain surgery in Phoenix and nine more hours of surgery in Montreal. He was permanently disabled in his left leg and arm. Later, in 1995, he was diagnosed with cancer of the colon and endured six months of chemotherapy, which had to be discontinued after two-thirds of the prescribed treatment. His weight dropped to 130 pounds, a 40-pound loss. Two years later, he had an operation to remove a match-size cancerous tumor next to his adenoid and lost his hearing in one ear. At about the same time, his youngest child, a beautiful daughter thirty-two years old, was diagnosed with multiple sclerosis. Through it all, I have never heard him utter a single word of self-pity about life being unfair or of having been dealt a miserable hand.

.   .   .

Law school was tough and boring. During the entire three years I was there, I was constantly flooded by doubts that I had chosen the right profession. Those doubts were ameliorated somewhat after I began visiting the Criminal Courts Building in Chicago, which I did with some regularity. There were always two or three murder trials in progress. The cases were exciting, and the tactics of some of the lawyers seemed brilliant to me at the time.

Professor Goldstein, our trial practice professor, knew how to make the course interesting. He had written the textbook we used. One day he asked me a question in class, and before I got four words out of my mouth, he said wearily, "Wrong."

I commenced again.

"Wrong," with his head in his hands.

I protested, "But Professor Goldstein, on page eighty-four of your book you say—"

He interrupted again. "Tear that page out."

I did very little job hunting my last semester, but the best offer I got was from the FBI. Two hundred and fifty dollars a month and a promise that I probably would not live in the same city for more than one year during my first ten years. It was an offer I had no difficulty refusing.

We were growing increasingly anxious to get started on whatever the future held when Betty awakened me at 2:00 A.M. and whispered, "I think I'm dying. I can't get my breath, and I feel like I'm going to pass out."

I ran to the phone and called the Chicago emergency squad. I checked her pulse, and it was racing at two hundred beats a minute. I called the operator at Passavant Hospital, where Betty worked as librarian, and told her I needed to call Dr. Flack, Passavant's premier cardiologist. I was shocked that she gave me his number, but better still, she called him for me. I told him who I was and gave him a brief description of Betty's symptoms. He said he would be there in fifteen minutes.

The emergency squad arrived within ten minutes. They streamed into our apartment like a Mongol horde. One put an oxygen mask on Betty, another monitored her heart, one went to the kitchen and started making coffee, and the others conversed about matters unrelated to why they were there. Neighbors began crowding in and silently, with their mournful faces and nodding heads, assured me Betty would never make it.

Dr. Flack arrived, and within sixty seconds he had listened to her heart and asked her, "Would you like to go to the bathroom?"

She said yes, went to the bathroom for about two minutes, and came out with her heart beating quite normally. The emergency squad and sullen neighbors departed, disappointed. Dr. Flack told Betty she had a condition called paroxysmal atrial tachycardia (PAT). He gave her pills to use if it occurred while she was shopping or working or whatever. He was reassuring and told her to go about her business the next time she had a similar episode.

We breathed a sigh of relief, believing it was to be an inconvenience at worst in her life. In reality, it turned out to be terrifying at times, dangerous a few times, and debilitating most times, wiping her out with stress and exhaustion. She would suffer such episodes over three hundred times over the ensuing forty years, some lasting for hours and several requiring visits to hospital emergency rooms. There were almost as many "cures" for her runaway heart as there were doctors who tried to stop it: holding her breath, straining, gagging, putting her hands in a big pan of ice water, and (most effective) putting pressure on the carotid arteries in her neck. The episodes began in an instant, almost always between midnight and sunup, and ended the same way. Over a period of years, I became the world's authority on carotid artery massage. Betty would sit on the floor between my legs while I sat on the bed or in a chair. I would use two to four fingers to press the carotid artery in the right side of her neck until she raised her finger, a system we devised, indicating she was getting faint. I would let up for a bit and then begin again. The object was to force blood back into the partially filled atria so the heart didn't have to race trying to pump enough blood from a half-filled chamber. I was successful in converting her heart to normal about 95 percent of the time. We went to the hospital emergency room the other times. It was a living hell, especially when she became pregnant or when I was in the middle of a hot campaign and she was in one part of the state and I was in another.

In 1995, Betty made an appointment to see Dr. Bernard Gersh, chief cardiologist at Georgetown University Hospital. After hearing her forty-year history of periodic terror, he prescribed a new drug for her, and she hasn't had an episode since. In addition to becoming our savior, Dr. Gersh later became a close friend.

He is now back at the Mayo Clinic from whence he had come to Georgetown. Constantly living with the stark terror we knew was always near is indescribable, just as is the relief we have enjoyed the last seven years.

Chapter 8

A Financial Disaster

Betty and I were packed and ready to head for Arkansas when I finished my last class. I didn't wait for my diploma. It was mailed to me later with a note enclosed that said I was also entitled to a juris doctor (JD) degree, but that it would cost twenty dollars. I couldn't spare twenty dollars, but a few years later, Northwestern sent it to me gratis.

When I received my law license, I became the entire South Franklin County, Arkansas, Bar Association and was flat broke. Charleston had three and sometimes four lawyers when I was a lad, but as they died off, nobody replaced them, and now there were none. I had no idea of how to begin practicing law. I had no office, no library, and no clients, and, of course, advertising was prohibited.

When Dad died, we sold his 50-percent share of the Charleston Hardware, Furniture and Appliance Store to his partner, Herman Adams. Now, two years later, Herman was desperate for cash because a separate manufacturing business he had started, similar to the one he and Dad operated during World War II, was headed belly-up. The store was the only asset he had left, and as it turned out, it was not an asset until I stupidly bought it and made it one, for Herman, not me. I had never known much about

Dad's business, but I knew there was a lot more inventory when we sold it to Herman than there was now, two years later.

Betty and I had been living from one GI Bill check to the next, plus my small income from part-time work and her income from designing and modeling dresses for Reliance Manufacturing Company. I learned from her that thousands of dollars could be saved by reducing the sweep of skirts by an inch or two.

My experience in the business world was limited to dealing with businessmen in a strange, part-time job I held my last year in law school. It was with the National Taxpayers Equality Association, a lobbying organization financed mostly by banks and agricultural businesses that wanted their competition, namely savings and loan associations and agricultural cooperatives, to pay taxes at the same rate they did. The association operated a phone bank, and my job was to raise money for the association by raising the hackles of these disgruntled people by calling and telling them how unfairly the government was treating them. It was an early version of today's telemarketing.

I could work whatever hours I chose, and I always chose afternoons following my last class. We were paid three dollars an hour, which was exactly twice the most money I had ever made in my life (I had worked in a laundry my first semester, for which I was paid half that amount). Because of time zones, we always started with calls to the East Coast and moved westward with the clock. A solicitation letter signed by a Mr. Taylor, the president of the organization, preceded our calls by a week or two, so we all used the name Taylor. When the operator got the party on the line, she would say, so the other party could hear, "Mr. Taylor, I have Mr. Jones on the line," whereupon I would go into my scripted spiel: "Mr. Jones, my name is Taylor, T-a-y-l-o-r. You recently received a letter from me . . ." It was all scripted, but by the time I made a few calls, I knew it so well that I began improvising and engaging in friendly banter and discussing topical events.

It was a nerve-racking job, and I soon hated it. I slept fitfully, dreaming of the script and hating the repetitiveness of it all. The supervisor was drunk most of the time. Some people became irate if they felt we were calling too often or complained that we weren't accomplishing anything. One of my first calls was to a cotton compress owner in Amarillo, Texas. By the time I got "My name is Taylor" out of my mouth, he yelled, "You people waste so goddamned much of my money on mail and phone calls, no wonder you can't get anything done. The next time you call me I'm going to personally come to Chicago, tear off one of your goddamned legs, and beat you to death with it."

I had heard that phrase many times, but this time I believed it. I had one conversation with an acquaintance who was a banker in Ft. Smith, Arkansas. He never recognized my voice, and I never revealed my identity.

One afternoon about six months later, the downtown operator said in her syrupy sweet voice, "Mr. Taylor, I have Mr. Reynolds for you."

I said, "Mr. Reynolds, my name is Taylor, T-a-y-l-o-r," and that's all I got out before Mr. Reynolds screamed, "Goddammit, Taylor—!" I suddenly remembered his name and voice and knew he was the man in Amarillo. I silently disconnected him, took off my earphones, hung them up, and walked out, never to return.

I was desperate to start making money quickly and knew building a law practice would take time, so I started negotiating with Herman to buy back the store. He offered it to me for less than he had paid us for it two years earlier. I was to assume his outstanding accounts payable, which amounted to about ten thousand dollars. To say I was naive would be a monumental understatement. I didn't even bother to take an inventory to determine what I was getting. What I was getting turned out to be about a fifteen-thousand-dollar inventory, considerably shy of Herman's assurance that it was at least twenty-five thousand dollars. So when I paid fifteen thousand dollars for the business, I got an inventory worth the same amount, but I had also assumed ten thousand dollars in accounts payable. Thus, I was technically bankrupt to the tune of ten thousand dollars. I had borrowed all of the fifteen thousand dollars—two thousand from Babe, five thousand from Carroll, and eight thousand from the bank. This was a very auspicious beginning for the new lawyer in town. All I could do was pray nobody found out about my inexcusable incompetence. I was the new guru in town who had come to advise people on how not to get hornswoggled in business deals.

Herman was selling tent stakes and wooden pallets to the army. Three years after I bought the store, Herman was in dire financial straits. He said the army was slow in paying its bills. In his desperation for operating capital, he made a deal with the First National Bank in Ft. Smith. It was this: As he made shipments to the army, he would immediately assign the bank the payment he was to receive from the army. In turn, the minute the shipment was made, the bank would advance him 95 percent of the invoice, and the army would pay the bank the full amount of the invoice when it fell due thirty days later. So the bank would make 5 percent per month. At least, that was what they were supposed to make. But not long after the deal was made, the bank managers noticed the army was taking up to sixty days, and sometimes longer, to pay the invoices, so they called the army to complain. The army assured the bank that it was quite current on its bills. In going over the unpaid invoices with the army, the bank discovered it was holding over one hundred thousand dollars' worth of phony invoices from Herman on goods that had never been shipped.

I was representing Herman at the time, and since the case was cut-and-dried, we had no choice but to plead with the bank not to prosecute. The morning we walked into the bank to "confess" and plead, every adding machine—indeed, every machine except the air conditioner—fell silent. All eyes were riveted on us. Herman wept as the banker told him of his disappointment, but he made no excuses. The bank shut Herman down, but they never attempted to prosecute him. He would have had to plead guilty, but even the publicity of a plea would have been humiliating to the bank—when the public and its shareholders found out how

easily they had been duped. I felt better knowing the biggest
bank in western Arkansas was in my league when it came to getting conned.

I later represented Herman in a case against the government
in which he alleged that the arbitrariness of a government inspector had caused him to go broke. There were other factors
involved, of course, but Herman got lucky again, because the
inspector was indeed a certified nut. He routinely rejected shipment after shipment of wood tent stakes, alleging that either the
moisture content was too high or the measurements were off by a
"frog hair." Of course, tent stakes were made for one reason—to
be driven into the ground with a sledgehammer. I filed suit in the
U.S. Court of Claims, and after seven years and a one-week trial,
the court found the inspector's actions totally arbitrary and capri-
cious. We got a judgment for eighty thousand dollars. It took almost two years to collect because we had to get an appropriations
bill passed by U.S. Congress, and even then we did not receive
one cent of interest for our two-year wait.

I had started operating the store around June 1, 1951, and the
next six months were disastrous. Business in Charleston was terrible. There was one day when only three customers came in and
total sales for the day were twelve dollars.

For the first few years I owned the store, I owed more people
than I didn't owe, and many suppliers would only ship merchandise COD. My banker generously allowed me to run overdrafts
of as much as five thousand dollars until a state bank examiner
discovered the practice and demanded a halt to it. My life immediately became even more difficult. I was miserable, sleeping
about four hours a night, and my only option was to dig myself
out of the hole as best I could. That would require years, and I
was ready to quit thinking about a political career. As a matter of
fact, the business had become such a disaster, I wondered how I
could ever build a law practice.

Betty and I had moved into a rent-free, tiny house that belonged to her father. It was barely habitable. We sweltered in the

summer and froze in the winter, with cold air blowing in under the doors and around the windows. We had a few pieces of worn-out furniture that had been given to us by Betty's family. The living room had a couple of wooden chairs and a small coffee table. On Christmas Eve 1951, I brought home an ugly green sofa from the store, having concluded I would never be able to sell it. The retail price was seventy dollars. We were so happy with the pitiful green sofa that we never strayed more than a few feet from it. It is amazing how something as simple as a cheap piece of furniture can loom so large in one's life. December sales of eight thousand dollars provided a little breathing room. That was double the amount of any preceding month.

My first law office was an unenclosed cubicle in the back of the store. I had two homemade, four-shelf bookcases and four or five books from law school with which to fill them. I also had a desk and a personal secretary, who doubled as the store bookkeeper. It was not uncommon to be visiting with a client while within ten feet a customer would be weighing up a pound of nails or searching for a certain size bolt.

My first client was an elderly man who was selling a piece of property and wanted a deed prepared. When he came back the next day to pick it up, I told him the fee was five dollars. He threw a tantrum and temporarily refused to pay, saying, "Why, it ain't nothin' but a bunch of writin'."

Returning to one's small hometown to practice a profession dealing with people's lives and property can be a very bad idea. Too many people think of you as the towheaded kid they watched grow up. The most common remark from people who entered my cubicle was, "Ain't you a sort of a lawyer?" They didn't know how accurate they were.

After about three years, my annual gross (not net) income had gone from sixty to twelve hundred dollars, so I decided it was time to upgrade. I rented a vacant office in the back of the bank for fifteen dollars a month. Best of all, I got access to the bank's rest room.

One reason my law income was so sparse was that I was having to spend an inordinate amount of time just keeping the doors open at the store. It was a touch-and-go operation and remained so for several years. I had been technically bankrupt from the beginning, but my upbringing made declaring bankruptcy unthinkable. For the first eight years, I could practice law only part-time while running back and forth between my office and the store. If a customer came in wanting a new refrigerator or washing machine, he and a store employee would haggle over the price; finally, when the employee didn't feel authorized to make any further concessions, he or she would call and I would drop everything and run down and across Main Street and try to close the deal. Once the sale was made, the employee and I would load up the appliance in a dilapidated pickup truck and deliver it, usually to a rural area miles away. Occasionally I would lose a sale because I'd have a client in the office who I felt was worth more than the profit on a dinette, sofa, television set, or refrigerator. Even under such chaotic conditions, I was winning a few cases and my law income began to grow at a rather rapid clip.

My mentor when I first started practicing law was a stentorian-voiced country lawyer named Mark Woolsey, who practiced in the principal county seat, Ozark. He once told me about a jury trial in a criminal case that had deliberated for an undue length of time, obviously unable to reach a verdict. An old man came up to him and told him he was sure eleven of the jurors favored his client, but that a certain juror, whom he named, was holding out. Mark replied, "I don't understand that. I can't ever remember doing a favor for that feller." Perverse but unassailable logic.

Mark was an iconoclast, an agnostic, and maybe an atheist. When his wife died, I stopped by his home a couple of weeks later to express my condolences, and we were soon in a philosophical discussion on death. He was going through sympathy cards he had received and would comment on the messages on them.

"Now here's one that's interesting. Look at this. It says, 'She's not dead, she's just a-sleepin'.' Hell, she's not a-sleepin', she's dead as a mackerel and a-layin' in her grave." He prefaced many of his words, mostly verbs, with "a," pronounced "uh."

"Now, here's another one that shows her a-sittin' in the crest of a quarter moon, like it's a porch swing. But, Dale, she's not a-sittin' on the moon. She's dead and in her grave. Why in the hell do people send out trash like that?" One day he said, "Dale, if somebody made a twenty-four-hour movie that began with the beginning of time and ended today, by the time it got to Jesus, you'd be a-gettin' up to put your coat on to leave."

He remarried six weeks after his wife's death.

Mark and I were adversaries once in a divorce case, and court was to convene at 9:00 A.M. Mark didn't show until about 9:15 A.M., and in explaining his tardiness to the judge, he said, "Your Honor, I'm sorry about being late, but I had a man come into my office to discuss a case with me, and he was a-holdin' a twenty-dollar bill in his hand. And, Your Honor, it took me a little longer to get that twenty-dollar bill than I thought it would."

Mark chuckled, thinking the judge would find the story amusing. He didn't.

"Mr. Woolsey," the judge said sternly, "the next time you're late in my court, you will lose that twenty-dollar bill and four more just like it."

Mark once defended a woman and her lover who were charged with conspiracy to murder her husband. Ozark had a pool hall with a room in the back that was rented by the hour to anyone wishing to tryst for an hour or two. The prosecutor had the pool hall owner on the witness stand, describing his rental of the room to the defendants.

Prosecutor: What day of the week was it?

Pool hall owner: Saturday morning. Nice, clear day.

Prosecutor: Now, describe for the court and jury what happened.

Pool hall owner: Well, they come in about eleven in the morning to rent the room. So I let 'em have it for two hours for three dollars. Then I sold the guy a package of condoms. They stayed almost two hours and left.

Mark began his cross-examination of the pool hall owner.

Mark: Now, you say it was a clear Saturday morning.

Pool hall owner: Yes, sir.

Mark: And you rented the room for two hours?

Pool hall owner: Yes, sir.

Mark: For three dollars?

Pool hall owner: Yes, sir.

Mark: And you sold the man a package of condoms?

Pool hall owner: Yes, sir.

Mark: Is that what us ole country boys call rubbers?

Pool hall owner: Yes, sir.

Mark: Now, what brand were they?

Pool hall owner: What do you mean?

Mark: I mean just what I said. Were they Trojans, Sheiks, what brand?

Pool hall owner: I don't remember.

Mark: Now, isn't that interesting. You remember the day, Saturday. You remember it was eleven o'clock. You remember it was a clear day. You remember what you charged them, three dollars, and how long they stayed, but you don't even remember the brand of rubbers you sold them.

Pool hall owner: Hell, Mark, I don't even remember the brand I sold you the last time you came in.

Pandemonium broke out and the judge had to declare a recess.

●   ●   ●

The businessmen in Charleston had formed a Lions Club in 1925 but dropped the national affiliation during the Depression because they couldn't afford the national dues. They then changed their name to the Commercial Club.

In 1953, the Commercial Club decided that if Charleston was ever going to make it in the big time, we would have to install a stoplight at the one intersection on Main Street. The city council agreed. Nobody would respect a town that didn't even have a stoplight. Of course, there was no traffic that needed stopping, but the city fathers thought it would provide a more urbane and sophisticated atmosphere. Until we got our very own streetlight, we had to drive eighteen miles to Paris on Saturday night to watch their light change. We finally got the light, but it had only two colors, red and green—no caution light. Of course, there was seldom enough traffic for more than one car to ever have to stop. Even people in Charleston grew tired of stopping when there wasn't a car in sight in any direction, but when the Arkansas State Highway Department ordered it removed, we strenuously objected. Ultimately we lost the battle, and our pride was severely wounded.

When television first became popular, Tulsa was our closest station, but it was 150 miles away, and all we got was snow on our screens. We would stare at the snow for long periods, hoping for the outline of a picture. Trying to watch Adlai Stevenson's acceptance speech around midnight in 1952 was maddening, as his voice and face faded in and out. TV sets were primitive, built with cathode ray tubes, which were constantly burning out. Finally, Ft. Smith, only twenty-three miles away, got a UHF station that gave us a relatively good picture.

Bonanza, which aired on Sunday nights, was everybody's favorite show. If a TV set I had sold zonked out on Sunday, I might have to travel ten miles into the country with my repair kit, get the hell shocked out of me because I didn't know what I was doing, and get the TV up and running before *Bonanza* came on. A customer missing *Bonanza* on Sunday evening could result in a permanently lost customer. Betty, our two sons, and I would go to the store on Sunday night to watch *Bonanza* and invite our friends to join us. I could afford only two or three television sets at a time in my inventory. We usually attracted a crowd of up to twenty people. When I sold a television set, I also had to install it, and in the days before cable television, that meant putting a fifty-foot-long galvanized pipe pole on the cone of a roof, with an antenna mounted on top of it. Some roofs were metal, which made climbing around on them treacherous, but almost all of them were dangerous. My helper and I wore tennis shoes to minimize the risk of sliding off.

One morning I rushed home following an antenna installation, ran into the house to put on a suit and tie in preparation for a court appearance scheduled in Russellville, sixty miles away, and I was running late. As I ran out of the house, Betty shouted, "Where are you going?" I shouted back that I had a trial scheduled for one o'clock. "You idiot! You still have your tennis shoes on!"

Between weekly *Bonanza* episodes, I tried to build a law practice. Uncontested divorces were seventy-five dollars and contested ones a hundred dollars. If I represented the husband, I could usually get a fee up front. If I represented the wife, usually a homemaker who had never worked and was totally dependent on her husband, I had to get a court order to require the husband to pay support and the wife's attorney's fees. But getting a court order was one thing and getting the money was quite another. It was usually more trouble than it was worth, and even a judge's admonition to the husband that jail would be his next abode if he didn't comply with the court's order was seldom sufficient inducement to jar him loose from a hundred bucks. One reason husbands didn't honor court orders was that they didn't have the money and had no way of getting it. The husband often viewed his wife's lawyer as a co-conspirator with his ungrateful and sometimes adulterous wife. The lawyer was also seen as an aider and abettor in alienating the children from their father. The husband's unrelieved misery, wild imagination, and sleepless nights made him dangerous. His rage would often drive him to uncontrollable viciousness, landing the lawyer, the wife, or both in either the hospital or the morgue.

I once represented a woman whose story of abuse indicated to me that her husband was psychotic. I filed a divorce complaint for her without a dime up front. Three days later, I received a call from a prominent divorce lawyer in Ft. Smith named Martin Green. Martin told me he was representing the husband, whom he described as a very decent guy who loved his son above life it-self and was desperate to see him (I had obtained a restraining order that barred him from seeing the wife or child). Martin said the husband was in his office and wanted to talk to me and tell me personally how much he loved his son. I told Martin I didn't question his love for his son, but that I didn't want to talk to his client without my client being present. Before I could object fur-ther, the husband was suddenly on the line, chanting, "I wan' see my boy. I wan' see my boy." He was every bit as nutty as I had an-ticipated, and I now concluded he was also as dangerous as a one-eyed water moccasin. If a wife has been unfaithful, a husband is sometimes dangerous, but this case was not about adultery. Be-fore I could get a preliminary hearing to ask for my fee and sup-port for the wife and child, the couple reconciled, and I had not received a farthing for my efforts.

A few months later they separated again, and the wife again came to my office, sobbing uncontrollably. I declined the case, not because she had no money, but because I knew her husband was a lunatic. She obtained counsel in a nearby community and again filed for divorce. A few days later, at about 3:00 P.M., my secretary came running into the office, returning from the post office just a block away, and said she had just seen the Decker girl's husband trying forcibly to take her little boy away from her. The mother had managed to hang on to the child, jump in her car, and head for her parents' house, which was only four blocks from my home. As the story later came out, she arrived there with her husband in hot pursuit in his pickup truck. The wife's mother, seeing the husband coming down the narrow dirt street, took the child and hid in a bedroom closet. The husband jumped out of his truck, shotgun in hand, and walked into and through one side of the house. The wife ran frantically out the front door while her husband searched for her in a back room. He appar-ently heard the front door slam and hurried back to the front porch as his wife raced across the front yard, trying to escape. He raised his shotgun to his shoulder, aimed, and shot her down like a quail on the wing before she could reach the street. At about the same time, the wife's father, who had gone out the back door, came around the corner of the front of the house, only to be confronted by the husband on the porch, who summarily executed him. At about that time, the deputy sheriff, a practicing coward whose help the family had desperately sought all afternoon, came down the street in his pickup truck. The husband saw him coming, walked slowly out to the front of his parked truck, knelt, placed the barrel of the shotgun under his chin with the stock on the ground, and fired. The grandmother and her grandson were miraculously spared. Three people were dead.

I have never doubted for a moment that if I had taken the wife's case the second time, they would have both wound up in my office that fateful afternoon. I, too, would have been killed. I wanted to quit taking divorce cases altogether, but I couldn't. I needed the income.

·   ·   ·

Many years after we had grown up next door to each other, J. O. Lane Jr. returned to Charleston and, according to him, was a reformed alcoholic. He was desperate for a job, and I gave him one in the store. He was a super salesman and did well for about three months, but one morning when I got to work, J.O. was missing. I asked as to his whereabouts, but nobody had seen him. I went to the back of the store to the water fountain and happened to glance through the glass pane of the back door. There he was, standing barely visible in the partially opened doorway of his father's long-idle blacksmith shop, motioning to me. I crossed the alley, and he said, "I've got to have help. I can't sober up." He asked me to call Alcoholics Anonymous in Ft. Smith. The man who answered was a barber and asked me not to use anyone's last name. He gave me an address, and J.O. and I set off. Our destination was a former servants' quarters behind one of Ft. Smith's larger old homes. Two men arrived shortly and after a few amenities proceeded to concoct the most ungodly-looking conglomeration I had ever seen. Raw eggs, Worcestershire sauce, Tabasco sauce, and God only knows what else. J.O. went into the bathroom with the two men, who watched to make sure he downed it all, then closed the door and left him. In about sixty seconds, from within the bathroom came the most horrible sounds I have ever heard emitted from the mouth and throat of a human being. But try as he might, J.O. could not regurgitate what he had just swallowed. After about ten minutes, he emerged from the bathroom stone sober, and we headed home. I let him out at his family home and never saw him again.

•   •   •

In 1951, the school board hired Ruth Classen, daughter of my good friend Frank Classen, to teach fifth grade. Ruth was the first Catholic ever to teach in the public schools. She was beautiful and intelligent, had a charming demeanor, and was an excellent teacher. The rednecks muttered under their breath, but the episode was essentially a nonevent. By the end of Ruth's second year of teaching, however, the bigots surfaced and presented the school board with a petition signed by a goodly number of people demanding that she be fired. There were no allegations of misconduct, teaching deficiencies, or that she had injected any of her religious beliefs into her teachings. I was not on the school board, but I weighed in with such clout as I had in the community. The board and the superintendent were already outraged. My brother-in-law, Archie Schaffer, German to the core but a social liberal and an agnostic, was on the school board. He was steaming. The petition created a firestorm in the community, the storm being mostly in Ruth's favor, and the board voted unanimously to renew her contract. The rednecks scurried back into their holes. They would surface again.

The little town of Charleston would learn that standing up for Ruth Classen was a small harbinger of a much more courageous stand it would have to take later. That stand would set it apart as not just another small town, but a town blessed with many brave people who were willing to take a historic stand, and for which its school would later receive the designation "National Commemorative Site."

Chapter 9

Charleston Makes History

While I was struggling to keep the doors of the store open, Betty began teaching fourth grade. We didn't live in a different city every year, as we would have had I taken the FBI job, but we did live in five different houses the first four years. We didn't move every time the rent came due, but we came close. Rents ranged from thirty to forty dollars a month.

In October 1952, our first of three unexpected babies arrived. Brent was a healthy seven pounds fourteen ounces, with one side of his head caved in because doctors almost always used forceps in deliveries. I thought he was deformed for life. Bill followed in 1955, and Brooke came along in 1962.

Betty taught until Brent was three years old. Her teaching meant the difference between eating and not eating, because I was contributing very little to the household income. She finally decided she had to quit when she came home from school one day and asked Brent what he and Henny (Henrietta, our elderly baby-sitter) had been doing all day. He said, "Oh, just warshin' and arnin'," Henny's language for washing and ironing. Betty knew the time had come to stay home, even though we had no idea how the rent would be paid.

In our fifth year back home, we bought a house for fifty-five hundred dollars, paying two hundred dollars down and agreeing to pay forty-eight dollars a month forever. It had nine hundred square feet, a space that made us jealous of canned sardines.

Charleston had one cemetery where everyone was buried free. Each year there was a "decoration" day on the first Sunday in May, when relatives of persons buried there decorated their graves with fresh or artificial flowers. There would be a short singing of hymns, a sermon by a local preacher, a benediction, and a plea for money to maintain the place. The money collected was not nearly enough, but it paid for mowing the grass a few times during the summer. While there was an informally chosen board, it didn't function, and people were free to build dividers, plant shrubs, or take any other liberties they chose in decorating plots of loved ones.

Blacks were buried in a small segregated section that had no defined bounds, but they never attended decoration day. Their headstones were pitiful. Some were marked by wooden, rotting crosses, and the others were concrete, made in someone's backyard.

Perpetual-care cemeteries were coming into vogue, and when I was approached by the local mortician, successor to my father and his partner in the funeral home business, about our building such a cemetery and selling lots, it seemed like an idea that might work. The law required that only 10 percent of the sale proceeds had to be placed in trust for perpetual maintenance. Who could argue with anything that turned a 90 percent profit? So we each put up one thousand dollars, bought five acres east of town, and started trying to sell lots.

But people weren't accustomed to paying for a plot in which to be buried, and they weren't anxious to start. Why pay for a lot when you could be buried in the old cemetery for free? Sales were almost nonexistent. I decided it wasn't such a hot investment after all, so my partner paid me my thousand dollars back, and I was out of the cemetery business. Then my former partner hired a door-to-door, high-pressure selling group that would make today's telemarketers look like shrinking violets. Their sales pitch made owning a lot in "the Garden of Memories" a requirement to get into heaven. They took 50 percent of the gross sales. They did well, and it turned out to be a great investment— for my former partner.

·   ·   ·

On May 4, 1954, the U.S. Supreme Court handed down a decision in the case of *Brown* v. *Board of Education* reversing the old *Plessy* v. *Ferguson* decision of 1896, which had declared that "separate but equal" facilities for blacks was constitutional. At first, southerners only complained about it, not fully comprehending the magnitude of the decision. Even though the *Brown* decision stipulated that the change was to be carried out "with all deliberate speed," that mandate didn't seem to carry much urgency as far as southerners were concerned. There was a seeming sub-rosa feeling that the court wasn't really serious and that somehow the whole thing could be finessed given a little time. The nation was quiescent, and the South was routinely ignoring the decision.

Shortly after the *Brown* decision, the Charleston School Board sought my advice on what course of action or inaction they should pursue. It was heady stuff for the only lawyer in a one-horse town, three years out of law school and operating out of a cubicle in the back of the bank. I hadn't even read the *Brown* decision. My advice was made easy by the fact that both the board and the school board superintendent were inclined to comply with the decision immediately. It was also made easy by the fact that I knew the decision had to be honored sooner or later, and I knew sooner would be easier. Obviously, the decision for Charleston could be delayed, "but the day of reckoning would come." Better to do it voluntarily than under a court order.

Charleston had about forty blacks, of whom twenty were children. Most of a once larger population had long since departed for Kansas City, Detroit, and Chicago. They had always lived two miles east of town in the "settlement" in shotgun hovels, trying to scratch out an existence on sorry land. A few worked at the Acme Brick Plant in Ft. Smith, hauling bricks in wheelbarrows to and from the kilns. They were the lucky ones.

The settlement consisted of a small Methodist church (African Methodist Episcopal), sponsored by the all-white Methodist church in town, and a one-room schoolhouse where one teacher, paid by the Charleston School District, taught eight grades. The students in grades nine through twelve were bused through Charleston to the all-black Lincoln High School twenty-four miles away in Ft. Smith.

I told the board and the superintendent, Woody Haynes, that integrating now would be infinitely preferable to waiting for the national chaos that was sure to come. In addition—and this was a big incentive for a poor school district—they could save the three to four thousand dollars a year it was costing to transport the children to a Ft. Smith high school and to pay a teacher to teach the first eight grades.

The Commercial Club, to which all the businesspeople in town belonged, met twice monthly. The women of the Methodist church earned a little money preparing their lunches. Attendance was usually thirty to forty persons. The club members were told by the school superintendent at one of their luncheons that the board was planning to integrate both the high school and grade school that fall. Silence. The *Charleston Express* then dutifully reported the school board's plans, and while there was some undercurrent of resentment, the reaction citywide was amazingly tepid.

At an 8:00 P.M. school board meeting on July 24, 1954, a motion was made to "disband the colored school and admit the colored children into the grade and high school classes." It passed unanimously. The school board minutes of that evening further show that Archie Schaffer, a board member, was granted a year's leave of absence, and I was elected by the remaining four members to fill in for him. The board further voted to increase the superintendent's salary to forty-eight hundred dollars a year.

The only other school in Arkansas, indeed in the entire South, to integrate in 1954 was Fayetteville, which integrated its high school only, with nine black students, two weeks after Charleston integrated. Nobody on the board or in the city dreamed we were taking a historic step that would land the little town in the history books.

When school opened on August 23, 1954, thirteen black students (some say there were twenty-one) got off school bus number two and walked unmolested, and virtually unnoticed, into the elementary and high schools, thereby making Charleston, Arkansas, the first and only school in all of the eleven Confederate states to fully integrate its schools in 1954. Two other schools in Arkansas had voted to integrate that fall, but the hostility of the people, once they found out about the votes, forced them to rescind their decisions.

Things went smoothly. Initially, no black students tried out for basketball or football, but later, when they did, a number of schools refused to play Charleston. Two band contests in nearby communities also refused to allow Charleston's band to participate because Joe Ferguson, grandson of James Ferguson and one of our trombone players, was black. Instead of challenging the other schools, we made the black students stay home if the other schools objected. It took a lot of the luster off an otherwise compelling story of a courageous little community doing what was right. The second year, we stiffened our spines and insisted the black students participate in everything. The schools that had previously objected wilted.

Three years later, Little Rock's Central High School, the state's largest, began making elaborate preparations to accept nine carefully selected black students in the fall of 1957. Untold hours were spent in attempting to assure a smooth opening day, and obviously, people were prepared to accept the inevitable. The city was quiet, and there had been no organized opposition.

Orval Faubus was in the first year of a second two-year term as governor of Arkansas. He had been a rather progressive governor and enjoyed a respectable approval rating, but not since 1904 had Arkansas elected a governor to a third term, and Faubus was highly unlikely to repeat that feat.

As the time neared for school to begin, a few, very few, segregationists began to clamor for action to stop the "mongrelization" of the races. Their voices were loud but largely ineffective. But one person was watching and listening intently—Orval Faubus. The rabble-rousers presented him with a surefire ticket to a third term.

Faubus shortly announced that the Brown decision was unlawful, and proceeded to call out the National Guard to deny the nine black children admission to Central High. He, not the Supreme Court, would determine what constituted "equal protection" for black children in the future. He mentioned the long-since *repudiated* theory of "interposition," loosely based on the Tenth Amendment to the Constitution. That amendment provides that any powers not delegated to the United States nor prohibited to the states, were reserved to the states. The thrust of the interposition argument was that the state could interpose itself between the United States and the people of the state when the United States was usurping a right reserved to the state. The lower courts made hash of the argument, as the Supreme Court had done many times since the days when John Marshall was chief justice. The Constitution, of course, delegated to the United States the duty to see that all citizens were accorded equal protection under the laws of the United States. Faubus, not a lawyer, knew the politics of the issue, but had no conception of the magnitude of the constitutional crisis he was creating.

On the morning of September 23, 1957, the nine black students marched up the beautiful curved steps of Central High School to the entrance, where they were stopped and told by the National Guard commander that they would not be permitted to enter. The rest is history, and the only possible outcome ensued, but not until Faubus made a trip to confer with President Eisenhower in Newport, Rhode Island. There was nothing to discuss, and Faubus returned home saying he had tried to resolve the matter. Eisenhower was slow to act and had to be convinced by his attorney general, Herbert Brownell, that he was faced with a constitutional crisis and had no choice. As the nation's chief executive, he was sworn to uphold the law, and that included Supreme Court decisions, whether popular or not.

Brownell was the architect of what followed. First, Eisenhower nationalized the Arkansas National Guard, removing it from Faubus's control, and sent the men home. He then sent the 101st Airborne Division from Fort Benning, Georgia, to Little Rock. It is difficult, decades later, to relate to the fact that a crisis with the potential for major violence was brewing and nobody could foresee a peaceful outcome.

When Eisenhower announced that he had ordered one of the most, if not the most, elite fighting units in the United States Army to Little Rock, I felt immensely relieved. Until that time, a mob that was growing bigger and more unruly by the day had been in control. People across Arkansas were frightened.

Fort Chaffee, fifteen miles west of Charleston, was ordered to furnish much of the logistical support needed for the 101st Airborne. I was trying a case on the second floor of the courthouse in Paris, Arkansas. It was a hot September morning, and the courthouse windows were open. Suddenly, I heard the unmistakable and all-too-familiar roar of army vehicles on Highway 22, which ran beside the courthouse, obviously headed for Little Rock. It was the first time I felt that this crisis, probably the most serious since the Civil War, was about to be resolved in favor of the Constitution and civil order.

The tension that prevailed across the length and breadth of Arkansas was reaching fever pitch. People spoke in hushed tones. Open hostilities were a distinct possibility.

Shortly after their arrival, members of the 101st Airborne escorted the nine terrified students into Central High. The crowd, which had grown in both size and unruliness, was quickly made to understand the seriousness of the matter when the troops stuck their bayonets into the rears of a couple of recalcitrant rednecks. The mob began to dwindle and within three days had totally disappeared.

I knew Faubus's action in Little Rock, which had 80 percent

approval in the state, would spill over into the small community of Charleston, which had chosen the path of responsible compliance with the law and was entering its fourth year of peaceful integration. It didn't take long.

As two board members fanned the flames, tempers flared and one member resigned. That left the board split between two members who wanted to resegregate, one who did not, namely me, and one who would do whatever the next election dictated. Archie had never reclaimed his seat and I had remained on the board. The fifth position remained vacant because we couldn't agree on a replacement. I recruited a candidate to run for the vacant position with me in the next election, and the two segregationists did likewise.

The election to be held in March 1958 would be volatile and nasty and determine whether Charleston would keep its place in history or attempt to follow Little Rock's intransigence.

My running mate and I did no campaigning. Our opponents ran advertisements in the paper and worked hard by word of mouth to assure citizens there would be no violence or untoward events, that we could go back to the same system we had just abandoned. They "had a plan to resegregate" that would work and meet any legal challenge.

One evening just about dusk and two weeks before the election, Joe Ferguson, a well-liked and respected black man who worked at the brick plant in Ft. Smith, knocked on my door. He told me some people had been driving by his home, shouting epithets and making threatening gestures. They were not shooting or displaying weapons, but Joe and his family were terrified. I told him I would follow him home and stay with him and his wife, Miriam, for a while and see what happened. Joe and I both knew it would be futile to call anybody in law enforcement.

The hecklers came by shortly after I arrived, made a few catcalls, and never returned. Everybody knew everybody else's car in small towns, and they obviously recognized mine, a 1954 blue Pontiac. I don't know what I would have done if they had presented a serious challenge that night, but I've been content to let everybody think I was a latter-day Atticus Finch, assuming Atticus Finch was terrified.

When the smoke cleared, Charleston School District #9 cast almost 500 votes, compared to the customary 100 to 150. I defeated my opponent 317 to 169, and my compatriot defeated his opponent 308 to 173. Little Rock had served a purpose. People in Charleston wanted no part of what Little Rock had been through. The 1957 school year in Little Rock remained chaotic, and Faubus called a special session of the legislature, which under his guidance voted to close the Little Rock schools for the 1958 school year.

Unfortunately, the hostility of the losers in Charleston didn't end with the election. The night before school was to commence in the fall of 1958, the new superintendent, Edgar Woolsey, and the school janitor, Buel Lyle, came to my home on Sunday evening looking for all the world as if they had just seen the Holy Grail. They were pasty white with fear. The "diehards" had painted "NIGGER STAY HOME" in huge block letters across the full width of the high school, which faced the main highway through Charleston. Strangely, the perpetrators had used dark green paint. I told them to recruit some help, get a few gallons of turpentine, and scrub it off with stiff-bristled brooms and hand brushes. I furnished the turpentine from the store. I went to the high school the next morning and waited for the people I felt certain were the sign painters. Two of them drove by, and I have never seen faces more forlorn than theirs when they realized their handiwork was gone. Only seven or eight people ever knew it had happened.

By 1962, the Catholic church had accepted two black families and enrolled their children in their parochial school, which covered only grades one through eight. A year later, the pastor of the Methodist church came into my office and said, "I need fifteen hundred dollars to put a new roof on the nigger church. I've got you down for a hundred dollars."

I told him that not only was I not going to give him a hundred dollars, but I would resist repairing the roof. "It's unconscionable to continue the pretense of maintaining that church," I said. "You should go to their members and invite them to worship with us."

He was stunned.

"If they were to come walking into our church, it would create chaos. Mrs. Frensmeir and Mrs. Floyd will both walk out," he argued.

"No, they won't," I said. "They would be afraid they would miss something."

The pastor was amenable to the idea, but only if I put the question to the board of stewards at the next meeting. I told him I would not only make the motion to invite the blacks to worship with us, I would strongly advocate it. Every single board member was present at the next meeting. After a lengthy discussion, my motion carried on a vote of twenty to two.

Everything was in place for the most dramatic moment in the history of the church. On the following Sunday morning, except for the seats reserved for the blacks, you couldn't have squeezed another soul into the church with a shoehorn. When the three black families walked in there was total silence, then abject relief, followed by an immense sense of pride in having taken a bold step that everyone knew in their hearts was the exemplification of Christianity. Mrs. Frensmeir and Mrs. Floyd were both present in their usual pews. As choir director, I was elated to have two new sopranos.

Orval Faubus became the most powerful force in the history of Arkansas politics, going on to serve a total of six terms, always winning by lopsided margins except in his last race. In 1966 he chose not to run for a seventh term, but four years later, after two terms of Winthrop Rockefeller, a transplanted New Yorker and the first Republican governor of Arkansas since Reconstruction, Orval Faubus decided to come out of retirement and rid the state of this outlander once and for all. But Faubus had a minor problem. In order to challenge Win Rockefeller, he first had to defeat seven other Democrats in a Democratic primary. I would be one of them.

Chapter 10

The Body on the Road
and Other Trials

I didn't begin practicing law with the intent of being a trial lawyer. My goal was simply to build a law practice that would afford me a comfortable lifestyle. But the store purchase had been such a disaster, I didn't have any options as to what kind of law I would practice. I took everything that came in the door.

The first case that carried any notoriety, that I felt would give me a boost if I won, involved a prominent, recently divorced businessman charged with negligent homicide. At about 3:00 A.M. on a cool October morning in 1956, J. D. Raney ran over a large object in the middle of an old, little-traveled state highway.

J. D. had owned a grocery store, then later, a dry goods store selling mostly men's work clothes, shoes, and boots. He had made a comfortable living, thanks to both his and his wife's total devotion to the businesses. J.D. was about forty-five years old, a country-talking tobacco chewer, and a very decent, devout man. He was unattractive by any measure, while his wife was pretty, well dressed, rather sexy, and well liked. She liked to flirt and the men flirted back.

I had represented J.D. in a divorce from his wife of twenty-five years. He had been devastated but, as is often the case, shortly began seeing another woman in a neighboring community. As he was returning from a visit with his new love and came off a bridge that was much higher on each end than the highway, his headlights suddenly revealed the large object in the road. The thump as he hit it had an unmistakable and terrifying sound. He felt he might have hit a body.

His mind raced through all the possibilities, including a ruse by robbers waiting for him to stop to see what he had hit, but the rearview mirror revealed only darkness. He didn't stop—rather, he proceeded on to Charleston and sought out his best friend, who also happened to be the county coroner, though not of the county where the incident had occurred. They returned the ten miles to the scene, which by then had attracted a number of people, including the sheriff, other county officers, plus the state police, all pondering what or who could have killed the woman in the road. J.D. told them the simple story of what had happened. He explained that by the time his car lights shone on her as he came off the bridge, it was too late to avoid her, and he didn't know what he had hit until he returned to the scene.

The case became big news, with daily stories in the Ft. Smith paper reporting all kinds of speculation, generated mostly by the prosecuting attorney's office, about what J.D.'s relationship with the dead woman might have been. Neither the sheriff's nor the prosecutor's office had done much investigative work. J.D. insisted through repeated questionings that he had never met the woman and had no idea who she was or what she was doing on the highway. The little investigative work done by the sheriff's office turned up nothing connecting J.D. to the deceased woman.

While J.D. and I had spent hours discussing the case and whether or not he was likely to be charged, he had never formally employed me. When he finally got around to asking me what my fee would be, I told him $150. The fee was ridiculous even then, but I knew the case would continue to be publicized. When some of J.D.'s older friends admonished him about my youth and lack of experience, he said, "Well, you never know what's under a rock until you turn it over."

The prosecutor called me one Saturday morning and asked

me to bring my client to the Sebastian County Courthouse at 11:00 P.M. The late hour was calculated to add drama to the case and to further terrify J.D. When we arrived, there was already an assemblage of officers and prosecutors in a room with everyone standing. One officer and a deputy prosecutor, one after the other, started giving him the third degree, repeating the same questions over and over that he had answered a dozen times. Finally, exasperated, I told them we were leaving. They immediately told us they were charging him with negligent homicide, which they had obviously intended to do from the beginning.

I worked night and day trying to unravel this mystery. I wanted to be sure I knew more than the prosecutor did about the case. I first went to a bar that I had heard the woman frequented. The bartender gave me the name of a man who he thought she had left with on the night of her death. I finally found the man in a nearby community, and he was astonishingly candid about what had happened. The sheriff's office had never contacted him. He said he'd seen no reason to get involved voluntarily. He said he and two other men had built a deer camp and had planned to hunt on Monday, the opening day of deer season. On Saturday night, he called them and told them when and where to meet him, and that he thought the woman he had just met in the bar from which he was calling might come along with them. She was indeed agreeable, so when his buddies arrived they stocked up on beer and headed for the deer camp. They drank beer on the way to the camp and after they arrived. Since the woman had been drinking long before they left the bar, it soon became apparent that their plan to have round-robin sex with her wasn't going to work. She was very shortly too drunk to accommodate them. They then decided to take her back to Ft. Smith, and on the way, she apparently became incoherent and difficult, so, disgusted, they stopped just beyond the bridge and kicked her out of the car and into a steep, deep ditch that ran beside the highway. They didn't hang around to see what happened to her. The weather was cooler than usual for October, and the speculation was that she had crawled back up on the highway, which was warmer than the ditch, and went to sleep. J.D. said he had not met a single car the preceding eight or nine miles before he arrived at the bridge, so he may or may not have been the first or even the only car to run over her. The man I interviewed said he thought it was about 1:00 A.M. when they dumped her out. There was never any evidence that anyone else ran over her. Threads from her dress were found on the underside of J.D.'s car, but we had no way of knowing how many cars may have been ahead of him or at what time she crawled back up on the road. Her body had been terribly mangled.

The prosecutor had never sought these men out, never charged them with anything, gathered very little information about the woman, and concentrated solely on J.D. They were nobodies and J.D. was a prominent citizen. She was a barfly, but I could find no evidence that she was a prostitute.

After a two-day trial, the jury deliberated twenty minutes before finding J.D. innocent in a case that obviously should never have been brought to trial. His not stopping was bad judgment, but he was terrified, and his thought that it might be a ploy to rob him if he stopped was plausible. The prosecutor even tried to submit sex into the case by introducing a pair of women's panties found in the glove compartment of J.D.'s car. I strenuously objected because the prosecutor offered no connection with anybody or anything to the panties. The objection was sustained.

The case was a slam dunk, but it made front-page news anyway, and the next morning there was a crowd at my office when I arrived, and I never lacked clients thereafter.

•   •   •

Mr. Dunn was eighty-five years old and had been married to Annie White, eighty, for about two years. They were both well known in the community, he as a man who was in his dotage and she as a woman who talked incessantly in a grating, high-pitched voice. Annie soon grew tired of Mr. Dunn, because, while he was growing senile, he was still sane enough not to want anything if it cost money, especially if it was for Annie's benefit. She said he was as tight as bark on a tree. His children, sensing his impending death, thoughtfully arranged for him to transfer the ten thousand dollars he had spent a lifetime accumulating to a joint account with them. In joint accounts, the share of any joint holder goes to the survivors, so upon Mr. Dunn's death, the children would get the entire amount. This, of course, was done without Annie's knowledge or acquiescence. The question was whether Mr. Dunn understood the implications of what he was doing.

Shortly after the joint account was set up, the old gentleman died. Annie's son, on her behalf—and his—hired a lawyer to file suit, alleging that Mr. Dunn was incompetent at the time the joint account was set up and that Annie had been defrauded of her dower right—namely, 50 percent of the account. It would be tried in chancery court, which meant no jury.

My job was to prove that Mr. Dunn was quite competent and knew what he was doing, though everybody in town knew he hardly knew where he was most of the time. The children all testified that Mr. Dunn was quite competent and that the joint account was his idea. When it was my turn to cross-examine Annie's son, Herman, I wanted to show through him that Mr. Dunn performed normal chores around the house and conducted his own affairs. The cross-examination went thusly:

"Mr. White, didn't Mr. Dunn buy the groceries?"

"Yeah, and sometimes paid for 'em twice," he answered.

"Mr. White, just answer the questions yes or no, please. Now, again. Didn't Mr. Dunn buy the groceries?"

"Yes," he responded.

"And didn't he mow the lawn?"

"Yes."

"And didn't he make a garden?"

"Now, I'll tell you about that garden . . ."

I stopped him. "Now, Mr. White, just answer the question yes or no. Didn't Mr. Dunn make a garden?"

Again, "Now, I'll tell you about that garden . . ."

I turned with a pleading look for help from the judge. "Your

Honor, would you please instruct the witness to answer the question yes or no?"

"Mr. Bumpers, I will instruct the witness to answer the question yes or no, but if he feels his answer needs an explanation, he has a right to explain it," the judge said.

I should have dropped the "garden" question at that point, but I naively plodded on.

"Very well. Mr. White," I said, "I know you want to make a speech, so I'll ask you again, didn't Mr. Dunn make a garden?"

"Yes, he did," he answered. "The last time I saw him in the garden was January sixth. There was six inches of snow on the ground, the temperature was twenty-five degrees, and he was in the garden plowing."

I still won the case, because the judge held an elective office and the Dunns had a big family and they all voted. It was the last time I ever assumed that simply because someone was uneducated, unsophisticated, and shabbily dressed, he couldn't make a fool out of me.

.   .   .

A few years later, in the same courtroom in Greenwood, Arkansas, where I had defended J. D. Raney, I defended a seventeen-year-old boy, Sonny Swofford, who was charged with manslaughter in the killing of his stepfather, "ole Lige," the boy called him, short for Elijah. Sonny, his mother, Mattie, and all but one of his seven siblings were mentally deficient. None of them had been sired by Lige.

Lige was a brute when he was drunk, and he came home in that condition most Friday nights after being paid for his week's work at the furniture factory. The house was rather isolated in the country and was about a quarter mile down a lane off a main county road. Lige was a responsible man when sober, but that was rare on Friday nights. On this Friday night he came home roaring drunk and immediately began cuffing Mattie around, yelling at her and, among other things, demanding something to eat. She wasn't moving fast enough for him, and as the argument grew louder and more volatile, Sonny and the seven other children ran into the yard to escape being embroiled in the argument. On the way out, Sonny thoughtfully picked up Lige's rifle in the corner of the front bedroom. The children continued watching the escalating argument through an open kitchen window, and when Lige, in a rage, threw hot coffee in Mattie's face, Sonny fired. The bullet hit Lige in the neck, penetrating his jugular vein. He jumped up, cursing, seeming to know it was Sonny who had fired the shot, and shouted, "Sonny, I'll get you, you little son of a bitch!" Sonny took off running up the lane toward the main road. Lige bolted out of the house and started chasing him, but the faster Lige ran, the faster the blood flowed from his jugular, and within two hundred yards he fell dead. Sonny was charged with voluntary manslaughter. Heartsill Ragon, a Ft. Smith lawyer, and I were hired to defend Sonny.

I knew the prosecutor had had a Rorschach inkblot test administered to Sonny while he was in jail, and when I went to the jail to see him, I asked him about it—specifically, what he saw in the inkblots. In his loud nasal twang he said, "Oh, Mr. Bumpers, they just all looked like murder to me."

I said, "Sonny, you didn't intend to kill ole Lige, did you?"

"Oh no, Mr. Bumpers, I never meant to kill him. I was just watchin' him through the window, and when he throwed that coffee in my mama's face, it made me mad, so I just took me a good aim right at his heart and shot him." His aim was poor, but he made his point.

Obviously, we weren't going to let Sonny within a mile of the witness stand.

Later, I queried him about the family. I asked him how many members there were in the family. He silently began to calculate, muttering their names, counting on his fingers, and finally said, "They's ten of us." Then he thought a second and said, "No. They's just nine now, since I shot ole Lige."

We—my co-counsel and I—wanted to get Sonny acquitted

without having him declared incompetent, if possible, but it would be necessary to get someone, preferably one of the children, to describe the beatings and abuse to which they had been regularly subjected. None seemed up to the task until we queried Sonny's twelve-year-old sister. She seemed quite normal and told a heartrending story of Lige's abuses, which were monstrous. She told the story in a plaintive, quiet manner that would obviously be compelling to a jury, so, without coaching or prompting, we decided to use her.

On the witness stand, she was totally disarming, innocently describing how the whole family often had to sleep in the fields to escape the beatings and could return to the house only when Lige sobered up. Her voice was soft, and she spoke with wide-eyed sincerity and candor. She had no understanding as to the importance of her role. The jury was awash in tears when she finished. I thought of the biblical passage "And a child shall lead them."

The jury was out longer than I thought necessary but after three hours came in with an acquittal. Sonny showed no emotion. He only asked, "Can we go home now, Mr. Bumpers?"

.   .   .

A Baptist preacher, pastor of the second largest Baptist church in Charleston, and his wife went to Ft. Smith to shop. They were returning home about 3:00 P.M., and as they came around Darnell curve and entered the straightaway in front of them, a huge semitractor-trailer was bearing down on them on their side of the road. The preacher pulled toward the right shoulder, but the truck veered left and continued to come down on them. The preacher continued pulling to the right, crossed the shoulder, a shallow ditch, and finally tried to go up a steep embankment in an attempt to avoid the semi, still bearing down on them. But the semi continued driving straight at them as though it were a premeditated murder attempt. The preacher's car was no more than three feet thick after the semi ran over it. The preacher and his wife were killed instantly, while the driver of the semi didn't suffer a scratch. The couple left two sons, twenty-two and seven years old. The twenty-two-year-old worked in a shoe store in Little Rock, and after a short visit with him, he asked me to represent him and his little brother.

In his deposition, the driver revealed that he had served a Texas prison term for drug use and was still a frequent user of drugs to stay awake. The trial took only one day but started on a hectic note. The day began with a heavy rain. The courthouse was in a state of disrepair, especially the roof, which leaked like a sieve, and water began pouring into the courtroom in twenty different places. We put a bucket under every leak until it became almost impossible to move without stumbling over one. The judge scattered the jurors over a large area of the courtroom in order to avoid the leaks. By 11:00 A.M., the rain stopped, the court took a recess, the buckets were removed, and the jurors returned to the jury box. Here I was, trying the biggest personal-injury case of my life, and everyone, the judge, jury, and lawyers totally distracted with trying to stay dry.

The defendant never took the stand, a fact that can't be mentioned in a criminal case but can be brought to the jury's attention in a civil case. Even then, the plaintiff's attorney isn't permitted to speculate or dwell on the reasons the defendant didn't testify.

The verdict was eighty-three thousand dollars, a pittance compared to what the case would be worth today, but the biggest ever rendered in Franklin County. My fee was 25 percent.

·   ·   ·

I learned early in my trial career to go over their testimony with witnesses before putting them on the stand and not to ask questions to which I didn't know the answer. A prominent Little Rock attorney, representing the Missouri Pacific Railroad in a highway-crossing accident, had failed to "woodshed" the conductor (go over his testimony with him) of the train before putting him on the stand. The plaintiff had alleged, among other things, that the train was speeding, an act of negligence that contributed to causing the wreck. The lawyer for the railroad, to refute the speeding charge, asked the conductor how fast the train was going. The conductor asked, "You mean in miles per hour?"

"Yes," replied the lawyer, "miles per hour will be fine."

The conductor said, "Well, I couldn't rightly say in miles per hour, but, brother, we were skipping through the dew."

.   .   .

One day, Keith, a youngster about twenty years old, came into my office and told me he had been charged with raping Connie, a local harlot. Most people felt it would be impossible to rape Connie. Keith said he was working for her husband on the husband's farm, and they were baling hay. The baler broke down, and the husband sent Keith to the garage behind his house to get a part with which to repair it. Keith said he was looking for the baler part in the garage when, suddenly, it started to get dark. He turned around to find Connie closing the garage doors. She walked over to him and asked, without preliminary conversation, "Would you like to do it to me?"

He asked, "Do what?"

She said, "Oh, you know."

I said, "Well, Keith, what did you do?"

He said, "I done it to her."

Keith's problem stemmed from the fact that Connie's husband came in while he was "doin' it to her," and Connie started screaming that he had forced himself on her. It took about two weeks to get the charges dropped.

Two or three years later, Connie's husband employed me to file for a divorce on his behalf. The trial was mostly about Connie's numerous and mostly well-known sexual escapades. But when she took the stand, she immediately accused her husband of several misdeeds, including having sex with the chickens. The judge, head in hand and almost asleep, almost bolted out of his chair.

On cross-examination, I asked Connie if she was telling the court that "your husband preferred chickens to you."

"He done it. He done it. I seen him do it," she replied.

The husband was granted a divorce.

.   .   .

One of the most memorable divorce cases ever tried in western Arkansas involved a husband who was seeking a divorce on grounds of adultery. Army Evans, an attorney in Booneville, a nearby community, represented the aggrieved husband, who had actually seen his wife in the act of adultery. On direct examination, Army asked the husband to describe what he had seen. He was an uneducated man, but he graphically described how he had hidden on a hillside and watched his wife and her lover cavort along the bank of a stream at the foot of the hill. Soon, he said, "they began taking off their clothes, and the next thing I knowed, they wuz on the ground fuckin'." The judge went apoplectic, sternly gaveled his bench, scolded the witness, and warned him that he did not "tolerate such foul language in my court." He admonished the witness, telling him, "If your testimony requires you to describe the sex act, then you must use the word *fornicate*. Do you understand?"

"Yes, sir," the witness replied.

When the wife's attorney cross-examined the husband, he took the witness through the scenario again. When the witness got to the disrobing and the sex act, he said, "First thing I knowed they wuz on the ground . . ." He paused, then turned to the judge and asked, "Judge, what was that nickname you told me to use for *fuckin'*?"

.   .   .

Three young men were accused of stealing a hydraulic tractor lift. One of them sought my services. In the office interview, he told me they had all drunk a lot of beer the night of the theft and that as they drove out to the farming area, he lay down in the backseat and went to sleep. He said he was asleep when the theft took place, and he didn't know a theft had taken place until he was arrested. During my interview of the man, I asked, "Was the hydraulic lift attached to the tractor?"

"No," he answered, "it was just layin' out there in the grass."

By the time he finished the sentence, he started smiling, realizing he had just confessed.

I told him it would be best if he hired another attorney.

．　　　．　　　．

One of the two jury trials I lost over an eighteen-year period was a criminal case in which my client, Earl, was charged with aggravated assault. At a community picnic, he pulled a pistol on a perfectly innocent black man whom he neither knew nor had ever seen before. He didn't fire. Earl conjured up a story about being provoked or threatened, but in fact there was no provocation. Earl had a reputation for being a volatile man and a bully, especially when he was drinking, as he was on this occasion. His father was one of the men who fought in front of Doc's Café and Pool Hall on Saturday afternoons when I was a child.

I shouldn't have put Earl on the stand, but trial work is a veritable mother lode of learning experiences. On cross-examination, the prosecutor asked him to reenact the pulling of the gun. Earl had obviously seen too many episodes of *Gunsmoke*, and he happily stood up and, à la Matt Dillon, whipped out an imaginary pistol and went into a crouch. He said the man looked threatening to him but couldn't say why. Earl was found guilty and sentenced to two years in prison. There were eight women on the jury. Never again would I allow so many women on a jury in a criminal case. I appealed to the Arkansas Supreme Court and lost, a loss I richly deserved.

When the presiding judge signed the commitment order to take Earl to prison, the deputy sheriff, Moe King, also one of Charleston's three barbers, went to pick him up at his home and transport him to prison. Earl, as was his custom, had been drinking, and Moe knew Earl was capable of killing him if he tried to take him by force. Earl refused to go peacefully, and, terrified,

Moe finally gave up and left. Earl's wife had an acquaintanceship with the presiding judge, who lived in a community twenty miles away, and went to see him to personally plead Earl's case. She was a lovely, demure, and shy woman. I don't know what she said or what transpired; what I do know is that Moe never returned to take Earl to prison, and he never served a day of his sentence. I never went to the courthouse to check the file. I don't know whether the judge entered an order or whether the case died of inertia. I didn't want to know.

·   ·   ·

J. D. Stiles had rotten teeth, an articulate wife, an irresistible urge to take any piece of property that wasn't tied down, and a three-term prison record resulting from his irresistible urges, the last term being in San Quentin.

As his wife sat passively, J.D. described for me how he and his wife had started toward Ft. Smith from their home in Booneville to buy a refrigerator, washing machine, and other furniture, items he intended to buy to fulfill a longtime promise to his wife. He said his truck broke down just east of Charleston. A man, whom J.D. didn't know and whose name he never bothered to ask, stopped to lend a hand. The Good Samaritan also just happened to have a truckload of furniture and appliances and was headed to Ft. Smith to sell it to a used-furniture store. After they managed to get J.D.'s truck running, J.D. inquired of his new-found friend whether or not they might make a deal on the furniture. After all, the new friend had the very articles J.D. intended to purchase in Ft. Smith, and why not just cut a deal here and now and save both a lot of trouble? And so it came to pass that J.D. gave the man two hundred dollars, backed his truck up to the rear of the other truck, and helped the man shove the furniture and appliances onto J.D.'s truck. Then everyone departed happily.

J.D.'s wife showed no emotion or movement as J.D. un-corked the highly implausible story.

As luck would have it, one day later, a family in Branch, a

community about five miles east of where the alleged trade took place, returned from a short vacation to find that the same pieces of furniture J.D. had purchased from the total stranger were missing from their home. When they reported the theft, the sheriff in Franklin County alerted the sheriffs in the surrounding counties of the theft. The sheriff in Booneville, J.D.'s hometown, knew of his record and called to suggest they get a search warrant to check out J.D.'s home. They found every piece of furniture, plus the appliances, that had been reported missing from the Branch family's home.

I took one or two criminal cases a year, just to stay boned up on changes in the criminal code and new Supreme Court decisions. Criminal cases always presented unique challenges. Even so, I took this case with great reluctance. First, I couldn't imagine any jury naive enough to believe J.D.'s story. Second, I knew J.D. would have to steal something else in order to pay my fee.

I delivered my opening argument with a straight face. I had only one thing going for me: J.D.'s wife was the most perfect witness I had ever seen or heard. She had had a lot of experience. In my office, even as I cross-examined her intensely, she remained composed, articulate, and unshakable; even her grammar was surprisingly good. I couldn't put J.D. on the stand to tell the jury he had spent most of his adult life in prison for stealing. She was all I had.

On the afternoon of the first day of trial, the judge ordered a fifteen-minute recess for everyone to use the rest rooms and stretch. One of the jurors, an ignorant "ridge-running" preacher who lived just north of town, came to me in great anxiety and said, "Dale, I saw that happen."

"Saw what happen?"

"I saw those two trucks out on the highway and those men taking the furniture off one truck and loading it onto another one."

I felt sure he was delusional, but who was I to look a gift horse in the mouth? When the judge returned to the courtroom, I called him and the prosecutor aside and repeated the story the juror had just related to me. The prosecutor insisted on moving for a mistrial, knowing the juror was about to deny him an easy win. But he also knew that if the judge granted a mistrial, the case would have to be tried again, and my new preacher friend would be my first witness.

Under Arkansas law, a trial may be resumed with only eleven jurors if both sides agree. The juror would obviously have to be removed from the panel, but the cause of justice mandated that he be allowed to testify. The prosecutor grudgingly agreed to continue the trial with eleven jurors.

By late evening, J.D.'s wife had been a superlative witness, unshaken by the prosecutor's cross-examination. The juror had testified as to what he had seen (or imagined he had seen), and J.D. dodged his fourth prison sentence. The jury took about two hours to find J.D. innocent.

About two years later, J.D. returned. He had been charged with stealing a motor off a boat on one of Arkansas's large recreational lakes in north central Arkansas. The state's case was not quite as open and shut as the furniture case had been prior to the juror's testimony, but J.D.'s wife's performance was, if anything, even more persuasive. She was so good, I don't think the jury ever wondered why J.D. didn't testify. The acquittal came after two hours of deliberation.

When J.D. came back a third time, charged once again with stealing a motor off a boat on another of Arkansas's premier lakes in southwest Arkansas (J.D. got around), I was thinking more seriously about a political race and declined the case.

The next time I heard from him was in a letter postmarked Grady, Arkansas, the small community that was the address of Arkansas's largest prison.

The prison term was a "bum rap," J.D. wrote. He said his attorney hadn't done a good job, and he hoped I could help. I couldn't.

•   •   •

One day Ira Flynn, a tall, lanky, illiterate man who worked for my father-in-law on his dairy farm, came to my office to have his tax return prepared. I did a lot of tax work, mostly short forms or fairly simple long forms, for which I charged five to ten dollars, depending on the complexity of the long forms. Ira told me he had ten children and had made two thousand dollars the preceding year. I assured him that with ten children he didn't need to file a return, but he insisted, so I asked him to give me the names of his children. He struggled mightily, came up with nine names, and finally gave up, saying, "I just cain't think of that other kid's name."

I assured him it was quite all right, nine was enough. He left dejected and began the long two-mile walk home. About three hours later, my secretary came back to my office to tell me I had a "guest" in the reception room. There I found a child no more than ten years old. I asked, "What is it, son?"

He said, "Pa forgot me."

I thanked him, and he, too, began the two-mile walk back home. It is still a sad reflection and I have lamented a thousand times not thinking to take him home.

Ira had another son, Ira junior. He was a surprisingly bright lad considering his circumstances, though his grammar and spelling were terrible. He began drinking rather heavily at a young age and wound up in prison with a life sentence for murder. One of the letters I received early in my first term as governor was from Ira junior. It read:

He was also in Cummins Prison and freely admitted that he and Glen Blaylock had indeed killed "ole Johnny Harris," but suggested I could ask "Bebe" (Babe), and he would assure me that ole Johnny needed "a good killin'." On my first visit to the prison, I saw Ira. He was dispensing food on the chow line. Ira was paroled after eight years, worked on a dairy farm for ten years, and then became a preacher. He's still preaching.

.   .   .

I knew, from my rural upbringing as well as usually knowing the client, when a case had an element of danger in it or when my chances of success were slim. But because I was continually

strapped for money, I took cases that were dangerous and involved little money, cases I wouldn't have touched had I been financially independent. Many were cases that had been rejected
by more seasoned or affluent attorneys.

My father was right in believing a law degree was the best
credential one could possess to pursue a political career. He was
wrong about knowing Latin and about Latin being a great asset.
It was virtually worthless. Trial experience was of incalculable
value in politics. Learning how to ingratiate myself and identify
with jurors proved invaluable later on, in campaigns.

Chapter 11

A Political Defeat and
a Tragedy Like No Other

In 1960, I decided to try the nursing home business on the advice of my cousin Bequita and her husband, Miller Huggins, who had learned firsthand that they were obscenely profitable. The federal government put up most of the money to care for the poor, and 90 percent of nursing home residents were poor. Miller said that in Oklahoma the program was administered by the state, the state was administered by the legislature, and the legislature was administered by the nursing home operators—a license to steal if ever there was one.

Building regulations were almost nonexistent, and the construction cost per nursing home bed was as low as two thousand dollars. When one considered that Medicaid paid fifteen hundred dollars per year for indigent care, and nursing requirements were minimal, one didn't have to be broke out with brilliance to know it was like finding a bird nest on the ground.

Bill Hensley came to Charleston in 1954, having just finished a one-year internship, and became the first doctor Charleston had had in years. Bill and I became good friends, and in 1960 I told him about this golden opportunity. Nursing homes were springing up all over Oklahoma in every village and hamlet, and there were virtually none in Arkansas. Bill was wary, fearing a fifty-fifty partnership would result in gridlock. He wanted a third partner, which was fine with me. He had gotten to know a registered nurse named Thelma Martin, who had tended her husband during his last illness, and Bill believed her to be an ideal choice to be our administrator. He believed she could run the place efficiently, and she also had a little money. I visited with her and found her to be shallow and totally inexperienced in business, but I wanted to get started.

I didn't have a dime, but my next-door neighbor did, and he loaned money at 6 percent, which was 3½ percent more than banks paid on savings. He asked little in collateral if he liked you, and he liked and trusted me, which was a happy circumstance for me because I had no collateral. He agreed to loan me eight thousand dollars, in exchange for which I would assign a ten-thousand-dollar life insurance policy to him, which was no collateral at all—unless I died, which I had no immediate plans to do.

The first twenty beds would cost forty thousand dollars. I put up eight thousand dollars, the good doctor eight thousand, and Nurse Martin four thousand. We borrowed twenty thousand more as a construction loan and converted it to a permanent loan upon completion. Unhappily, the forty thousand dollars proved to be insufficient, so we gave the builder a note for the seven-thousand-dollar cost overrun.

At the end of two months, we had eight residents and were losing money faster than the U.S. Mint could print it. The good doctor almost stroked out. Nurse Martin had not a clue about administering the place, and the few residents we had were quite vocal about their unhappiness with her. We finally filled our twenty beds, but then discovered that twenty beds was only a break-even point. Nurse Martin was not the reason we weren't making a profit, but she was obviously in over her head. She wanted out anyway and was willing to leave voluntarily as long as she got her four-thousand-dollar investment back. I wanted to buy half of her stock and let the doctor buy the other half, but he had become increasingly apprehensive about our venture and didn't want to invest any more money in it. The problem was that he didn't want me to, either. I asked Archie Schaffer if he'd like to get involved. Strangely, the doctor, who didn't want me to own 50 percent, was willing to let my brother-in-law and me own 60 percent. However, one of Archie's conditions was that he would be allowed to buy enough stock from the two of us, if he could ever afford it, to make us all own one-third each.

We quickly added twenty more beds, all with borrowed money, and Maggie, Archie's wife and Betty's sister, became administrator. The profits I originally envisioned began to accrue. However, while we were planning a third addition, the doctor, early one October morning, fell asleep at the wheel on his way to the hospital, twenty miles away in another town. He was killed in a head-on collision with a semitractor-trailer.

Archie and I would have been happy to have the doctor's widow as a partner, but we also wanted to add thirty-two more beds for a total capacity of seventy-two, and she strongly resisted the idea. We finally negotiated a deal to buy her interest, but it wasn't pleasant.

By 1962, the hardware and furniture business had grown to the point that I was no longer buried under a staggering debt and could hardly wait to dip my toes in the political waters. I was thirty-six years old and had the foolish and totally mistaken notion that I had to start at the bottom and await my turn for higher office. I announced for the Arkansas House of Representatives, to the loud applause of no one. Franklin County had only one representative, and the incumbent was not seeking reelection. A twenty-seven-year-old county clerk named Mike Womack would be my opponent. The Ozark district, where Womack lived, had twenty-seven of the thirty-two voting precincts in Franklin County. Charleston had five. The voter distribution was also tilted seventy to thirty. Only if one had been eating "dumb pills" all his life would he not have foreseen the outcome. On hindsight, I can't think of a single thing I had going for me except the five Charleston precincts and a big ego. Not only had my opponent spent four years smiling and shaking hands with every person who walked into the Ozark courthouse, but he made much of the fact that he had lost his parents when he was about twenty years old and was running as an "orphan," an unbeatable platform in rural Arkansas. By his definition, I was also an orphan.

In a rural, sparsely populated county, candidates were expected to shake every hand, knock on every door, laugh at every joke, and attend every function to which they were invited, though the crowds seldom exceeded fifteen people.

Virtually every rural county in Arkansas was sharply divided between two and sometimes three political factions and dominated politically by either the sheriff or the county judge or both. The county judge was not a judge at all, but the chief administrative officer and road builder. If the two were political cohorts, and you weren't on their unwritten slate, then you had best stay home. The sheriff dominated Franklin County politics in 1962. He had nothing against me, and I had supported him in the past, but some of my strongest supporters were archenemies of his, and that made me his enemy. He still had to hold his cards close to the vest, though, because everyone in the Charleston district was a strong supporter of mine, and he didn't want to alienate them.

Twenty years prior to my first run at politics, my uncle Bill Jones, Mother's brother, was county judge and too close for comfort to a very dramatic event. He and the sheriff, Champ Crawford, had dominated Franklin County politics for twelve years. Terms were only two years, so politics dominated most conversations year-round in coffee shops.

In 1940, Uncle Bill and Champ were again running as a team, as they had the preceding five elections. Champ's opponent, Jim Wilson, who had been county treasurer until 1938, had more than a political interest in defeating him. Rumors were rife that Champ had been trysting with Wilson's wife. Though Wilson had been county treasurer, he had never been a real player in county politics, and when the votes were counted, Champ was once again a handy winner, as was my uncle.

Uncle Bill once told me how he and Champ took the ballot boxes to the courtroom on the second floor of the courthouse a few days after each election, usually late at night, dumped the ballots out on a table, and looked them over, especially ballots of people they suspected of lying to them about their support.

On February 26, 1942, Champ walked into the local barbershop at about 9:15 A.M. for his usual morning shave. Shaves were twenty-five cents. The barber would tilt his customer back to a horizontal position and, with a finely honed straight razor, make quite a twenty-minute ritual of what most men today try to put behind them each morning in about three minutes.

Before getting into the barber's chair, Champ took off his belt and holster, which housed his pistol, and hung it on a hat rack. The barber, Mollard Jacobs, laid the chair back to a horizontal position, lathered Champ's face, and started the shaving ritual. Champ and the barber, along with a second barber, who was idle, were the only people in the barbershop when Jim Wilson walked in and announced, "I'll finish this man."

When the barbers remonstrated, Wilson told them they had better leave. Mollard raised Champ back to a sitting position. Champ, sensing a desperate situation, said, "You're all wrong about this, Jimmie. Let's talk this over."

Wilson said, "There'll be no talking."

The two barbers ran out the door, and gunfire erupted immediately. Wilson fired five shots, and Champ, who had managed to get to his holstered pistol hanging on the hat rack, also got off five rounds. Each man was hit three times. An ambulance arrived, and both would have been put in the same ambulance, but Champ's father, a former sheriff himself, arrived and declared that his son would not be placed in the same ambulance with Jim Wilson. Champ died at the scene, and Wilson died two and a half hours later. Uncle Bill decided to retire from politics.

It took almost a week for it to soak in that my decision to run for representative was a bonehead stunt that would haunt me forever, but I felt I had to see it through. I stayed in my office till 1:00 P.M. each day and then took off for the mountains north of the river to go through the motions of pretending to think I would win. I knocked on every door, listened to every inane story imaginable, and, after wasting twenty minutes on some hopelessly ignorant mountaineer, would often be told he was committed to my opponent or wasn't eligible to vote. I could take some comfort in the belief that he was not likely to vote.

The campaign was not a total waste. I learned a lot about the pervasiveness of poverty and ignorance, how manipulative people can be, and, most important, that many people don't have a prayer from the day they crawl out of their mother's womb. A lot of the children in homes I visited would have been better off almost anywhere other than where they were. I saw one family living in what had been a livestock barn, another where incest was obviously rampant, and perhaps most odious of all, people with a superior attitude because of their particular brand of religion.

There were no issues. It was a campaign of smiles, telling jokes, and making sure you never uttered a profanity. Republicans seldom bothered to field a candidate in Arkansas, and as the press faithfully reported after every election, "the Democratic nomination is tantamount to election." In this case, being on the sheriff's slate was tantamount to election. I never solicited or received a single contribution. By election day, I knew from personal knowledge how most of the electorate would vote, and all I could do was smile and wait for the impending disaster. I didn't bother to endure the ritual of going to the Ozark courthouse on election night, where, traditionally, a large crowd gathered to hear the results from each precinct announced from the courthouse steps. I got 93 percent of the votes in the Charleston district and 33 percent in the Ozark district. The vote was roughly 58 to 42 percent. I was only mildly embarrassed, but I went back to my office the following day and resolved to put politics behind me forever.

In 1963, a one-thousand-dollar gift from my sister, along with the small savings I had accumulated, enabled Betty and me to build a larger house with central heating and air-conditioning, built-in appliances, and a small courtyard, where we planted grapes and developed an impressive arbor.

The store had begun to generate a small profit, and my law practice was beginning to flourish. Sales of RCA television sets were large enough to win an all-expense-paid trip for Betty and me to Acapulco. It was our first trip outside the United States. Though politics and what was going on in Washington were my favorite subjects, most of our companions on the trip had no knowledge of or interest in Washington, but they still spent a lot of time condemning its inhabitants. They were interested in TV sales and profits. So I engaged Mexican shopkeepers in dialogues to learn all I could about politics in Mexico. It was the first time I had heard of the one national party, the PRI, which dominated every facet of Mexican politics.

On our return home, we stopped in Dallas to meet Archie, Maggie, and John McConnell, the contractor who had built both my law office and the nursing home, and his wife, Auda Faye. They had come to Dallas to meet us and spend a couple of days and nights shopping and eating at fancy restaurants. The Sunday paper was heavily devoted to the impending visit by John F. Kennedy on the following Tuesday. Most comments were negative by both citizens and the press.

I had actively supported Jack Kennedy and was captivated by the family's glamorous lifestyle on Cape Cod. But, more important, I wanted this country to overcome its anti-Catholic bias. Kennedy's passionate speech to a large audience of Protestant ministers in Houston had stirred the nation as few speeches ever had and dampened the anti-Catholic hostility that had been almost palpable. He was only eight years older than I was, so my admiration for him was also partly generational.

We drove home Sunday, but just to have been in Dallas two days before the assassination made the whole tragedy even more personal for me.

When we got home, Henny, who had baby-sat our children since our first son was born, told us that Brooke, our youngest child and only daughter, now almost two years old, had been stumbling and also seemed to be experiencing some inexplicable, episodic pain, which caused her to scream and pull her arms against her side. We immediately made an appointment with our pediatrician in Ft. Smith, Dr. Roger Bost, who, along with his wife, Katherine, would become two of our dearest friends.

He couldn't find anything to be alarmed about, but after another visit or two, he said her stumbling could be a problem caused by some trauma or lesion affecting the central nervous system. He wanted to hospitalize her for tests, the first of which was a myelogram, a definitive test to see if there was an obstruction in the spinal canal. The test involved injecting a dye into the canal, and the result could not have been clearer. I always had difficulty spotting a problem on an X ray, even after doctors pointed out some anomaly to me. However, this X ray was a crystal-clear heart stopper that showed Brooke had a tumor of some kind that totally blocked the spinal canal. The blockage was located at what the doctors call T-7, or the seventh thoracic vertebra. Only surgery could determine the nature and extent of the tumor.

There were only two neurosurgeons in Ft. Smith, one of whom had recently moved there following a residency at the Mayo Clinic. We chose him. He had to perform eleven laminectomies (removal of part of the vertebra that allowed the spinal cord to be exposed) before determining the extent of what was later diagnosed as an "intra-medular astrocytoma," which meant a lesion embedded in the cord itself. Astrocytomas are usually malignant, on or near the brain stem, and almost always fatal. This one was in a much lower position and was not only benign but a grade four, which is a classification denoting the slowest growth. Dr. Bost said when the surgeon opened the dura, the membrane housing the spinal cord, the cord mushroomed. Tragically, after getting a couple of tissue samples, the surgeon packed the cord, tumor and all, back into the dura and closed it. The damage that had been done, and would continue to be done, was caused by pressure on the tumor, which, though benign, was a "space taker." Packing the cord back into the dura was probably the worst thing that could have been done.

No one seemed to know what the treatment should be. The surgeon had never seen such a condition before. He recommended radiation, simply because he considered the tumor inoperable. Dr. Bost opposed radiation as did the chief radiologist at Sparks Hospital, who said he had strong reservations about radiation because it would probably do more damage than good. He was absolutely correct.

For a $2.30 phone call to the chief radiologist at Boston Children's Hospital, Dr. Bost got superb advice, which was that radiating the tumor was the very worst thing that could be done, because a grade four tumor was almost totally insensitive to radiation, while the damage to good tissue would be devastating.

Dr. Bost referred us to Dr. Don Matson, chief of pediatric neurosurgery at Boston Children's Hospital and author of the definitive textbook on pediatric neurosurgery. Virtually every pediatrician in America had a copy of his book.

We flew to Boston and met with Dr. Matson, who told us he wouldn't operate on Brooke immediately because the tumor was indeed very slow growing. He said that we should watch her closely for any deterioration in walking or any bowel or urinary problems, and return quickly once we were convinced her condition was deteriorating. We watched her constantly, but the degeneration, if there was any, was insidious and difficult to discern, though she continued to suffer unspeakable pain from periodic muscle spasms.

We endured two hellish years hovering over Brooke, often imagining things that weren't there. In March 1966, I had a case in the U.S. Court of Claims in Washington and was away for almost a week. When I returned, I decided there was a marked degeneration in her condition, and we headed immediately for Boston.

I had no idea what this whole nightmare would cost, but I had just won a verdict of eighty-three thousand dollars in the personal-injury case involving the preacher and his wife. My fee, twenty thousand dollars, provided a temporary respite from our always strained financial condition.

We checked into the hospital on Saturday, and Brooke was put in a ward with about twenty other children. The charge was forty-four dollars a day, which we considered outrageous. We were allowed to spend two hours each day with her. She was almost four years old and traumatized about being left alone twenty-two hours a day. I would have picked her up and walked out, but I knew if she was to be saved, we were probably in the only place in the United States where it could happen. I ate no solid food from the time we checked Brooke into the hospital until we first talked to Dr. Matson following her surgery four days later. I couldn't force a morsel down my throat.

Dr. Matson was fifty-two years old at the time and looked fully ten years younger. He was a most impressive man in appearance and demeanor. When he walked the corridors of the hospital, he was obviously held in awe by both doctors and nurses. He told us the surgery was going to be immensely difficult. He would use "loop lens," a form of microscopic surgery. The operation lasted seven hours to remove what Dr. Matson described as a teaspoonful of tumor. The prognosis included the chance of a normal life span. We were rhapsodic. We had arranged for special nurses around the clock, so we indulged ourselves the luxury of going out to dinner at one of Boston's best restaurants.

Our euphoria was short-lived. Two weeks after her surgery, Brooke began running a very high fever. Three efforts at spinal taps failed before a fourth finally yielded fluid. She was diagnosed as having aseptic, as opposed to viral, meningitis, caused by "debris" resulting from the surgery. The treatment was simple—an oscillating fan blowing on her naked body. It seemed incredibly primitive to us, but not to Brooke. Before it broke, her fever hovered around 105 degrees for a week, but the cool air from the fan felt good to her.

After almost six weeks in the hospital, we were approaching the long-awaited day we could leave. There was one more procedure to endure: fitting Brooke for a back brace. That's when we came to know Dr. Arthur Pappas, a widely respected orthopedic surgeon. He supervised the fitting, which was done by covering Brooke with plaster of Paris from her neck to her waist. She was required to stay as still as possible until the plaster set. Then it was cut off her. The following day, she was fitted with a brace, the purpose of which was to keep her from developing scoliosis, or curvature of the spine. But for a little girl to grow up with such a contraption as a companion almost twenty-four hours a day, and to be unable to wear the kinds of cute clothes all her friends wore, was a terrible social onus and a constant torment to us. While she never complained or lamented her plight, we could only guess at her feelings. She was allowed out of the brace two hours a day.

The Boston weather in March and April had been much colder than we had been accustomed to in Arkansas. I hadn't even taken a topcoat to Boston and wound up buying a three-quarter-length coat for $7.50 at Filene's Basement, a popular discount clothing house in Boston. I wore it for twenty years, mostly when I worked on the farm.

When we arrived home, a huge iris bed that Betty had tended laboriously for three years was in full bloom. They were the most beautiful flowers I had ever seen, and I thought surely they were an omen of a beautiful life to come.

Brooke was in a wheelchair for a few months. Before we left the hospital, Betty had been given detailed instructions on the physical therapy she must be given religiously, twice daily. Stretching and pulling, with Brooke protesting loudly, was a daily ritual. Discipline was difficult but imperative. Within six weeks she could crawl, and in the evenings after dinner, we chased each other around the living room floor on all fours, which was a joy to her and also strengthened her legs.

There were no laws then requiring handicapped access to public places, so I carried Brooke and the wheelchair over steps, curbs, and every conceivable obstacle. We had a local carpenter build a contraption, a boardwalk about ten feet long with handrails. It was a surprisingly effective device. Brooke improved quickly by walking endlessly from one end to the other, holding on to the handrails. Within four months she took her first step without holding the handrail. It was an overwhelming moment.

While we were in Boston, I made an irrevocable promise to myself—I was going to get rid of the hardware and furniture business if I had to sell it out the front door, one item at a time. Happily, I didn't have to. My competitor was anxious to be the only hardware and furniture dealer in town, and God knows, I wanted him to be. I conducted a heavily advertised sale and was able to sell off about 50 percent of the inventory. I sold him the balance at cost. It was the end of an ordeal that had cost me untold misery for fifteen years and kept me in a never-ending financial bind. I had taken very little in salary from the store. Rather, I put every spare nickel back into the business by building inventory. I reaped the reward when I sold the business.

.   .   .

I had a growing law practice and money in the bank, and I promptly bought a 210-acre cattle farm with the proceeds of the store sale. I filled it with registered Black Angus cattle and proceeded to enjoy cattle farming as I have enjoyed few things in my life. One year later, I flew to California with Brent, now fourteen years old, to meet with a woman who owned 160 acres adjoining my property, with the intent of buying it if at all possible. The woman met us at Los Angeles Airport and, after a brief discussion, agreed on a sale price. However, it was essential that her husband, from whom she was separated but not divorced, sign the deed. She told us he was a derelict and ventured a guess that we would find him in a bar in Long Beach the next morning. The following morning, she picked us up at our motel and took us to a street that had nothing but bars on both sides. She took one side of the street, and I, with Brent in tow, took the other. We would stick our heads in each bar and shout out the man's name. About halfway down the street, she found him, only half-drunk. We retrieved him from the bar and headed for the office of a lawyer whom the woman had previously used. His office was the seediest dung hole I had ever seen, an appropriate setting for the seediest-looking lawyer I had ever seen. The husband happily signed the deed, asked nothing in return, and headed back to the bar. Brent enjoyed an unforgettable learning experience, and Betty and I were beginning to feel that we had reached what for years had seemed hopelessly elusive—a reasonably secure future financially, a daughter whose future looked more promising than we ever dared dream, two fine, bright, healthy sons, and a mortgaged home with affordable payments. My thoughts finally began again to turn to a political race, one bigger than a race for the state legislature.

Chapter 12

A Rockefeller Comes to Visit
—and Stays

Winthrop Rockefeller moved to Arkansas in the 1950s to take advantage of Arkansas's relatively liberal divorce laws. He had been encouraged to choose Arkansas as the venue for his divorce by Frank Newell, an Arkansas insurance executive with whom Rockefeller had become close friends when they were in the army together. The residence requirement before filing for a divorce in Arkansas was sixty days, and only a ninety-day residency was required prior to a final decree being entered. It was one of the easiest states outside of Nevada in which to obtain a divorce. The cause of Rockefeller's breakup with his wife, BoBo, daughter of a West Virginia coal miner, was a subject of considerable speculation by the country's gossip columnists. Win, as Rockefeller was popularly known, quickly fell in love with Arkansas and decided he not only wanted a divorce, he wanted to live and die there.

Rockefeller was one of five sons born to John D. Rockefeller Jr., called Junior, and Abby Aldrich Rockefeller, whose father had been a powerful senator from Rhode Island. Win's brothers were David, Nelson, Lawrence, and John D. III. Nelson served fourteen years as governor of New York and later became vice president.

Win scoured the state looking for a place to settle down. He finally chose a big spread of about two thousand acres on top of Petit Jean Mountain, a mountain that was not part of a chain but simply rose from a completely flat plain in central Arkansas. The Arkansas River ran along the base of the north side of the mountain. The vistas from Petit Jean were breathtaking, so beautiful, in fact, that the state had created a state park on top of it. Win built a runway on top of it to accommodate his jet. He filled his acreage with expensive, registered Santa Gertrudis cattle, purchased mostly from the famous King Ranch in south Texas. He built a beautiful home for himself and one almost as beautiful for his cattle. The birthing barn was as sterile as most hospital delivery rooms. He became an exemplary citizen, and among other demonstrations of his love for the state, he headed up the Arkansas Industrial Development Commission, a position to which (then) Governor Orval Faubus appointed him. The appointment caused some grumbling among old-line Democrats, because Rockefeller had also been working assiduously to build the Republican Party in Arkansas. There was another school of thought, which was that with Rockefeller's connections and wealth, we would soon have more industry clawing to get into Arkansas than we could accommodate.

In addition to his wealth, Win was an imposing figure physically, standing about six feet four inches tall and weighing about 240 pounds. He was thin haired and fair complexioned, and while not handsome, he had a pleasant countenance and demeanor. He wore custom-made cowboy boots with his personal monogram, *WR*, neatly tooled on them. Guessing their cost was a pastime, and speculations ranged up to five thousand dollars.

In 1964, he made the long-anticipated announcement that he would run for governor and try to prevent the incumbent, Orval Faubus, from winning a sixth term. The campaign was unusually rancorous. It was a horse race until Faubus leveled a charge against Rockefeller that his farm workmen had desecrated a cemetery on another farm he owned just east of Little Rock, by bulldozing graves, allegedly to provide more cropland.

Television was rapidly becoming the political medium, and Faubus produced a thirty-second TV spot showing bulldozers hard at work destroying a cemetery. Apparently one of Rockefeller's bulldozers did accidentally knock over a tombstone, in a cemetery grown over in weeds. The allegation proved deadly to Rockefeller, but Faubus's victory in this, his sixth race, was close enough that it sent a clear and unmistakable message to him that the halcyon days of winning with a wink, a nod, and all the racial code words were over.

Two years later, in 1966, Faubus announced that he would not seek a seventh term, and Rockefeller, who had already made his plans known following his defeat in 1964, kept his word and announced that he would run again.

On the Democratic side, Arkansas's number one old guard segregationist, Jim Johnson, resigned from the state supreme court to run. Frank Holt, another supreme court justice, considered a moderate, also announced his candidacy, but Holt, an eminently decent man, refused to resign from the court. His drawing a salary from the public coffers while running for governor would not have been an issue but for the fact that Johnson had resigned and made a big issue of Holt's not following suit. Holt created an even bigger problem for himself when he was seen leaving the office of Witt Stephens, one of Arkansas's all-time power brokers, who controlled Arkansas's biggest natural gas utility but whose support was becoming a mixed blessing. Costliest of all to Holt was that a lot of Republicans crossed over to vote for Johnson, as did a few liberal Democrats, in the belief that he would be much easier for Rockefeller to defeat in November. The strategy worked, and Johnson, to the joy of Republicans, became the Democratic nominee.

There was yet another factor at work for Rockefeller. Arkansans had always suffered from low self-esteem because they believed the rest of the country perceived them as backward. Rockefeller's move from New York to Arkansas would go a long way toward erasing that image. Why would a scion of one of

America's most prestigious and wealthy families, and whose brother Nelson was governor of their home state of New York, choose Arkansas as his home if it wasn't a highly desirable place to live? He had forsaken the city and state of his birth, where he had lived his entire life, to become an Arkansan.

While Faubus had played the race card to perfection, as the years wore on, people who had originally been wildly enthusiastic became ambivalent about what he had done. They mostly approved of his segregationist policies, but they deplored what his actions had done to fortify Arkansas's reputation as a backward state filled with rednecks. In addition, economic growth had come to a halt. In the decade following the year of the Central High School crisis, not one new industry had located in Arkansas. The Jacuzzi brothers finally broke the ice in 1967.

Arkansans had elected J. William Fulbright to the U.S. Senate over and over, not because he reflected their thinking or tended to their needs or "brought home the bacon," but because he had been a Rhodes scholar and university president, and they believed his being in the Senate ameliorated to some extent the national image of Arkansas as a poor, race-baiting state.

Rockefeller made no bones about being an avowed champion of civil rights and an advocate of the 1954 Supreme Court decision ordering a speedy integration of the nation's schools. Blacks had a certified champion, a man in whom they could place their trust. Win stood on the steps of the capitol at a black rally, held hands with them, and sang "We Shall Overcome." It was an act utterly unthinkable for a politician after what had transpired nine short years earlier. Blacks, normally a reliable Democratic bloc, gave Rockefeller approximately 90 percent of their votes on election day, and on that day he became not only Arkansas's thirty-fourth governor by thirty thousand votes, but also the first Republican governor since Reconstruction. It was the dawn of a new day.

The state legislature was still almost totally Democratic. The thirty-five-member Senate had one Republican, and the one-hundred-member House had three, so poor Win, with all his grandiose plans for reorganizing state government, raising taxes and teacher salaries, and implementing a host of other progressive ideas, was thwarted at every turn, and his first term became a virtual throwaway.

The *Arkansas Gazette*, the oldest newspaper west of the Mississippi and the only liberal statewide paper in the South, did its best to help Win get his proposals passed, but to no avail. The *Gazette* had ritualistically condemned Johnson during the campaign and written favorable editorials for Win, but its Democratic tradition ran too deep for it to formally endorse Rockefeller even against the hated Faubus. Its excellent political cartoonist, George Fisher, was probably as important in Rockefeller's victory as the *Gazette* editorials, and while they were also powerful during the legislative session, they weren't enough to give Rockefeller any victories.

In addition to the mass confusion at the capitol during Rockefeller's first term, his drinking, his notorious habit of being late for every function, and his interminable absences from his office, sometimes for ten days at a time, were becoming legendary. The barbers were especially chagrined with his allegedly jetting to New York to get his hair cut.

I once attended a Sebastian County Bar Association meeting in Ft. Smith just to hear Rockefeller, the scheduled speaker. I wanted to observe his stage presence and general demeanor firsthand just in case the stars someday aligned themselves in my favor. When the crowd of roughly one hundred lawyers had finished lunch, he still hadn't appeared. By 1:15 P.M. the president of the bar announced that they had checked on his whereabouts and that he was "high" someplace between Little Rock and Ft. Smith. The crowd roared with laughter, but that turned out to be the only entertainment. Rockefeller never showed up.

Rockefeller was a pitiable speaker, whose constant pauses in search of a word were nerve-racking. The few times I heard him, I had an almost irresistible urge to jump up in the audience and

shout out the word to him. He was uncomfortable with a microphone in front of him, and I never detected the slightest improvement in his speaking ability or his poise. He leaned on the
podium if he had one and constantly crossed and uncrossed his
legs as he spoke, sure signs of being ill at ease.

As Rockefeller prepared for a second-term bid, the best-
known Democrat likely to run was a veteran old guard state legislator named Marion Crank, and while he was a personable man
with whom I later became friends, he was considered a part of the
Faubus machine. The Republicans couldn't have chosen a better
candidate to oppose Rockefeller. People were increasingly turning their backs on the past.

Crank was a poor speaker with an unappealing voice. In addition to being a seasoned legislator, he had been manager of the
Foreman Cement Plant, owned by the Stephens brothers, Jack
and Witt, whose political clout had been dominant during the
Faubus era. If anybody ever owned a politician, they had owned
Orval Faubus. But now their support was becoming a liability,
though most pols still found their money irresistible.

From 125 miles west of all this political intrigue, I sat in my
windowless office, in the old renovated blacksmith shop in a
town now grown from a Depression level of 851 to 1,200 citizens—where I was still the entire South Franklin County, Arkansas, Bar Association. I pondered whether this might be a golden
opportunity to finally keep faith with my father and jump into
the jungle of statewide politics against what would obviously be
overwhelming odds. Normally, stepping up to the plate against
such odds would have been naive at best and insane at worst. But
I had developed a growing trial practice and in fifteen years had
lost only two jury trials. A few of the wins had been at the expense
of some of Arkansas's best trial lawyers. Why would the same
style and technique not work on a much bigger jury if I could get
the money to visit with them in the intimacy of their living rooms
via television?

Rockefeller had quickly squandered a lot of goodwill in his

first term. Few people felt openly hostile toward him, but he was increasingly perceived as an inept leader. While a second term was not likely to be more successful than the first, people still weren't ready for a return to the Faubus era. The voters were beginning to feel cheated for lack of a choice. It seemed an ideal time for a progressive candidate with no skeletons in his closet, who spoke about the future of our children in a warm and believable way. While Faubus had shattered the strong anti-third-term tradition, there was still an equally strong tradition for granting governors a second term. Only once since the turn of the century had a governor been denied a second term.

I called Woody Haynes, the same Woody Haynes who had been superintendent of the Charleston schools during its perilous integration crisis and who was now farm manager for the College of Agriculture at Arkansas State University in Jonesboro. ASU was three hundred miles away, so we agreed to meet for dinner in Conway, which was about equidistant. Woody gave me the name of Martin Borchert, mayor of Little Rock, whom he had come to know while lobbying the legislature for ASU. He described the mayor as middle-aged, respected, diligent—one of the "better operators."

I called the mayor a couple of days later and told him I would like to visit with him as soon as possible. I gave him the gist of why I wanted to see him but didn't elaborate. He suggested a date, which was one day before the filing deadline.

Betty's father, whom I had kept apprised of my plans, knocked on our door at 6:00 A.M. the morning I was to go to Little Rock. We were sound asleep, and we both staggered, half-asleep, into the kitchen.

He said, "How much is the gate money?"

"What do you mean, gate money?"

"I mean how much does it cost to get in that goddamned Governor's race?"

"You mean the filing fee?"

"Whatever."

"Fifteen hundred dollars," I replied.

He pulled out a wad of bills and peeled off fifteen hundred-dollar bills and handed them to me.

"And I'll bale your hay for you, too," he added.

I had a forty-acre meadow on my farm that had to be baled, and the hay was crucial to winter feed for the cattle. I had given no thought to the farm, the cattle, or who would tend them while I was campaigning, and now I suddenly began to think of all the other things that would have to be tended to should I actually decide to run, such as pending legal cases. As Babe, Betty, and I sat drinking coffee and discussing a lot of other things I hadn't thought about, I realized just how stupid this whole ego trip was becoming. People run for office for a lot of reasons, and altruism is seldom one of them. Ego satisfaction tops the list. They want to be known, admired, deferred to, and catered to, not unlike the officer corps of the military services. But, as one year follows another, ego satisfaction begins to become less important than what the historians are likely to write, though the former is never totally sublimated to the latter.

As I began pondering why I wanted to be governor, the only thing I could come up with was that my father expected it of me. Even if I lost miserably, as long as I gave it my best and adhered to his sense of honor, decency, and good values, he would be proud.

Babe could hardly conceal his enthusiasm that his son-in-law might one day be governor. After all, that would make him an important person at the livestock sale barns; plus, he figured he would have first pick of state prison parolees to work on his farm, pay them whatever he pleased, and threaten to turn them in to the parole officer if they squawked.

As I drove to Little Rock with my good friend and superintendent of Charleston schools, Guy Fenter, I worried about another potential candidate. A bright young lawyer named Ted Boswell from a small community south of Little Rock was also considering the race. He was the only other possible new face, and I had heard that his philosophy would be pleasing to the *Arkansas Gazette*. The fact that the field of Democratic candidates, except for Boswell and me, would be anathema to the *Gazette* meant that we would probably split the moderate to progressive vote and guarantee the nomination to Marion Crank.

I walked into the office of Little Rock mayor Martin Borchert, introduced myself, and told him as precisely as I could that my main objective was to erase the stigma and humiliation that Arkansas was still suffering as a result of the integration crisis. I pointed out that economically, Arkansas was dead in the water. We were still suffering educationally, and tourism was almost nonexistent. In short, Arkansas had become a pariah among the fifty states. He listened attentively, though he had never heard of me prior to my phone call.

He began telling me about the problems he had had with riots in Little Rock following Martin Luther King's assassination. He believed that although things were becoming more tranquil, the problem was going to require much more attention. He felt it would constitute an abdication of his first responsibility to the people of Little Rock to leave his position and join my campaign.

I have thought many times about how bizarre that day was for the mayor and me. Here I was asking the mayor of Little Rock, whom I had never laid eyes on before, to leave his prestigious and demanding position to run a campaign for a man he was meeting for the first time in his life and was totally unknown outside a community of twelve hundred people plus a few lawyers around the state. As I later reflected on the scene, I realized how charitable and polite he had been—and how naive I had been.

When I later thought about the fifteen hundred dollars in hundred-dollar bills burning a hole in my pocket, and about how I was prepared to go immediately to the Democratic Party offices and plunk it down to campaign with a manager I had never seen before and, as was discovered two years later, with a whopping 1 percent statewide name recognition, I determined that my later detractors were right—my ego was exceeded only by my naiveté.

My maternal grandmother, Elizabeth. Everyone called her Lizzie. Her stern countenance belied a gentle soul, and my grandfather adored her. She always referred to him as "Mr. Jones."

The Oak Valley baseball team. Dad is third from the left in the second row, and his oldest brother, my Uncle Joel, the "drinking uncle," is third from the left in the first row.

One of the eight grades Dad taught in a one-room school in Oak Valley. Dad is standing on the right in the back row. Teaching was the love of his life next to politics. He walked a total of six miles each day to and from school.

Dad, with customers and employees, in the Charleston Hardware Store, which I would later own and operate for fifteen years.

Me in my typical summer
attire. I was seven.

All of the first grade and part of the second at the Charleston Grade School. I'm
first on the left, seated in the front row, with overall bib hanging and sole
detatched from my shoe. Betty is third from the right in the second row.

Family photograph, 1939. Mother and Dad are seated, and standing from left to right are me, Carroll, and Margaret.

Me at age fourteen or fifteen.

Mother and Dad, around 1942.

Carroll (left) and me, around 1940.

Betty Flanagan,
age twenty-two, a student
at the Chicago Academy
of Fine Arts.

Me, all decked out in
borrowed "dress blues."
Nobody wore dress
blues during the War,
but street photographers
had them to loan for
pictures to impress parents
and girlfriends back home.

The photo used on all billboards and campaign literature in the governor's race of 1970. Out of 300 pictures taken, this was the only one we felt was acceptable. It turned out to be a big factor in the race.

Family photo taken in 1981. Betty and Brooke in front, and, left to right, standing in back, Bill, me, and Brent.

The mayor saved me from what surely would have been a losing and probably humiliating defeat.

Mayor Borchert was a native of Stuttgart, Arkansas, which was settled by German immigrants on what is called the Grand Prairie. Arkansas produces 43 percent of all the rice grown in the United States, and most of it is produced in the Grand Prairie. Stuttgart also calls itself the "duck capital of the nation." The national duck-calling contest is a major annual event, and it is an amazing thing to witness and hear.

The mayor had made the eminently sensible point that since I was totally unknown in eastern Arkansas, I should give up the notion of running in 1968 and wait until 1970. He said he would be happy to schedule speeches for me before a few Rotary Clubs in eastern Arkansas and Little Rock and let me try out my talents on people from a culture quite different from that of the mountainous, virtually all-white area from which I came. I left in a melancholy mood, disappointed but knowing the mayor's decision was the correct one for him. I returned Babe's fifteen hundred dollars the following day.

The outcome of the ensuing race was highly predictable. The Democratic candidates were Virginia Johnson, wife of the race-baiting former supreme court justice whom Winthrop Rockefeller had defeated in 1966, plus Marion Crank, Ted Boswell, and three others who wound up as also-rans. There was a common belief that the Democratic runoff would be between Virginia Johnson and Marion Crank. But, predictably, Boswell began to emerge as a viable contender for two reasons. One, nobody knew him, and two, he was getting strong support from the *Gazette*. Johnson and Crank, though front-runners, were too well known, and they represented the past, which people were increasingly anxious to leave to the past.

In the first primary, Crank led easily, and Virginia Johnson was second, but only three hundred votes ahead of Boswell. As the votes were counted and recounted, the Crank forces worked overtime trying to make sure Boswell was not their opponent in the runoff. They had a lot of help from the Rockefeller forces, who were praying that Virginia Johnson would get in the runoff, maybe beat Crank, and become their general election opponent. They did not want to face a new young upstart named Boswell, who had momentum going for him, and they succeeded in not getting him. Virginia Johnson edged Boswell out by about four hundred votes and became Crank's runoff opponent. Two weeks later, Crank handily defeated her and became Win Rockefeller's opponent. All to no avail. Rockefeller defeated him by sixty thousand votes in the general election, but nobody seemed particularly happy about it.

Rockefeller's second term was, predictably, as acrimonious as the first. Absolutely nothing happened, and people, while not sympathetic with the legislature, were also growing increasingly impatient with Rockefeller's lack of leadership. Five-thousand-dollar cowboy boots or no, WR still found it impossible to corral the legislature, and that, combined with the still relatively strong tradition against a third term, especially after Faubus's six terms, and all the never-ending gossip about him, made his political future bleak indeed.

A line began to form among the well-known Democratic politicos, including Orval Faubus, now reputed to be interested in making a comeback. He had divorced his wife of thirty-seven years and three weeks later got himself a new young wife, Elizabeth, who wore a trademark beehive wig and had visions of presiding over elegant parties at the Governor's Mansion. She was strongly urging her new husband to run.

The possibility of a Faubus candidacy was having a greater influence on my thinking than it should have, but the thought of fulfilling a lifelong ambition and taking Faubus out at the same time was too powerful to resist.

‖ *Chapter 13* ‖

It Was Sheer Madness

Arkansas's prisons had become a national scandal. There were only about thirty "free world employees" at our largest prison, which had seventeen hundred inmates. The prisons were run by the inmates, called trustees, and were averaging one escape per day. Stories, probably apocrypha, were rampant about people in southeast Arkansas almost daily seeing inmates running across their backyards with prison personnel and bloodhounds in hot pursuit. I later learned that tales of barbarism by inmates against inmates were true. There were too few guards to do anything about it. The prisons had become so unconscionably scandalous that a challenge to the constitutionality of the prisons succeeded and the federal court took over supervision of the entire system. Whoever got elected governor would inherit this mess.

On New Year's Eve 1970, a white inmate was locked in a maximum security cell with two notorious black inmates, one of whom had a grudge against the white. I later read a detailed report on the torture and murder of the white inmate, which was the most gruesome and minutely detailed report of barbarism I have ever read. The torture went on for two hours while the screams of the inmate were drowned out by the shouting and singing of other inmates in adjoining cells who knew what was happening.

Rockefeller deserved high praise for his valiant efforts to dismantle the Faubus political machine. He also deserved high marks for stopping rampant, wide-open, illegal gambling in Hot Springs. But he deserved even higher marks for his futile efforts to bring about prison reform, though the people he hired to accomplish it virtually guaranteed failure. He personally paid Peat-Marwick a handsome sum to study and make recommendations on how Arkansas's state government could be streamlined, reformed, and made more efficient. State government was saturated with boards and commissions, many serving no useful purpose except to tickle the egos of appointees. But the legislature stymied all efforts to implement the study, especially the recommendation that would have reduced the number of agencies reporting to the governor from sixty-seven to thirteen. It was becoming obvious that the issues that would dominate a campaign were growing more numerous by the day.

The governor's fights with the legislature, and vice versa, made daily headlines. While the people were largely disinterested in such arcane subjects as government reorganization, they generally agreed with what the Governor was trying to accomplish. They still had not fully adopted his liberal policies on race, which included appointing large numbers of blacks to state jobs, boards, and commissions. But mostly, Arkansans were tired of the bickering. Teachers wanted raises, parents wanted their children to learn, and people in southeast Arkansas wanted to get a night's sleep without worrying about prison escapees breaking into their homes. The U.S. Supreme Court had ordered busing to achieve racial balance in some places across the country, a decision that heightened resentment of Rockefeller's racial policies. Even so, I was betting that their antipathy toward Rockefeller still didn't make them yearn for the return of Orval Faubus.

It was time to take Mayor Borchert's suggestion that I start

making a few speeches in east and southeast Arkansas, agricultural areas with heavy black populations, where a plantation
mentality was still prevalent. I was also invited to a few communities to speak to bar groups about what it was like to be a solo
practitioner in a small town. I found the accents of east and south
Arkansas to be quite different from that of the west. The economies were also different. Strangely, even the humor was different. The blacks lived in shanties for the most part, and while
racial prejudices were not as intense as I would have imagined,
the lives of blacks were little different from what they had been
a hundred years previously. My speeches were well received, especially the point that our common goal should be to change
Arkansas's national image from a backward to a progressive state.
In order to do that, the changes had to be real, not cosmetic. I
stole Hubert Humphrey's line: "This will never be a good place
for any of us to live until it's a good place for all of us to live."

·   ·   ·

Humor, particularly self-deprecating humor, is a must for successful politicians. It conveys a strong message that the speaker
doesn't take himself too seriously, doesn't consider himself superior, has stumbled on occasion, and is not incapable of learning a
thing or two from his audience. But I learned early on that
humor can be a bane or a blessing, and there's often a very fine
line between what is acceptable and what isn't. Much depends on
the kind of audience one is addressing. I developed an understanding of regional humor, how to deal with a liberal as opposed
to a conservative audience, and where the threshold lies on
slightly off-color humor.

I once told a joke to about a thousand people, almost all
women, from all over the southeastern United States that netted
me one of the harshest letters I ever received. The joke was about
a gas station that placed a huge sign out front that read FREE SEX
WITH EVERY TWENTIETH FILL-UP. One man eagerly and regularly
pulled into the station but was always told by the attendant that

he was eighteenth or nineteenth or twenty-first, but never twentieth. Finally, utterly disgusted, he came home one evening and told his wife, "You know that service station on the way home that has the free sex sign out front?"

"Yes," his wife replied.

"Well, that's the biggest fraud I've ever seen."

"No, it's not," his wife said. "I've won three times."

Now, admittedly, the story was a little bold, but it was obviously designed for women and to point out how it never occurs to men that women might also be interested in such a contest.

The author of the letter, a devout Arkansan, chastised me as an aider and abettor of the permissive sexual attitudes our teens had adopted, and how could we expect Christian conduct from our children when they hear their leaders treat such a serious subject with such abandon and indifference just to get a laugh? It was "disgusting," she said. I wrote and apologized profusely, but I also pointed out that while it was her privilege to respond as she pleased, I felt her reaction was a bit excessive. The other 999 women present had seemed to love the story.

The other shocker I richly deserved. I was invited to speak to an organization in Boston. It was very early in my political career. The audience was well dressed, sophisticated, well educated, and very liberal. The story I told resulted in a wake-up call to just how unsophisticated I was on the changing agenda and attitudes of women. In the South, the story had always evoked uproarious laughter, but not in Boston.

Story: A guy couldn't decide which of two women to marry. One was beautiful, a great body—the personification of grace and beauty. The other was a homely, unattractive woman, but she had a beautiful mezzo-soprano voice, knew every aria from every great opera, and sang them to perfection. The man was an opera buff and was positively captivated by her voice. Finally, out of deference to his love of opera, he chose the great soprano over the much more beautiful woman.

Two months later, he got out of bed one morning, went to

the window, and, lo, the beautiful woman he had rejected was walking by his house, beautiful as ever, the personification of grace in motion. He looked back at his wife, still asleep, hair in curlers. He looked out the window again, then walked over to the bed, shook his wife, and said, "For God's sake, Helen, get up and sing something."

The chorus of *boos* and *oohs* might not have been total, but it was close. Betty was as appalled and fully as unforgiving as the audience and aided the booers.

One of the stories (totally fabricated) I used to good effect when I first ran for governor was about seeing a man coming across the street toward my law office the day I moved in. I quickly picked up the phone and, as the man entered, said with contempt in my voice, "Listen, I wouldn't take your case for a thousand dollars. As a matter of fact, I wouldn't take your case for two thousand dollars," and slammed the receiver into the cradle. I looked up and asked the gentleman if I could be of help.

He said, "No, I'm from the telephone company. I just came to hook up the phone."

The other story my consultant in the governor's race told me not to ever use again after he heard me tell it the first time was about overhearing two women in another aisle of the grocery store. The story was designed to get a laugh out of being the only lawyer in a very small town. One woman asked another, "Who's the best lawyer in Charleston?"

"Dale Bumpers when he's sober," the other answered.

"Who's next best?"

"Dale Bumpers when he's drunk."

One story I told many times on Strom Thurmond, and later myself, was about campaigning in a nursing home. He stopped by an elderly woman seated in a rocker and asked, "Do you know who I am?" "No, but if you'll go down the hall to the front desk, they can probably help you find out," she replied.

Another story I told after the campaign for governor began almost put my consultant, Deloss Walker, in a coma. I told it to a large and rather staid audience. It was about a New Yorker moving to Arkansas and buying a run-down farm from a farmer who was so elated over pawning his farm off on a neophyte, he told him he was going to throw his old sow in just as a token of friendship. The New Yorker said, "What will I do with a sow?"

The farmer said, "Raise pigs, of course."

"And how do I do that?" the New Yorker asked.

"Well," said the farmer, "you put the old sow in a wheelbarrow and cart her up the hill to farmer Jones's place. He's got a boar hog, and when that old sow and boar spend a day together, you'll get little pigs." The New Yorker dutifully loaded the old sow up and took her up the hill to farmer Jones, left her all day, and went back that evening to bring her home.

The next morning, he went out to check to see if he had any little pigs, which, of course, he didn't. So he loaded the sow up again, carted her back up the hill, and returned to retrieve her that evening. Same story. No pigs. He continued this ritual until finally, on Saturday morning, he told his wife he was exhausted from hauling the old sow up and down the hill, and asked her if she would go out and check to see if there were any little pigs. She checked, and came back and said, "You still don't have any little pigs, but the sow's in the wheelbarrow waiting for you."

I never told the story again—until I left office.

·   ·   ·

Faubus was easily the best-known and most formidable candidate seriously considering the governor's race. He and his new wife, Elizabeth, were beginning to make appearances around the state. Elizabeth had taught Orval, an inveterate cigarette smoker, to use a long cigarette holder, and the two were regularly seen smoking using the holders. People might have accepted such from blue bloods like FDR, but from Orval and Elizabeth Faubus it was a wholly unacceptable affectation. I was incredulous that they were oblivious to the sniggering, especially since Faubus had long projected an image of a "good ol' country boy."

Then there was the respected attorney general, Joe Purcell, whose speaking style and gestures were robotic. Like Harry Truman, he chopped the air incongruously when he spoke, and his syntax was confusing; but even so, he was considered the top challenger to Faubus. Before filing, he went to what came to be called "charm school" in Dallas. If anything, it made his style worse.

The other potential candidates included House Speaker Hayes McClerkin; Bill Wells, a near winner in the lieutenant governor's race two years earlier; Ted Boswell; Bob Compton, a prominent south Arkansas attorney; Jim Malone, whose father had been a political player during the Faubus years; and Bill Cheek, a West Memphis oil distributor who may have had even less name recognition than I had.

The Arkansas Jaycees (Junior Chamber of Commerce) numbered about five thousand in 1970, and they were a raucous bunch, full of energy and naiveté. Though Rockefeller had ingratiated himself with them, we concluded they were a potential fountain of energy that just might be harnessed on my behalf and wouldn't be intimidated by the conventional wisdom—that I was a "nice guy but didn't have a chance." I also knew that all the so-called power brokers in the state would be aligned with one of the well-known contenders and that, as a total unknown, I would have to seek out people who, for the most part, had never been involved in a political race before.

The Jaycees state convention was to be held in Hot Springs, and we decided to go, invite everyone to our suite, post pictures everywhere, and set up a well-stocked bar. But it suddenly dawned on us that we didn't even have a photograph with which to decorate a hospitality suite. Archie Schaffer, a native of Allentown, Pennsylvania, never understood much about Arkansas politics, but he loved what he did understand. He was enthusiastic about my running for governor and had the perfect solution, inspired by a mail-order catalog that featured enlargements of snapshots. At the time, I didn't know there were political consultants who did all those things, such as yard signs, billboards, policy ideas, literature, anything from which they could extract a 15 percent fee. Anyway, we didn't have two pesos to rub together and couldn't have hired a consultant if we had known one, which we didn't.

I put on what I considered the best of my four suits for our photography session. Archie got out his Polaroid, only slightly superior to a Brownie, and we went into the courtyard of our home and began taking pictures beneath our grape arbor, which hung over the courtyard as a perfect backdrop. We took four or five pictures, all equally awful. One problem that had never been noticed before was that I seemed to have a droopy left eye. Archie concocted a remedy. We decided we could prop open the recalcitrant eyelid with a finely crafted toothpick. We began again, and the results made the droopy eye look as though it had just seen Frankenstein's monster—which then left the right eye looking droopy. We returned to au naturel. Finally, everyone agreed that one of the pictures was not awful, and off it went to the mail-order house. A few days later, we received three prints, each of them two by three feet; we pasted each print onto an identical-size piece of cardboard and set off for Hot Springs and the Jaycees convention. It was then three weeks before the filing deadline.

Amazingly, not one other potential candidate attended or even put in an appearance. As I attempted to ingratiate myself with the Jaycees (thirty-five was the maximum age), many of them suggested that I hire Deloss Walker, a former president of the organization, as my consultant and television producer. I had never heard of him, but he showed up on Saturday evening, the last night of the convention, and came by our suite. We liked each other immediately, visited for about three hours, and at midnight adjourned to an all-night café until 4:00 A.M. He was desperate to make a name for himself, and I was anxious to be the vehicle for him to do it. He had handled one successful statewide race for an Arkansas supreme court candidate, and one congressional race for Bill Alexander, who would go on to serve twenty years in the House of Representatives. When I told him I had no money except my own limited resources plus what I could weasel out of my brother and sister, he was undaunted. As a matter of fact, nothing seemed to daunt him. I was buoyed by his seeming sophistication and especially by his enthusiasm. I told him I would be back in touch. If nothing else, I knew his familiarity with the Jaycees could be a great asset.

When I returned home, I called Carroll, who was living in Winnetka, Illinois, a suburb of Chicago. He was moving up the corporate ladder and was president of Greyhound Computer Corporation, a leasing company and subsidiary of the Greyhound Corporation. I told him of my plans and asked if we could meet at his house the following Sunday. He was agreeable and even mildly enthusiastic.

I then called my sister, Margaret, who in a divorce settlement had wound up with a very profitable vending business she and her husband had owned. Her husband got the loser, a Dr Pepper bottling business in Elyria, Ohio, a city of about thirty thousand just west of Cleveland. Margaret had been phenomenally successful building the business and was rapidly becoming one of America's most prominent businesswomen. She would later be admitted to the Sales Marketing and Executives Association of Cleveland, thereby becoming the first woman in the nation admitted to the organization. In 1960, she and ten other vending companies merged to form a company called Servomation. Margaret's share shortly became worth three million dollars on the New York Stock Exchange, a fortune in 1960.

Since Margaret was worth several million dollars and would shortly be worth much more, I felt sure she would want to spend a big wad of it to see her baby brother become governor of Arkansas. Nothing could have been further from her mind. It was Sunday, May 30, 1970, when we gathered around Carroll's breakfast table, roughly two weeks before the filing deadline, June 16. Margaret thought the idea of taking on Orval Faubus in the Democratic primary, and then, if successful, facing Win Rockefeller and his unlimited supply of money, was pure madness. She was right, but Carroll and I didn't know it. After three hours of wrangling, baby brother came away with the following commitments: Margaret, twenty-five thousand dollars; Carroll, fifteen thousand; and me, ten thousand. I began to suffer something akin to stark terror as I slowly reached the point of no return, and I would wake up in a cold sweat, contemplating the impending disaster. My mother's genes told me my family would starve, my children would go uneducated, I would die still trying to pay off the debts, and, most of all, hardly a living soul would remember at my funeral that I had once run for governor and finished a slow fourth or fifth in a field of eight.

There would be ample time in the immediate future while staring at motel room ceilings to agonize or regret my decision and ask, "What the hell do you think you're doing?"

Chapter 14

The Campaign Begins

I decided to file on Friday, four days before the deadline, rather than wait until the last minute. I wouldn't make the Sunday papers, but Saturday was next best. And just as I had felt a sense of inner peace the day we had sailed out of San Diego for an unknown destination and unknown destiny, so did I now, having made the irreversible decision to run, feel calm and at peace with myself.

We recruited a small band of about fifty friends, mostly from Charleston but a few from Little Rock, to assemble for a 10:00 A.M. press conference on the mezzanine of the Lafayette Hotel, a fleabag that was about done for but had been prestigious in its day. I began by uttering a few unremarkable and immediately forgettable words. The media, mostly the writing press, one popular radio commentator, and one television station, turned out for what Charlestonians considered an earthshaking event. Mayor Borchert had been able to recruit one elderly black man, who recruited another one. On hindsight, it would be difficult to conjure up a more pitiful, inauspicious beginning for somebody running for sheriff, let alone the highest political office in the state.

Following my mercifully brief statement, the UPI reporter and the radio commentator burrowed in.

"With no political experience outside the Charleston School Board," why did I think I could blah, blah, blah.

"Specifically, what do you propose in the way of prison reform?" Good question, and I didn't have a good answer, but I assured everyone I would get the prisons out from under the federal court's jurisdiction. Being forced to relinquish control over our prisons, no matter how deplorable they were, had been immensely unpopular.

"Do you favor the proposed new state constitution?" Some of it, yes—some of it, no. I was catching on. It was, of course, highly controversial. I didn't say so, but I strongly favored changing that part of the 1874 constitution, amended in 1879, that set the governor's salary at ten thousand dollars a year. It had originally been five thousand. As lawyers love to intone, "Since the memory of man runneth not," New York had had the highest governor's salary and Arkansas the lowest. It was true in 1970, and it's true today.

"How are you going to raise Arkansas teachers' salaries from the second lowest in the nation without raising taxes?" queried a reporter with a self-satisfied look.

"We'll have to explore all possibilities, but I believe the people of Arkansas are tired of having to continually say 'Thank God for Mississippi,' I answered, also with a self-satisfied look.

The press left the Lafayette underwhelmed and I left depressed, but there was no such thing as Prozac. I assumed I had just torpedoed any chance I might otherwise have had of being governor. The serenity I had felt earlier was gone. Mother's genes took hold. I later learned that nobody was paying attention.

That afternoon the *Arkansas Democrat*, an afternoon daily in Little Rock, carried a small article on the bottom of the front page with a picture of me that I felt sure the public would take for that of a serial killer. My mother wouldn't have voted for me. My spirits couldn't have been lower.

For lack of something better to do, I went home, but not before mindlessly going to the Lafayette Barber Shop for a haircut. Surely in a big city like Little Rock, barbers would be more sophisticated than Ed Haney, my Charleston barber, who cut my hair for seventy-five cents. I came out looking like a Nazi skinhead, and it would be at least three weeks before I would be presentable for television. The barber had to have been on Orval Faubus's payroll. Adding insult to injury, it cost $1.25. After looking in the mirror, I decided the picture in the *Democrat* looked pretty good. One good thing about the press conference was that no editorial writer or columnist of any consequence had attended, so no damaging pieces were going to be written. I comforted myself with the knowledge that I could avoid televison for a while and my hair would ultimately grow out. At least, it always had before.

When I first met Deloss Walker at the Jaycees convention in Hot Springs about three weeks prior to the press conference, he had insisted I come to Memphis and do a few thirty-second television run-throughs to determine how I looked and sounded. I was pretty impressed with the spot I did on education. I sat on a stool with a few notes on a legal pad and emoted for what I hoped would be twenty-eight seconds, the time usually required for a thirty-second spot.

When I finished my first attempt, Deloss said, "Listen, champ,"—that was to be my name for the next five months—"if I invited you into my living room for a visit, would you start shouting at me?"

"Of course not," I said.

"Well, that's what you just did. Now, let's try it again. Don't change anything except the decibel level."

Four or five of Walker's staffers thought it was great, but I thought I was so-so at best. I considered their opinions suspect, because if they could get me in the race, they got 15 percent of all radio, television, and newspaper ads. Huge up-front fees weren't in vogue yet. After my announcement, I had wanted to start running TV spots immediately, but we didn't have the money, plus the Lafayette barber had done too much damage.

As my nephew and I drove back to Charleston after the press conference, I made a few calculations. I had seventy-four days until the first primary, and if I survived it and became one of the top two Democratic candidates, I would have fourteen days until the runoff. If I won the runoff, I would have fifty-six days until the general election, a grand total of a hundred and forty-four days. Not much time for someone nobody ever heard of and who had fifty thousand dollars for staff, yard signs, bumper strips, and literature, to say nothing of television.

The next morning, I awoke to find my picture on the front page of the *Southwest Times Record*, the Ft. Smith daily that blanketed western Arkansas and parts of northwest Arkansas. It was the very flattering picture we had chosen from three hundred taken by a couple of professionals about a week previously and handed out to the press at my announcement. My spirits soared. I couldn't have been happier if I had just won an Academy Award. I felt certain that picture was going to land me in the Governor's Mansion, and as it turned out, it played a major role. We put it on our yard signs, all our literature, and all the highway billboards we could afford.

Reflecting back on how our hearts sank one minute and how elated we were the next over what were, in retrospect, meaningless and trivial incidents, I know now it was the very essence of politics. Every politician scans every story about him- or herself and, almost without exception, attaches far too much importance to its likely impact.

Our morale soared mightily when we received word on Monday that Ted Boswell, who had come so close to making the runoff in 1968, and Sid McMath, another former governor who was also considering a comeback, had opted out. Deloss decided we should spend ten thousand dollars on early television spots, mostly on Little Rock stations, which covered most of the state. Hopefully, it would save me a lot of time introducing myself to every voter, telling who I was and why I was running. A ten-thousand-dollar television buy would be laughable today, and it was pretty ludicrous then. But placed carefully on the local evening news, the spots were cheap and would have some effect.

We had liked the spots in Memphis with me sitting on a stool. Deloss decided I was talented enough to simply sit on a stool with a legal pad on my lap and, with a blacked-out background, speak extemporaneously for as close to twenty-eight seconds as I could. We did spots on prison reform, education, doctors for rural areas, and the deplorable condition of our state parks. Amazingly, each was a "take." They were fresh, my voice was better than usual, and as they were shown over a three-week period, they began to have the desired effect. People still tell me they remember these early TV spots with the yellow legal pad.

Much of the fifty thousand dollars we started with had been committed. But within thirty days, the TV spots had raised me to about 10 percent of the vote in the Little Rock "popcorn" poll. It was a meaningless but traditional poll taken at a popular Little Rock theater, where people who bought popcorn were allowed to pick the popcorn bag with their favorite candidate's name on it. It amounted to nothing, but it was good for our morale. Unhappily, an authentic statewide poll taken at the same time had me at 4 percent. But even that was a 400 percent improvement over day one.

The first real break was a 7:00 P.M. Sunday evening primetime special produced by the widely watched Little Rock NBC affiliate, which decided to do a one-hour program on the governor's race. The station gave each candidate four minutes, and best of all, the lineup would be by alphabetical order, which placed me first. I surely had a friend at the station. I knew that after the first two or three candidates spoke, thousands of Arkansans would be twisting the knobs off their sets getting back to Ed Sullivan to watch a dog bark "Home on the Range."

I spoke without notes, and it was my best performance of the entire campaign. I agonized over the death penalty but could not bring myself to oppose it, because I knew the terrible trauma families suffered from a wanton murder. It was my first opportunity to share my father's belief in the political system and talk about our solemn duties to one another. I closed with a somber plea to "join me. . . ."

The feedback from the show was great. The next morning, our phones were jammed with people calling our headquarters asking for literature and yard signs. Our problem: We had precious little literature and no yard signs. Worse still, we had no money to buy them. But the show produced a trickle of money, too, so we hurriedly replenished our depleted stock.

The strategy of the campaign was simple: Try to finish second. This sounds like Coach Lou Holtz's great story about when he first started coaching. He said he always told his hapless team before the opening kickoff, "If they kick off, try to recover the fumble. If we kick off, try to block the extra point." We knew Faubus would lead.

One of the best things I had going for me was that the other candidates didn't take me seriously, so at political rallies they beat up on one another and ignored me. Bill Cheek was the exception. Running dead last, he would go through the peccadilloes and misdeeds of each of the other candidates and end with, "Now, I don't know much about this fellow Bumpers, but the folks in his hometown tell me he's to the left of Hubert Humphrey."

About four weeks before the election, we started running as many newspaper ads as we could afford, saying, "The dark horse is moving up." I thought it was trite. We dreamed up a few salient points on why people were "switching" to me, and to my surprise, the ads proved effective. Everybody loves a dark horse. At that point I was at 7 percent in most polls, Faubus was at 44 percent, and House Speaker McClerkin and Attorney General Purcell were tied at 14 percent, precisely where they were when the campaign began. From the beginning, I was the only candidate who moved a single point. While 7 percent seems insignificant, it wasn't bad considering where I started, and the small momentum was becoming a topic of conversation. None of the other candidates seemed to notice.

Campaigning is a unique experience. Every day something memorable and totally unexpected happens. One of the most dramatic and unforgettable moments of my life occurred one afternoon in Springdale, a city of about fifteen thousand. I walked into the office of the *Springdale News,* the local daily paper, and asked the receptionist if the editor, Chuck Sanders, was in. She said no, but that the assistant editor was and to go right in. The assistant was a fine-looking young man, and I held out my hand.

"I'm Dale Bumpers, candidate for governor."

He took my hand and said, "I'm Bill Elderton."

"Are you Bill Elderton Jr.?"

"Yes, I am."

I was overwhelmed by my emotions and flooded with memories of Bill Elderton, my best friend in boot camp, who had been killed in the invasion of Pelelieu and who had told me his greatest fear was that he wouldn't live to see his yet unborn child, now standing in front of me. I spent an hour with him, sharing stories about his father and our experiences—stories he would never have heard if I hadn't stumbled onto him by the sheerest coincidence. He and his mother later attended several political rallies.

At an east Arkansas political rally, on a hot Sunday afternoon ten days before the election, Deloss and I anxiously awaited the arrival of House Speaker McClerkin. We had heard that he was to receive a poll the previous evening, and we felt sure we could determine by the look on his face and his general demeanor whether the poll was good or bad. When McClerkin showed up, he sat in his car for fully ten seconds without moving. He then slowly got out of his car and walked toward the crowd like a condemned man being led to his execution. We were ecstatic. Two days later, he canceled a big television buy, and we knew then that the race for the runoff spot against Faubus was between Purcell and me. Only one week after the poll showing me at 7 percent came out, an independent poll showed me at 11 percent. I had ten days left.

Deloss, without my knowledge, called Carroll and told him

in glowing and exuberant terms, "We've got a real shot at this sucker. We can win it. But to win, you and Margaret have got to come up with another thirty-five thousand dollars." Carroll was willing and immediately called Margaret. She said, "I'm not putting another damned dollar into that big ego trip our brother is on. This gets more absurd by the day." Carroll cajoled, argued, pleaded, and refused to hang up. After thirty minutes he had twenty thousand dollars from Margaret and fifteen thousand from himself, enough to make a dent with warm and fuzzy TV spots in the last week of the campaign. I again sat on the stool and spoke with all the heartfelt emotion I could muster.

Because of the chaos that had prevailed between the legislature and the governor's office the preceding four years, we had adopted the slogan "Let's get our state together." It had begun to take hold. I began reminding people that because nobody had given me a chance to win, no favors had been sought, nor any promised. I would assume the office of governor free to do what was best. A small, unreliable sampling of voters two days before the election indicated I was at 14 percent. It also showed Purcell still at 14 percent. McClerkin had dropped to 11 percent.

Friday afternoon before the election on Tuesday, I was handing out literature in front of an office building as people poured out, rushing for home. One of Faubus's best friends, adviser, and chief counsel during the Little Rock school integration crisis was last to leave the building. We shook hands in the foyer, and he lauded me for my conduct during the campaign. He said I shouldn't be discouraged because I had come close to making it but had been barely nosed out. He spoke in the past tense, as though the votes had been counted. He indicated that Faubus had just completed a poll showing as much. He said I should consider trying again someday, because I showed promise. I was much cheered by his words and attitude. He reminded me of the little boy whistling as he walked through the cemetery late at night. I knew I was the candidate Faubus least wanted in the runoff with him.

I later learned of an interesting story that had occurred earlier at a political rally in North Little Rock about midway through the campaign. Faubus had spoken before I did because I was late in arriving, and strangely, the huge crowd stayed after he spoke. They usually left after he spoke. It was one of the biggest audiences I had had a chance to address.

Faubus later told me this story: When he left with his friend Bill Smith, he expected the audience to follow, but they didn't. And he and Smith didn't leave, either. They pretended to leave but then hid behind a hedge to hear what I had to say. When I finished, Faubus turned to Smith and said, "You know, that son of a bitch may beat me."

The election was held on a typical hot and humid August day. At our headquarters that evening, people were dripping perspiration and their clothes were soaking wet. Our small headquarters was packed with people, and the air-conditioning was hopelessly inadequate. Some of the people were well known to me, but many had worked very hard in their own way in their own neighborhoods without seeking recognition and were unknown to me. I felt guilty that I hadn't had a chance to thank each of them. Of course, some were political hangers-on who sensed that I just might get in the runoff and it would be wise to hedge their bets by putting in an appearance.

At 10:00 P.M., with about 50 percent of the precincts reporting, Faubus had 36 percent, Joe Purcell had 21 percent, and I was a close third with 20 percent. That 1 percent difference was about two thousand votes at the time, and it looked as though it would hold up. I was disappointed but gratified to have come so close.

An ABC political commentator from Washington, who was not widely known but was something of a celebrity in Little Rock that evening and who thought much more highly of himself than he had a right to, was holding forth doing interviews with each of the candidates in what had been the lobby of the old Marion Hotel, now closed. He had been in town for about five hours and was making sagacious observations on Arkansas politics, about which he knew virtually nothing. He interviewed me with questions that bordered on being contemptuous and demonstrated a strong Rockefeller bias. I tried to be statesmanlike in saying that even if I didn't make it, it had been a worthwhile undertaking; that I had appealed to the best instincts of people and encouraged young people to honor their civic obligation and participate in the political process; and that, above all, I had kept faith with my father. When I got back to the headquarters, Carroll was still teary-eyed. He said, "What you just said makes me certain this was all worth doing regardless of the outcome."

While I was doing the television interview, returns from Sebastian County (Ft. Smith), which abutted my home county of Franklin, began coming in, and by the time I got back to our campaign headquarters, I had taken a two-thousand-vote lead over Purcell. Pandemonium had broken out, as only those who have been closely associated with a campaign on election night can fully appreciate. The lead not only held up, but by about 2:00 A.M. it had grown to almost four thousand votes.

Faubus	142,869
Bumpers	79,108
Purcell	75,211

We began calling officials, mostly sheriffs, all over the state, pleading with them to protect the ballot boxes in their counties. Faubus was strong in the mountainous regions of north central Arkansas and was strongly supported by all the county officials in them. In one of those counties, I had about nine hundred votes. At about 3:00 A.M. I phoned the sheriff, whom I had come to know as an ardent Faubus supporter, and told him that I wanted only the votes that were mine and nothing more. He assured me there was only one precinct that hadn't reported, and it was a small one-church community with thirty-two votes in it. He gave me a solemn promise that I had nothing to fear.

By Wednesday night, my lead was down to just under two thousand votes. Obviously, vote fraud was taking place. My vote in the county in which the sheriff had given me his solemn vow had dwindled to a little over four hundred.

I did not personally dislike Orval Faubus, but I felt he had badly tarnished the state's reputation for the most lamentable and self-serving political purposes, and for which we had all suffered and would continue to suffer for decades to come. I wanted to prove to the nation that Arkansas was turning its back on the most insidious, shameful part of its past. There was no brilliance or originality in it, but there was a lot of sincerity. What Faubus had done was crass, devastating, and divisive, and it appealed to the basest instincts in people. Sadly, it had been immensely popular and had the calculated effect of making him a political icon. Now, thirteen years later, people were beginning to appreciate the different rhetoric and to believe we could indeed be better and act better.

In the three days following the election, newscasters reported changes in the returns each evening, and each change showed my lead dwindling. I knew precisely what was happening, and we sent attorneys into the counties where the changes were occurring, mostly to serve notice on officials that we were monitoring their actions. A massive effort was being made to count me out. The Faubus people had made all their plans in anticipation of having Attorney General Purcell as their opponent. They had even placed newspaper ads to that effect for the following Sunday. Now, they were clearly unsettled by the results. By Thursday evening, the unofficial returns still had me in second place, but by only 950 votes.

The results had to be formally certified by noon the next day. We were terrified at what was happening and our inability to stop it. But on Friday noon, when the formal figures were certified, I was still in second place, and by 4,443 votes, which meant those who had been trying so hard to manipulate the results simply couldn't pull it off. They had obviously decided there was no point in risking federal prosecution for a losing cause and ultimately reported the accurate figures.

I strongly felt that our last surge in the waning days of the campaign was a result of letters we sent out about two weeks before the election. A strong supporter who owned a computer operation and had the names and addresses of every voter in Arkansas offered to mail 150,000 letters for us if we would pay the postage. We finally scraped up the money, but then the question was to whom we should send the letters. In our household, Betty had always opened every piece of junk mail and read it religiously. I had a feeling my household was not unique, so I elected to mail letters to every female voter in a five-county area of central Arkansas. I believe it was a major factor in getting me in the runoff.

One week before the runoff against Faubus, we decided I probably couldn't do better than spend an evening going out to see a Travelers game. The Travs were a triple-A team and drew up to three thousand fans.

A young black lad came over to where I was seated and asked, "Mr. Bumpers, do you know my mama?"

"I don't know. I may. What's her name?"

He told me and I said, "No, son, I don't believe I know her."

He said, "Yeah, you do. You sent her a letter."

The media, which had been most shocked of all by the results, took off for Charleston to find whatever they could about any indiscretions or shenanigans I had been involved in, whether or not I had been a breech baby, maybe dropped on my head at birth, or maybe a molester of children. One reporter was stunned when he visited my farm and found one lone cow, because I had alluded in many speeches to the fact that I had sold my cattle to help finance my campaign. I would later get a little mileage out of a small joke about the fact that I had had to sell my cattle to raise money for my campaign and Governor Rockefeller hadn't had to sell his.

One story an enterprising AP reporter came up with almost

derailed my campaign. He found the mother lode when he interviewed members of a Sunday school class I had taught in the First Methodist Church for many years. It was the "Bumpers class," named for my father. Joe Hiatt, the son of the local banker and a class member, told the reporter:

"He was talking one time about the Red Sea and the story about how it parted to let the Israelites through and then drowned the Egyptians. Then Dale said something like 'You know, I don't any more believe God had anything to do with that.' He put out some suggestion about how it could have happened—an earthquake or a landslide, some other act of nature. It sure leads to some lively discussions when you say something like that to people who have believed something else all their lives."

The story was dutifully reported but buried in a long feature article in the *Gazette*. When I saw it, I knew how the people on the *Titanic* must have felt. Faubus immediately began alluding to it in speeches during the week, at first with little effect. But then, on Saturday morning prior to the runoff on Tuesday, the *Jonesboro Sun* carried a big Faubus ad: "What about the Bible, Mr. Bumpers?" it demanded. Then followed the full quote from Joe Hiatt, and it concluded with, "If the Bible isn't all true, can any of it be true?"

It is a truism in politics that if a story such as this one is raised by an opponent, it is only marginally effective, especially when the candidate running the ad is behind in the polls. It is considered to be an act of desperation. Not so of a story dug up by a reporter from a perfectly innocent person—indeed, a good friend. We tried to ignore the story, but I knew it couldn't be ignored and could be devastating in a Bible Belt state. I also knew a reporter was working intently on an article for the Sunday editions. I could think of only one possible tack. I called Bishop Galloway, Methodist bishop for all of Arkansas and a longtime family friend. It was 7:00 P.M. Saturday evening.

"Bishop Galloway, this is Dale Bumpers."

"Yes, Dale, I've been expecting your call."

I told him the story was spiraling out of control and that a big story was likely for the Sunday morning paper, and I would be eternally grateful if he would call the reporter writing the story and give him a finely honed theological rationale for what I "undoubtedly meant" by the statement. He was happy, even anxious, to oblige. The story was a front pager, and Bishop Galloway was quoted:

"To seek flaws in a man's church work seems unfair. . . . All the Bumpers family are a good, fine, faithful people. And I've never known their theology to be out of line. . . . I know him and his family. He attended my church while a student."

We quickly added an addendum to a thirty-minute television show scheduled for Monday evening, election eve, in which a voice-over said, in referring to what had become a major flap: Dale Bumpers's "faith was strong enough to allow him to rationally consider new ideas and concepts without being shaken. It is not men of faith, but men of secret doubts who are afraid of new ideas." The voice-over also pointed out that in the Red Sea flap, I was quoting from a book that contained speculations about the parting of the Red Sea.

The enterprising reporter had, in fairness to me, also dug up a quote from Faubus from his earlier race against Rockefeller when he chastised Rockefeller for getting a divorce, saying the Bible said, ". . . that you have one wife, and that you do not love whiskey. . . . Marriage is ordained by God and that marriage should be observed." Now, as he stood beside his new and adoring wife, he denied saying those words.

On Sunday afternoon, Faubus announced he would hold a press conference on Monday morning. He built it up as a real "blockbuster," and all the staff and I assumed it would be on the Red Sea. We had Ed Lester, a prominent Little Rock attorney, attend with instructions to call as soon as he knew the gist of the announcement. I was in Malvern attending the groundbreaking of a new vocational technical school, and when Ed called, he said, "Dale, Orval says he has irrefutable and conclusive evidence of a plot against his life. It hinges on his election. If he is elected, he will be assassinated within thirty days. It is a radical left-wing plot." I was immensely relieved to hear such utter nonsense.

Faubus didn't reveal any of his sources or the rationale for the plot, but the clear implication was that he was so important to the cause of segregation that the left wing would have to eliminate him if he was elected. The other implication, of course, was that I was behind it. But what was really shocking was the slam dunk he left me.

That afternoon, both Faubus and I appeared at a huge political rally in Pine Bluff, sponsored by employees of the Cotton Belt Railroad. It was Labor Day. Virtually all the railroad workers were for Faubus, but of the roughly one thousand people in attendance, we had a sprinkling of support. One woman, however, did her best to whop me over the head with her huge Faubus sign as I walked to the platform (a truck bed). She had an angry, violent look on her face that was convincing. A state trooper intervened. I began reiterating Orval's claim, because I knew most of them hadn't heard it, plus I wanted to preempt Faubus, who would follow me.

"Orval Faubus says his life is in grave jeopardy. He says he's making a great sacrifice to make the race again in order to oust governor Rockefeller and reclaim the governor's office for you folks. This morning he announced just how great that sacrifice might be, because he says there's a gigantic plot afoot to assassinate him if he is elected. He has refused to name the source or the reason anyone would want to assassinate him, but I know many of you are his friends and supporters, and I'm asking you, as his friends, to help me save Orval Faubus's life. Elect me your next governor."

Even Faubus supporters roared with laughter.

The outcome was never in doubt from the moment the first precincts reported. By midnight, it was over. The vote was 58 percent to 42 percent. People in our headquarters were going berserk. I had carried fifty-five of Arkansas's seventy-five counties. Two weeks earlier, when I had received 21 percent of the vote, 50 percent of the people in Arkansas had never heard of me. I was alternately saddened because Dad couldn't be there and euphoric about the victory, especially the size of it. I went back to a small, unoccupied office, meditated a few moments, and wept for my father.

The sheriff with whom I had pleaded to save my votes on the night of the first primary, and who had later taken over four hundred away from me, was now in our campaign suite with his friends, who had come down from the mountains to join up and contribute money for the race against Rockefeller. I said, "Sheriff, after pleading with you to guard those ballot boxes and getting your assurances you would, you still tried to take over four hundred votes away from me."

Quick as a flash, he said, "Next time we'll do it for you."

One thing in the campaign that I found shocking and, indeed, troubling was the number of people who asked me, "Are you a Christian, Brother Bumpers?" or, "Have you been saved, Dale?" or, "Have you confessed Jesus Christ as your Lord and Savior?" I was unprepared for such questions. At first I stumbled, but I soon developed two or three standard answers: "I try to be," or, "I'm willing to trust God with the answer to that." The questioners never considered the questions intrusive or offensive, and I did my best not to show my resentment.

The general election would be on November 3, fifty-five days away. The Rockefeller camp was as overwhelmed by the fast-moving events as had been the Faubus camp. We had spent a hundred and twenty-five thousand dollars in the first primary, eighty-five thousand of which was Margaret's, Carroll's, and mine. We spent the same amount in the two-week runoff, but none of it was personal. It would take much more in the upcoming Rockefeller campaign.

The general election campaign was anticlimactic. The first poll taken two weeks after the primary showed me with over 70 percent of the vote. One of the first things I did after winning the

Democratic nomination was to recruit a man I had met and instantly liked during the Faubus campaign. He was Hall of Famer George Kell, one of the all-time great third basemen, who spent most of his career with the Detroit Tigers. George was an icon in Arkansas and enjoyed tremendous respect throughout the state. Four days after the Faubus election, I named George as my statewide campaign coordinator. I could probably have been elected in Michigan, too.

The first move by the Rockefeller campaign was to call a few of their supporters in my hometown for any information about me that might be detrimental. They then sent a team of investigators to scan the courthouse records to determine my legal competence, scan the files of cases I had tried, and, in general, seek evidence of skulduggery. They meticulously went over the minutes of school board meetings for the twelve years I had served, interviewed teachers, and generally scoped out the entire community. They found that a small town like Charleston offered very little opportunity for hanky-panky, but in politics there's never a problem with making something out of nothing. Happily, the Red Sea story had run its course. But the gossip about the doctor's wife was just emerging. The town's one doctor and his wife were our next-door neighbors. The wife was beautiful.

One night in El Dorado, Bill Lewis, a senior reporter for the *Gazette*, was waiting for me as I came out of my motel room on the way to a rally.

"Dale, I hate to ask you this, but my editor says I have to. Did you ever have an affair with a doctor's wife?"

My immediate thought was, No, but I always wanted to.

But my answer was a simple no, with no elaboration. The Republicans in Charleston were obviously trying to associate me with another case that had been common gossip. It failed.

Rockefeller was a pathetic campaigner. He had never been able to learn the names of the hundreds of small towns in Arkansas and was totally at sea in his attempts to carry on conversations with strangers. He could never find common ground on which they could relate to him.

One story that was legendary in Arkansas was of Rockefeller on a high school stage, speaking to the Wynne Chamber of Commerce and starting his speech with, "I'm delighted to be here in . . ."

He paused, obviously drawing a blank as to the name of the community. His aides offstage started whispering, "Wynne, Wynne."

He whispered back, "Dammit, I know my name. Where am I?"

One Sunday afternoon about sixteen days before the election, I was scheduled to cut a couple of thirty-second television spots at a local studio. As I arrived at the television studio, Rockefeller was leaving. His seersucker suit was soaking wet with perspiration, and he was obviously tired and frustrated. I asked one of the people who had helped produce a Rockefeller TV spot what was troubling him. He said it had taken over an hour to produce a single thirty-second spot.

About six weeks prior to the election, Rockefeller began challenging me to debate him. I thought I was smarter, more articulate, and better looking and was itching to accept. Fortunately, cooler heads prevailed. Deloss Walker was adamantly opposed, maintaining that four things could happen and three of them were bad. One, I wouldn't be as good as I thought; two, Rockefeller might be surprisingly better than anticipated; three, I might be perceived as ostentatious and generate sympathy for Rockefeller; or four, I might win hands down. We ducked, dodged, and procrastinated until we knew it was too late to schedule a debate and then called a press conference to accept the offer.

Nothing the Rockefeller forces did had more than a negligible impact. At one time, my rating dropped into the high fifties, but on the night of November 3, 1970, the results confirmed the polls:

Bumpers	62%	382,889
Rockefeller	32%	196,770
Carruth	5%	34,513
(Am. Ind. Party)		

My vote was the largest ever received by a gubernatorial candidate in Arkansas.

.   .   .

I had hardly gotten my governor's seat warm when I had one of the most memorable experiences of my career. In the spring of 1971, the Arkansas River Navigation System, which had made the Arkansas River navigable from Tulsa to the Mississippi, was dedicated. The cost had been $1.2 billion. Senators Kerr of Oklahoma and McClellan of Arkansas had spent years keeping the project on track. Congress named it the McClellan-Kerr Navigation System—because Senator Kerr, the powerful, longtime Oklahoma senator, had the misfortune of dying just before the project was completed and named.

President Nixon came down for the ceremony, as did Anita Bryant, who once again sang "God Bless America" to the smiling nods of approval from Nixon. The dedication was at Catoosa, a small community a few miles from Tulsa, where the project ended. Navigation didn't actually reach Tulsa.

During the ceremonies, someone passed a note to me asking if I would like to spend the rest of the day on the Pedernales River at Lyndon Johnson's home. The answer was yes. So David Hall, governor of Oklahoma, and I, along with two aides, crawled on a jet belonging to the American Milk Producers, Inc., and landed on a strip that took us to LBJ's back door. AMPI later was reputed to have once given Richard Nixon three hundred thousand dollars in cash in the Oval Office.

When we arrived, Johnson was sitting in a lawn chair in his front yard with two or three aides. He was working on his memoirs and regaled us with two or three passages. Then we all piled into his Lincoln convertible with the top down and drove around the ranch, listening to him talk of his long political career between stops to spray red-ant hills. He would drive up beside an anthill, open the door, take a huge spray can from the floorboard, and spray the ants, saying, "That'll fix them little sons a bitches."

Lady Bird had gone to Austin for a bridal or baby shower but was due back by the middle of the afternoon. Johnson soon began calling back to the house to see if she had returned. Silence. Finally she answered the phone and in her familiar, sweet voice asked, "Lyndon, were you trying to get me?"

"You know damn well I've been trying to get you," he stormed.

He told her where to meet us, that we were "going to the Messican's house" and to bring jelly beans. It was a big two-story house occupied by a large Mexican family, all of whom did indeed enjoy the jelly beans.

Lady Bird stayed with us until we left, and she was a delight, charming, intelligent, and interesting. But Johnson did virtually all the talking, and this went on from around noon until 10:00 P.M. I felt certain when I left that he didn't know either of us, David Hall or me, by name. He never asked either of us how we liked being governor, whether we had families, questions about our backgrounds, or anything else of a personal nature.

That evening, Johnson uttered the most memorable words of the day. As we prepared to leave, he said, "Now, if you boys don't remember anything else I've said today, I want you to remember this: When I was majority leader, and later president, I spent all my time pulling every power string I could find to pull, trying to pass bills that helped people, that made their lives better and the country stronger. That's what Democrats stand for. Republicans. Republicans just stand for two things: protectin' the rich and investigatin' Democrats."

Two stories, one true, one almost surely apocrypha, demonstrate much of the Johnson psyche. Prior to becoming vice president, Lyndon Johnson was Senate majority leader, and Everett

Dirksen, the gravel-voiced Republican senator from Illinois, was minority leader. The Senate furnished each of them cars and drivers. But in order to provide the majority leader a small perk not available to the minority leader, Johnson's car was outfitted with a mobile phone. Car phones were rare. It rankled Dirksen, and Johnson knew it. Quite often, to add insult to injury, Johnson would call Dirksen from his car phone while on his way home, ostensibly to discuss the schedule for the ensuing day, but in reality to rub it in.

Dirksen began insisting that he, too, be provided a car phone, and the Senate Rules Committee finally relented and agreed to provide him with the highly prized phone. The first day it was installed, Dirksen watched until he saw Johnson leave, then rushed to his car, started for home, and promptly called Johnson in his car.

"Lyndon," he said, "I'm on my way home in my car and I thought we might discuss—"

Johnson interrupted, "Hold on just a minute, Ev, my other phone's ringing."

Hubert Humphrey once told me that when he was vice president, he had an idea for a housing program that he thought would be a big success and that Johnson could boast about when he ran again. He went to the Oval Office to describe his idea to the president, and when he finished outlining the whole proposal, Johnson said, "Hubert, get out of here with that. That's the craziest idea I ever heard."

"Yes, sir, Mr. President," Hubert responded dutifully. "I just thought it was something we could get going on before the next election and use to our advantage."

"Well, forget it," Johnson said.

Hubert exited. A few days later, he received a call from Johnson.

"Hubert."

"Yes, sir?"

"Come in here a minute."

He walked into the Oval Office and Johnson said, "Hubert, I've been thinking about that idea you had the other day. After considering it further, I've decided it's a pretty good idea. I think it might work. I think we ought to try it."

"Well, I appreciate that very much, Mr. President. I'll go to work on it immediately." Hubert turned to leave, and as he got to the door, Johnson stopped him.

"Hubert!"

"Yes, sir."

"Hubert, remember. This was my idea."

"Yes, sir, Mr. President."

Two years after visiting the Johnsons at the ranch, I was seated by Lady Bird at a Southern Governors' Association dinner in Austin. She had been in Little Rock two weeks previously and told me she had stayed at the new Camelot Hotel overlooking the Arkansas River. She then described the scene from her upper-story window. She said there was a sand-and-gravel operation on the riverbank and a county jail. She said, "Governor Bumpers, I believe Little Rock is the only city in America located on a major river that doesn't have a park or even landscaping on it."

I reported this to the Little Rock city fathers, and today there is a beautiful city park where the sand-and-gravel operation and county jail were located. An amphitheater is heavily used during the summer months, and the Spring Riverfest is a statewide attraction.

‖ *Chapter 15* ‖

The IRS Comes Calling

Every political writer in Arkansas wrote a postelection analysis on how the stars had lined up for me, how an unknown country lawyer had, just months apart, pulled off two of the biggest political upsets in the state's history. Most of the stories were flattering but highly embellished. My own analysis was more accurate and, unhappily, much less flattering. I had simply spoken, with passion but without getting maudlin, about how we had squandered our opportunities in the past by allowing ourselves to be distracted by race. We were dead last, or nearly last, in many categories because we had chosen to be. I harped on the deplorable condition of our state parks and the inexcusable low pay of teachers. I injected the environment into the campaign, the first politician to ever make it an issue. Since they hadn't heard it, people saw it as a visionary concept, and more and more heads, especially of hunters and fishermen, began to nod affirmatively when I talked about it. I often closed my speeches with, "When families in Arkansas sit around the dinner table and talk about what they love most, it isn't that big car in the driveway, or that posh office downtown, or the big fields of rice and soybeans out back. It is their children." Nothing else resonated nearly as powerfully as this short appeal to people's best instincts.

I never walked away from a voter without calling him by his first name. It told him I had been paying attention—plus, there's no sound as beautiful to a person as the sound of his name.

Years before I ran, but in anticipation of running for high office someday, I attended the dedication of the Ozark Lock and Dam, one of the giant dams that would one day make the Arkansas River navigable in addition to providing a lot of electrical power. It was a miserably hot summer day in the midst of a hot governor's race. At least one thousand people were present, about three hundred of whom were seated in folding chairs. I watched Bruce Bennett, then attorney general and a major contender for governor, as he walked up and down the lines of folding chairs, shaking hands with the mostly elderly people who occupied them. He would hand each person a piece of literature, saying, "Hi theah, how you? Hi theah, how you?" like an automaton. By the time the recipient of the literature and the "Hi theah" had time to look up to see with whom he had just shaken hands, Bruce was on a "Hi theah" two people away. I'm sure he boasted to his wife and staff that evening that he had shaken twice as many hands as any other candidate. What he didn't know was that he had probably not gotten a single vote for his efforts. I will be eternally in Bruce's debt for teaching me how not to campaign.

I had very little knowledge or understanding of what a governor did. I had no legislative experience and knew very few members of the legislature on a first-name basis. In short, the dog that caught the car knew a lot more about what to do with the car than I knew about what to do with the governor's office. I knew the legislature had made toilet tissue of a million-dollar study, for which Rockefeller had personally paid Peat-Marwick, on how our state government should be reorganized. The state had sixty-seven departments. My brother, then group vice president for the Greyhound Corporation, had told me that no executive could be effective with sixty-seven department heads reporting to him, so I readily understood the part of the study that recommended they be cut to thirteen. I had nothing else much in mind, so I took the study and made it my own. Why waste a million dollars? In the end, there was blood all over the floor, but we passed it—and it has remained largely intact.

Rockefeller did me a gigantic favor before yielding the governor's office. His mother, Abigail Aldrich Rockefeller, was a strong proponent of world peace and, apparently, was also strongly opposed to the death penalty. She had even intended to name her fifth son Winthrop Aldrich Rockefeller but, realizing his initials would then be WAR, decided against it and simply named him Winthrop Rockefeller. When Win ran against Faubus in 1964, the Faubus forces had said "Win" stands for "Wants Integration Now."

On the evening of January 2, 1971, prior to my inauguration the following morning, Rockefeller commuted all thirteen men on death row at Cummins Prison, lifting a gigantic burden from my shoulders. Remarkably, there were no protests. Win had never concealed his antipathy for the death penalty, and people respected his strong convictions on it. I never had to make the soul-shattering decision as to whether or not a human being should live or die.

I had been governor only a few months when one of my worst fears became a reality. We discovered that a member of the parole board had been selling paroles. He used a simple technique: Get the list of inmates likely to be paroled at the next board meeting, go to their parents or parent, and tell them he might be able to get their son paroled at the next meeting but would have to "settle with the man," meaning the governor or someone in the governor's office. We were told the story by a destitute and distraught mother who desperately wanted her son released but had no money. I can think of nothing more horrible than a mother whose sole goal in life is to see her son freed from prison and then, when the opportunity comes, can't meet the price of a despicable son of a bitch trying to extort money from such a wretched soul. We arranged for the state police to have an officer hide in the woman's home, and when the parole board member came calling, he taped the entire conversation.

After listening to the tape, I called the board member to my office and told him, without revealing the whole story, that I was constrained to ask for his resignation. He was visibly shaken and incoherent but didn't protest. He agreed and was almost out of the building before an aide decided we needed a written resignation. He was called back and readily signed a resignation we prepared for him. The prosecutor in the county where the bribe was solicited never got around to filing charges. The parole board member controlled a lot of votes in the county. Jim Guy Tucker, who later was lieutenant governor and would become governor when Bill Clinton was elected president, was the prosecutor in Little Rock at the time and tried valiantly to get the case removed so he could file charges, but he was unsuccessful.

.   .   .

One of the first delegations to call on me in the governor's office was a group of Texans. They wanted to get my reaction to a possible proposal that Arkansas sell water to Texas. I found the proposal interesting, but I was neither favorably inclined nor averse to the proposition.

Nothing ever came of this idea, but when I told Gerald Fisher, president of one of our community colleges, about the Texas proposal, he said, "I would make an offer to sell them all the water they want and can transport through a quarter-inch line. If they complain about the size of the pipe being ridiculously small, tell them that if they can suck like they can blow, a fourth-inch line will be plenty big."

.   .   .

I quickly learned one of the ways governors had been making it on ten thousand dollars a year. About a month before my first Christmas in the governor's office, one of my cabinet members came in to ask me what kind of car I would like for Christmas. I first thought the question had been asked in jest, then quickly realized not only that the offer was serious, but that it had been fairly common for state officials who owed their jobs to the governor to occasionally pony up for a new car for the governor. I'm sure no such offer was ever made to Rockefeller. Since I was new, I was eligible. The cabinet member apologized but said that owing to his age and tenure, he had been selected to inquire, though he assured me he had told his colleagues what the answer would be. One never knows until one asks.

Shortly after I took office, Betty was shopping in a Little Rock department store, and as she walked by the men's clothing department, she was hailed by a salesman who told her he had a suit "awaiting the governor." She asked what he meant, and he told her that a man, whom he named, had left money with the store to be used for a new suit for the governor. Interestingly, I knew the purchaser as a former political player in the state during the Faubus era but had no recollection of ever having met him. The salesman said he had twice left messages at the governor's office, but I hadn't responded. Apparently, my staff had considered it a ploy of some kind. Betty assured him he could return the money to the donor, that I wouldn't accept the suit. He said, "I can't tell you how pleased I am to hear that."

.　　　.　　　.

Betty was a very popular First Lady. Her accomplishments during my four years as governor were remarkable. Her liberalism was not based on political theory or history courses in school (she had been an art major). It stemmed from the misery she and her family had experienced growing up in abject poverty. She knew the First Lady of the state would enjoy considerable prestige, so she spent the first year looking for a meaningful way to use that clout and not squander it pouring tea. She soon discovered that Arkansas's childhood immunization levels were the lowest in the country, and she immediately knew that rectifying that problem would be her calling. After a year of planning, she recruited hundreds of volunteers, commandeered the Arkansas State Health Department, the Agriculture Extension Service, and two or three other state agencies, plus the Arkansas National Guard, and immunized over three hundred thousand children on one Saturday. The immunizations covered polio, measles, mumps, tetanus, diphtheria, pertussis, and rubella, and, remarkably, not one single child had a reaction. She never slowed down after that and became a national leader in promoting childhood immunizations. The new thirty-five-million-dollar vaccine research center on the campus of the National Institutes of Health is named the Dale and Betty Bumpers Vaccine Research Center. She deserved the honor. All I did was keep the money flowing.

·   ·   ·

I had been governor for two short months when I received an invitation to deliver the Truman Day dinner address in Kansas City, Missouri. While I had had remarkable success with the state legislature, things were growing more contentious. I told the caller I would have to decline for fear "those guys [legislators] will unscrew the dome off the capitol if I leave town." The caller was persistent and phoned again the following day. He said that if I accepted the invitation, they would arrange for me to spend an hour with the Trumans in their home. It was an irresistible offer. Betty was anxious to go, too. Her father was often told he was a "dead ringer" for Truman, so he thought Truman was the greatest. He also admired Truman's profanity.

I went to the private air terminal I always used, and where a plane being sent by the Truman Day committee was to pick me up. I was expecting a jet, but the only plane on the tarmac awaiting a passenger was a twin-prop Beech Baron, a good but slow plane, and the only person in the terminal was a seventy-five-year-old cowboy who looked like anything but a pilot. He came over to shake hands and tell me he had come to get me. "I'm Claude," he said.

"Where's your pilot?" I inquired.

"I'm aiming to take you myself."

The prospect was terrifying. The folks at the dinner in Kansas City were going to get home early that evening unless we could find another pilot. In an effort to avert this impending disaster, I told my staff to call the Highway Department to see if their grand commander and a pilot were available. Both were, but I decided that rather than have the press write about my commandeering a state plane to take me to an essentially political event, we would recruit Bill Miller, head of the state police and also a licensed pilot, to accompany us. He knew the Baron well enough to land it should our pilot succumb, which seemed a distinct possibility. When I asked Claude about the weather in Kansas City, he said, "They're expecting thunderstorms about the time we get there."

Betty, who was in her best long dress and already terrified at the prospect of Claude flying us, heard Claude's weather report and immediately fled across the tarmac toward the car with her dress tail flying, headed for the Governor's Mansion. Many people already believed she was the smarter member of the duo.

Claude seemed to know his plane well, and he also seemed to know every small airport operator between Little Rock and Kansas City. He would switch to the radio frequency of a small airport below and say, "John, you down there?"

"Hey, Claude, is that you up there?"

The conversations back and forth were personal, banal, and endless.

Claude never removed his cowboy hat the whole trip.

The weather held off, and we arrived without incident. Archie Schaffer, my chief of staff, Bill Miller, our host, and I immediately headed for Independence and the Truman home.

When I arrived, Mr. and Mrs. Truman came down the stairs to greet me; she looked like every picture I had ever seen of her, but he looked quite different. It had been over eighteen years since he'd left the White House, and he had become rather feeble. He had used a cane as a prop on his jaunty morning walks around the White House, but now he needed it. Mrs. Truman greeted me with, "Oh, Governor Bumpers, we're so glad you beat that ol' Rockyfeller. We saw your television and just loved it."

The former president asked if I was enjoying being governor.

I told him no, that I was just a country lawyer, that the pace was hectic and dealing with the legislature was difficult to maddening, and that I was unaccustomed to dealing with the press, whose relentless search for scandal was unnerving. I told him I spent a lot of nights staring at the bedroom ceiling in the Governor's mansion. I rambled on about what a tough job it was, until it dawned on me that I was telling my troubles to the man who had made the decision to drop the atomic bomb on Hiroshima. I realized how parochial my problems must have sounded, so I changed the subject.

Mrs. Truman kept the conversation going. She was charming, much more intelligent and engaging than I had anticipated, and she seemed genuinely interested in my background and family. As the time for our departure grew near, Truman became more philosophical and proceeded to give me a few suggestions that he obviously thought would make life a little more bearable and maybe even enjoyable.

"Son," he began, "I'll tell you how to make your job easier and less worrisome. You should always remember that the people elected you to do what you think is right. They're busy with their own lives, and they're depending on you. You said you spent a lot of sleepless nights looking at the ceiling out at the Governor's Mansion. I'll tell you how to get more sleep. Get the best advice you can find on both sides of the issues, pick out the one that makes the most sense to you, and go with it. That's all people expect of you.

"Secondly, trust people with the truth. Politicians always have a hard time telling people the truth, rather than telling them what they think they'd like to hear. People can handle the truth, and you can trust 'em with it."

Truman's contempt for Nixon, who was sitting in the White House at the time, was well known. He paused, waved his hand toward the east, and said, "The only time this country ever gets into trouble is when there's some lying SOB sitting in the Oval Office."

None of this was very profound, and had I heard it from somebody on the streets of Little Rock, I would have listened politely and never given it another thought. But coming from a man for whom I had developed such great respect, especially for telling people unpleasant truths, it made an indelible impression. Few days have passed since then that I haven't remembered Harry Truman's words. My respect for Truman had soared the day he fired General MacArthur. I had stood with the throngs on the outer drive in Chicago as MacArthur rode past my dormitory and waved from the back of a convertible. It was a welcome home parade following his firing. I didn't applaud and was one of a small number of Americans who fully supported Truman's decision to fire him. And I, of course, fully shared Truman's contempt for Senator Joe McCarthy.

It was only later that I came to understand how the Marshall Plan had saved Western Europe from communism and how courageous and visionary the decision had been. I have always believed it to be the single greatest foreign policy success of the twentieth century.

The trip back to Little Rock was uneventful, except that as we taxied into position for takeoff at around 11:00 P.M., I saw a 727 bearing down on us for landing. I shouted to Claude, "There's a 727 coming in on us!"

Claude, without hesitation, said, "I'll feed him a little prop wash." With that, he shoved the throttle full forward, getting the little Beech Baron off just ahead of the 727 and barely averting a disaster. He reminded me of Slim Pickens riding the bomb in *Dr. Strangelove*. Neither Claude nor Bill Miller noticed that the landing lights were still on until we were halfway home.

.   .   .

In October 1971, Missouri governor Warren Hearnes, chairman of the National Governors' Conference, invited seven governors to join him on a trip to the Soviet Union. The cold war was white hot at the time, and I had some reservations about accepting, thinking my constituents might think I was defecting, or at least consorting with the enemy.

The revelation by the press that I was going generated no hostility or adverse comment, but it did rankle one oldster from Cabot, a small community thirty-two miles north of Little Rock, though not because he thought I was a Communist sympathizer. A local radio station had a popular noon-hour show where each day a roving reporter would select some busy downtown inter-section where pedestrian traffic was heavy and pose one or two questions on hot topics. One of the questions on the day follow-ing the announcement that I would go to the Soviet Union was, "What do you think about Governor Bumpers going to the So-viet Union?"

When the question was posed to the old gentleman, without hesitating he responded, "I don't know what he wants to go to Russia fer. He ain't been to Cabot yit."

When we landed at JFK on our return trip from the USSR, a State Department functionary met us and told us the president (Nixon) wanted us to come to his office the following morning and brief him on our trip. It would obviously be a photo op, be-cause we had gleaned no information worthy of reporting to the president.

When we walked into the Oval Office, Nixon greeted us and began telling me what a great game I had missed the preceding Saturday between Arkansas and Texas. He was full of praise for Bill Montgomery, Arkansas's quarterback, and described him as the best all-round athlete since some player, whose name I forget, who had played at Harvard.

Al Haig, who was Deputy Assistant to the President for Na-tional Security at the time, sat in a chair away from where Nixon and the governors sat. We were requesting assistance in the use of government aircraft to transport our Soviet counterparts when they paid a reciprocal visit to the U.S. the following year. Nixon would respond to every request with, "Sure. Yah! Yah! We can do that, can't we Al?" Haig would dutifully agree.

Other than seeing the Oval Office for the first time, it was uneventful. Of course, we would all make it as important-sounding
as possible when we held our first press conference back home.

.   .   .

Shortly after I returned home, I got a call from my accountant,
who had received a notice that the IRS wanted to audit my tax returns for the preceding three years. I had not yet filed a return as
governor and had never been audited before. It was patently obvious that this would be a political audit. Scary! It meant somebody was playing hardball and that innocence or guilt would have
little to do with the outcome. But who was behind it? Some of my
strong supporters had already been or were then suddenly being
subjected to audits. The clear meaning was that someone feared
me as a potential opponent. My approval rating was in the seven-
ties. Even so, it can ruin your whole day to learn that someone
who has the power to have you audited wants you removed as a
political threat.

I had always been scrupulously careful in preparing my returns, even depreciating fifteen-dollar law books. The only political race coming up, other than my own bid for a second term,
was the U.S. Senate seat held by Arkansas's powerful senior senator, John L. McClellan. McClellan would be running for his sixth
term. As a very senior senator, chairman of the Appropriations
Committee, and member of the Judiciary Committee, he had almost total control over the appointments of both the U.S. attorney and the Arkansas director of the Internal Revenue Service.
In short, he had the power to put you in jail. There had been rumors for years that in 1954 McClellan had sicced the IRS on Sid
McMath, former governor, just before Sid announced that he
would challenge him in the upcoming election. Despite Sid's
being distracted by the audit, McClellan barely squeezed out a
win. Sid later told me he had no doubt about how he came to be
audited.

Later, when it was revealed that Nixon had an enemies list

consisting of two hundred names and that many of them had been audited, most of my friends felt sure that Nixon was the instigator of my audit. I never believed for a moment that Nixon had anything to do with it. I'm quite sure he hardly knew who I was, but I was quite certain of who had arranged for me to be audited.

The auditor was a perfect gentleman and seemed embarrassed about having to conduct the audit. After thirty or forty days, I paid the IRS thirty dollars, because of a mathematical error in computing the amount I had received in the sale of one of my cows.

·   ·   ·

In October 1973, I was chairman of the Democratic Governors' Association. The Watergate scandal dominated the news and most conversations. Nixon had fired Archibald Cox, serving as a special prosecutor in the Watergate case, and Attorney General Elliot Richardson resigned in protest. It became known as the "Saturday Night Massacre."

I called a meeting of the Democratic Governors' Association to discuss what our response should be. There were thirty-one Democratic governors, and twenty-seven attended. It was virtually unanimous that we should adopt a resolution, but the rather raucous meeting was mostly about how tough it should be. During our discussion, we got word that Nixon aides Haldeman and Ehrlichman had resigned. At the close, Jimmy Carter spoke, saying that we should be reasonably measured, and that the resolution should protect the office of the presidency. Phil Noel, governor of Rhode Island, stood up and said, "Jimmy, my old man taught me that when you get a son of a bitch down, kick the hell out of him." The resolution passed unanimously.

My second term was relatively uneventful. I continued my efforts to upgrade the Medical School by establishing a Family Practice Residency, providing money for a new education building, and establishing Area Health Education Centers in cities outside Little Rock, believing that if students had experiences in hospitals outside Little Rock, they might choose to go there to practice.

I failed utterly in trying to establish a State Wilderness System. The state owned a lot of land, some of which would qualify as wilderness. But it was a new and mysterious concept to most of the General Assembly. One senator said in a speech on the Senate floor, "We don't need no wilderness. If we ever get to needin' a wilderness, we can always grow one."

We established a system of two-year colleges over the strong objections of the four-year-college presidents. They were crazed about the additional competition for scarce educational dollars. I argued that there were too many children who couldn't afford a distant school and pay room and board plus tuition. If the college was in commuting distance, they could find out whether college was the right option for a very small cost.

Today, there are twenty-two two-year colleges in Arkansas, enthusiastically supported by local taxes, in addition to state funds. Many of their graduates find out they are indeed college material and continue their studies in four-year schools. The program has been a howling success.

The time had arrived when I had to make a decision soon over how I wanted to spend the rest of my life. Dad had said there was no reason I couldn't be president, but I doubted he thought it could happen from the governor's office.

Chapter 16

Third Term? Go Home?
Challenge an Icon?

In early 1974, Senator J. William Fulbright, author of the Fulbright scholarship program and ardent, unrelenting opponent of the Vietnam War, announced that he would seek a sixth term in the U.S. Senate. Even after thirty years, Fulbright was still Arkansas's junior senator to John L. McClellan. He often referred to himself as the "seniorist junior senator in the U.S. Senate." It always drew laughter but was not quite true. Senator John Stennis of Mississippi was the longest-serving junior senator to his senior senator, James O. Eastland.

Fulbright was a political anomaly. He was widely admired for his intellect and courage, didn't suffer fools gladly, and was often considered aloof, diffident, and sometimes petulant. He was a Rhodes scholar and former president of the University of Arkansas. His detractors referred to him as "Sir William" when he once suggested the United States should consider replacing our political system with a parliamentary system. It was a perfectly plausible item for debate but didn't resonate well with the American people, and especially with President Truman, who felt it was a slap at his leadership. As a University of Arkansas Razorback football player, he kicked the winning field goal against Rice

University in the 1929 homecoming game, and everyone in Arkansas recognized the action photograph of the kick, which was featured prominently in all his political literature every six years.

Fulbright's constant drumbeat against the Vietnam War netted him the animosity of Lyndon Johnson, a former close friend, but gained the adoration of a younger generation who knew they were the ones who would do the fighting and dying. He later told me the worst vote he ever cast was his vote for the Gulf of Tonkin Resolution, which did indeed irreversibly commit the United States to a horrible mistake. Wayne Morse, a Democratic senator from Oregon, and Ernest Gruening, Democratic senator from Alaska, were the only dissenting votes.

There were a few ardent Fulbright supporters who were deeply saddened when he signed the Southern Manifesto, which was an attempt to justify segregation, but there was also a spirit of forgiveness among many, who knew his refusal to sign would have surely cost him his seat. The manifesto was a hokey political document calculated to appeal to the ardent southern segregationists but that had little effect on the tide of the times. Those are the choices members of Congress must sometimes confront.

My strongest supporters, along with a few people who didn't care for me but intensely disliked Fulbright, urged me to challenge him. I had been an admirer and fervent supporter of Fulbright and had little reason or stomach for such a race. But I had no stomach for a third term as governor, either. I had no interest in the House of Representatives, which was out of the question anyway because it was the one race I probably couldn't have won against the very popular Republican congressman John Paul Hammerschmidt. Virtually all contested races in Arkansas were in the Democratic primaries.

My political guru, Deloss Walker, was hot for me to make the Senate race. So we did what all politicians do: We took a poll. We received the results in late January, prior to a March filing deadline, and the results were astounding. It not only showed me

beating Fulbright 52 percent to 26 percent, it showed him neck
and neck with a couple of "has-beens." It demonstrated his incredible weakness, and barring a catastrophe, I would win should
I choose to run. It was difficult to understand the deep-seated
antipathy for Fulbright. My analysis was that, on the one hand,
veterans and ultraconservatives resented his opposition to the
Vietnam War, and an increasing number of voters resented his
being right about the war when they had been wrong for so long.
But perhaps a bigger reason was that many people resent opposition to a war once American troops are committed, no matter
how wrong the war may be.

Another group, friends of mine and Fulbright's, were either
opposed to my running or were ambivalent. They understandably didn't want to be forced to choose. The *Arkansas Gazette* was
going bonkers at the thought. They worshiped Fulbright. I concluded that it was either challenge Fulbright or return to Charleston, which wasn't terribly appealing. Most of Fulbright's closest
friends were older, upper middle class to wealthy. Several who
had been supporters of mine came to the mansion to feel me out
about my intentions, having been sent by the senator.

It was fairly well known among political observers that Fulbright had returned to Arkansas only five or six times the year before. He had never been enthusiastic about retail politics. The
Gridiron Show, produced by the Arkansas Bar Association, did a
skit showing him getting off a plane in Little Rock wearing a
tweed sportcoat and sunglasses with a *Wall Street Journal* in his
coat pocket. He gazed around, obviously upset by the poor sur-
roundings, and, not knowing where he was, said, "This is deplorable! Do these people realize they're entitled to foreign aid?"
Funny, but politically devastating.

About two weeks before the filing deadline, Carroll was waiting to be introduced as a lay speaker in the First Methodist
Church in Phoenix when he suddenly fell against the shoulder of
the woman beside whom he was seated and who was waiting to
introduce him. It was a serious stroke.

He was rushed to the hospital and a few days later underwent
nine hours of brain surgery. X rays showed the operation was
not fully successful, so Greyhound, his employer, put him on its
corporate jet and flew him to the Montreal Neurological In-
stitute, affiliated with McGill University, where he endured an
additional seven hours of surgery. This time the surgery was successful, as far as saving his life was concerned, but he was left severely impaired in his left arm and leg.

I was in abject agony, because I considered Fulbright both a
friend and a great senator. I didn't want to oppose him. On the
other hand, I would never forgive myself if he was defeated by
someone whose views were anathema to me.

On March 12, 1974, I held a press conference in the governor's conference room of the capitol to announce my decision.
The weeks of conjecture about whether I would run for the Senate had resulted in a press frenzy, and the room was packed with
press, friends, and the curious. When I uttered those necessary
words—"Therefore, I will run for the United States Senate"—a
few wept, but many more cheered. Brownie Ledbetter, who had
coordinated Pulaski County (Little Rock) for me in my first race
for governor, ran sobbing from the conference room. Fulbright
immediately held a press conference to say it was tragic to see
such a promising career cut short. He was very unpopular with
the Jewish population, and he indicated that he expected to
drown in out-of-state money. I immediately announced that I
would accept out-of-state money only from family and former
classmates.

Following the press conference, I went to the airport, flew to
north Arkansas, and campaigned all afternoon in Harrison. The
following day, I flew to Montreal to spend two days with Carroll,
though he was still hallucinating and never knew I was there.

The Democratic women of Pope County, about seventy
miles west of Little Rock, had a traditional Saturday night dinner
for Democratic candidates following the ticket closing. It was
a big "must" event, attracting four hundred people. I had scored

well at their dinner four years earlier as an unknown gubernatorial candidate. On that evening in 1970, the guest speaker had been Senator Harold Hughes of Iowa, a strident, former alcoholic truck driver and then a vocal opponent of the Vietnam War. He was paid five thousand dollars by the American Milk Producers, the same group who jetted David Hall and me to Lyndon Johnson's ranch. He delivered a forty-five-minute not-so-well-received tirade against the war in his famous stentorian voice. He then proceeded to sleep, or give a good imitation of it, with his eyes closed and his head draped on his chest, as every candidate, from justice of the peace to governor, either simply announced his name and the office he sought or spoke for the allotted four minutes, depending on the importance of the office. I considered Hughes's inattention insulting at the time. Years later, having endured many similar evenings, I understood just how bored he had been. In 1983, when I was considering a race for president, Hughes agreed to be my campaign manager in Iowa, if I chose to run. I forgave him for sleeping through my speech.

Now, on this March evening in 1974, the Pope County women had engaged Senator Robert C. Byrd of West Virginia as their featured speaker. Fulbright had arranged for his appearance, but Senator Byrd said nothing negative about me or anything particularly positive about Fulbright. I knew little about him, but he gave a traditional Democratic "tub thumper," covering everything from the New Deal down to that moment. The Vietnam War was not mentioned, and neither Fulbright nor I said anything memorable that evening. We were like one-eyed roosters dancing around each other. What I vividly remember about that evening was a young law professor from the University of Arkansas who was a candidate for the U.S. House of Representatives. In four minutes he delivered one of the most beautiful, eloquent speeches I ever heard, pushing every emotional button on every value Americans cherish. He spoke of our solemn duty to our children and the peace, education, and economic security to which they were entitled. He spoke without a note and without a single hesitation or grammatical error, which I found remarkable. I later realized the speech had been memorized when his staff handed out copies of it after the dinner. I especially remember that as my staff and I drove the seventy miles back to Little Rock, I said, "I hope that guy never runs against me." His name was Bill Clinton.

The Fulbright forces attempted only two mildly exciting ploys during the campaign, neither of which worked. They purchased a small newspaper that few people had ever heard of, called the *Arkansas Sportsman*. It allegedly had a statewide circulation of about twenty-five hundred. The paper was designed for hunters and fishermen in Arkansas, which included most males. Suddenly, about 250,000 of them appeared on the counters of every crossroads country store in Arkansas with a banner headline proclaiming GOVERNOR OPPOSES HUNTING! Our headquarters was immediately inundated with calls from friends and enemies alike.

We quickly discovered that the genesis of the headline stemmed from a proclamation that had been signed, as had many others, with an auto pen in the basement of the capitol, where routine mail, proclamations, photographs, and other unimportant papers were signed. The staff had wide discretion over what could be signed with the auto pen. The proclamation had been sent to us by a New York group called Friends of the Animals. The proclamation seemed innocent enough and was not nearly as dramatic as the headlines, but when we called their New York office to find out what they really stood for, we got an earful. They essentially believed the only good hunter was a dead hunter. It was the nadir for us. Happily, two good friends from Pine Bluff, with whom I had duck-hunted, had thoughtfully taken photographs of me both alone and with others, holding up our limit of ducks for the photographer. We had the best one reproduced and circulated it all over the state. The caption read, "Does this look like a man who opposes hunting?" The photograph was very similar to one of Fulbright and Adlai Stevenson, whom Fulbright had brought to Arkansas for a duck hunt several years before and which showed them stepping out of a boat with their duck kill for the morning. The damage was mitigated, and by election day the whole affair had been largely forgotten.

The other ploy was perpetrated by a well-known Fulbright supporter, who told the press that, though the governor only made $10,000 a year in salary, people who were sympathetic should bear in mind that he also received a $25,000 annual expense account to run the Governor's Mansion, and a $10,000 public relations fund that went to the governor's office. It had never occurred to me that anybody might feel sorry for me because I did indeed receive the lowest salary of any governor in America. In fact, I had gotten a lot of mileage out of a story I frequently used that, when my first paycheck arrived after my election, I left it on the dresser in my bedroom, where the maid saw it, thought it was hers, and quit.

The suggestion was that people were entitled to an accounting of these monies. We heartily concurred. In the past, some governors had reputedly pocketed any amounts left over in the expense accounts, but paid taxes on them, which was technically legal but obviously violated legislative intent. Some well-intentioned friends had suggested I do the same when I was first elected, but I rejected the idea out of hand and, at the same time, took the simple precaution of having both the Department of Finance and Administration and a private CPA perform a monthly audit of the mansion account, and another CPA do a monthly audit of the public relations account. The Fulbright supporter obviously assumed I had followed tradition.

A few days following the first story in the paper, we spread out all the expense accounts on the dining room table at the Governor's Mansion and invited one and all to look at them as long as they wanted. The story died in the dining room, except for one story the following day. The afternoon *Arkansas Democrat* carried the headline GOVERNOR USES MONEY TO ENTERTAIN ORPHANS. Each year, I had taken money from the public relations expense account to take the children from St. Joseph's Catholic orphanage in North Little Rock to an Arkansas Travelers baseball game. We fed them hot dogs, popcorn, and candy until they threw up. I couldn't have purchased a full-page ad that would have had a greater impact.

Fulbright and I debated only one time, and that was on CBS's Sunday morning *Face the Nation*. It was dull and uninteresting, and, happily, everybody in Arkansas was in church. The questions were mostly national and international in scope, and of course, I was not nearly as well prepared or experienced in either as was Fulbright. It didn't seem to influence anyone, and on May 25, after the votes were tallied, the results were decisive:

> Bumpers   65%
> Fulbright   35%

The seven-month period between the night the votes were tallied and my becoming a senator was the most relaxed period of my adult life. I had intensely disliked most of my time as governor. My mother's genes and her teachings that the abyss was directly in front of me haunted me every waking moment. I spent more time trying to make sure bad things didn't happen than I spent trying to make good things happen. The governor, unfairly, is held accountable for every two-bit boodler some reporter can uncover—from someone padding expense accounts to someone else selling prison paroles. I admonished all my appointees that if they got caught in unethical (to say nothing of unlawful) conduct not to look to me for solace. I served in the Senate with many former governors, from Strom Thurmond on down. I was the only one who hadn't loved the job.

Senator Fulbright was visibly upset on NBC's *Today* show the morning after the election. Privately, he was bitter and unforgiving. He had appeared on a statewide television show on my behalf during the Rockefeller campaign and was said to believe I was an ingrate. I fully understood his anger.

I saw Fulbright from time to time over a fifteen-year period, and while he was always cool and aloof, he was never rude. One day, as I was walking out of the Senate chamber, I ran into Lee Williams, Fulbright's longtime trusted administrative assistant, who had long since become a very good friend of mine. He asked if I would have lunch with Fulbright. I told him I would be delighted, but that he should clear it with the senator. He said, "He sent me." The senator, Lee, Mary Davis (my chief of staff), and I had a two-and-a-half hour luncheon at the 116 Club, a club started many years ago by former and current Senate staffers, that was immensely enjoyable and gratifying. Fulbright was aging and became easily frustrated when he couldn't remember a name, date, or place. He was intensely interested in my analysis of what was going on in Congress. He seemed shocked at such things as how much defense spending had increased. We obviously had everything in common, and I regretted, as I believe he did, wasting so many years.

Harriet Fulbright, the senator's wife, later told me that Fulbright simply could not deal with his defeat and brought it up at least once a week. She finally told him that he was only hurting himself, that I had been a respected governor and senator, and that he should sit down with me and have a discussion. She said all she got for her effort was a contemptuous look. About a week later, he told her he had been thinking about what she said and that he was willing to try her advice. She suggested calling Lee because he was well schooled in how to handle such matters. Thus, the luncheon.

We saw each other a number of times after the luncheon, and our meetings were always most enjoyable. I have always hoped the reconciliation was as therapeutic for him as it was for me. He died as a result of a stroke on February 9, 1995, and I was honored that Harriet and the Fulbright family asked me to deliver one of the eulogies at his memorial service in the Old Main Auditorium at the University of Arkansas. I told of my longtime admiration and support of Fulbright, especially for his efforts to end the Vietnam War. I also shared our reconciliation with the audience.

.   .   .

Exactly forty years after our family trip to California in 1937, Southern California Edison Electric Company invited me, by then a U.S. senator, to address a prestigious audience of officers and employees in that same Biltmore ballroom where I had been embarrassed as a child by my clothing. The Biltmore had been closed for several years, but following a thirty-five-million-dollar renovation, it had been reopened. Again, the women were in long dresses and the men were in tuxedos, as was I. I told the audience that that evening was not the first time I had ever been in that ballroom and proceeded to tell the poignant story of how, in 1937, I had stepped on padded carpet in that room for the first time in my life, of the humiliation my brother and I had experienced, and of how my father's soothing explanation had made everything all right, as had happened so many times in my life. As I told the rest of the simple story, heads nodded and a few tears were shed. I have told the story to young audiences many times in an effort to provide hope and ambition to those who had little of either.

.   .   .

Orval Faubus and his wife, Elizabeth, moved to Houston in the fall of 1978. Jimmy Carter was president. Orval came to my Senate office seeking my help in getting a grant from the Labor Department to fund a jobs program he was setting up that he said was designed to train minorities and other disadvantaged youth for gainful employment. I told him I would be helpful if I could and asked him who in the Labor Department was in charge of the program. He said Ernie Green. I flinched and Faubus smiled.

Ernie Green was assistant secretary of labor and also one of the nine black children who integrated Central High School in

1957 under the protection of federal troops after Faubus had mo-
bilized the Arkansas National Guard to prevent their entry into
the school. What a paradox. Now Faubus was a common suppli-
cant for government funds, while one of the nine children was assistant secretary of labor, to whom the former governor must
plead.

I said, "Orval, surely you jest."

He grinned and said, "I saved his life."

I replied, "I don't think Ernie would see it that way."

I made no promises, made no calls, and no grant was approved.

According to the definitive biography of Faubus, written by
Roy Reed, former *New York Times* reporter and later journalism
professor at the University of Arkansas, Orval and Elizabeth's
relationship was deteriorating, and by 1980, Faubus was spending most of his time in Arkansas. He sent money to her when he
could but was destitute himself.

She came to detest him and in the fall of 1982 filed for divorce. Faubus said she became increasingly irrational. On a Sunday morning, Elizabeth went across town looking for a small,
cheaper apartment. There she met a young man appropriately
named Killer, age twenty-four. He later said he had met her
when she came to inspect a vacant apartment in a complex where
he and a girlfriend lived. Learning Elizabeth had some furniture
for sale, he went to her house about 8:00 P.M., ostensibly to check
it out. Two other people were there also looking at furniture she
had advertised. When they left, according to Killer, she poured
herself another drink and started telling him about her problems.
She told him he was a good-looking guy. He said he bought some
jewelry from her. His version, and the only version, went as follows: He went outside to look at a bicycle, and when he came
back in, he said, she approached him closely and asked him to
stay a while longer. He slapped her, then struck her repeatedly in
the head with a large glass until she was dead. He then undressed
her, put her into the bathtub and filled the tub with water,
grabbed her bloody clothing, and left.

He was apprehended almost immediately, and the police check on him uncovered a long record of sexual assaults, although he had never served jail time. He was tried for rape and given a life sentence. He died in prison in 1994.

A few months after Elizabeth's death, Faubus called to ask if I had a safe deposit box in my office. I told him I did, and he said the FBI had found a key to such a box in Elizabeth's belongings and had concluded, and told Faubus, that it was a key to a U.S. senator's safe deposit box. Orval said John Tower and I were the only senators Elizabeth knew and he had no idea why she would have such a key in her possession but thought I might know. I told him I had no earthly idea how the FBI had reached such a conclusion, but that I would be happy to talk to them. He said he didn't know whether to pursue it or not. I said, "Orval, my safe deposit box has a combination lock, not a key lock, so I probably wouldn't be much help."

I never saw or heard from him again, and I have no idea what happened to the key story.

· · · ·

When Ronald Reagan talked about firing a nuke "across their bow," referring to the Soviets, he terrified a lot of mothers whose nurturing instincts quickly surfaced. Betty was among them. She went to work establishing her own peace organization, Peace Links. When she told me what she and a group of congressional wives were going to do, she said, "We're even going to put *peace* in our name."

I said, "I'll tell you what you're going to do. You're going to get your husband beat." Voters love to speak of peace at Christmastime, but when a politician speaks of peace at other times, he does so at his own peril.

She said, "Yes, and you men are going to get my children killed."

Peace Links was controversial in its early years. During an evening session in 1983, I offered an amendment to an unrelated "must pass" bill. The amendment, which proposed the establishment of a National Peace Day, did not meet with unanimous approval. Senator Jeremiah Denton of Alabama sensed a left-wing plot in the making and began filibustering the amendment. The debate grew white hot as he freely used the name of Peace Links in arguing against a National Peace Day. When Denton finished his speech, one senator after another felt obligated to speak in Betty's defense. Senator Paul Tsongas of Massachusetts suggested the moon must be out of alignment and was affecting Denton's thinking. As the hour grew late, Howard Baker, then majority leader, came over to my desk and pleaded with me to withdraw my amendment. He said he would love to speak for Betty, too, but he had to get the bill passed. I acceded to Howard's request.

In my next campaign, in 1986, a thoughtful reporter asked me if I believed Betty's activities would cost me votes. Since Betty had spent her entire public life on childhood immunizations, and after 1981 added the cause of peace, I had a well-thought-out answer. "I suppose it will among all the people who favor whooping cough and nuclear war." It was never mentioned again, and in 1986 I was reelected with 60 percent of the vote. Jeremiah Denton was defeated.

Peace Links, through its attorney, made a request of the FBI to see any information the Bureau had compiled on the organization. It took the Bureau several months to respond, and when they finally did, they sent two typewritten pages with everything blacked out except two words: "Detroit, Michigan."

·   ·   ·

Arkansas had suffered an unusually big snowstorm in January 1987. It had snowed twelve inches on Friday, but the sun rose on a crystal-clear, but very cold, Saturday. The Gillett Coon Supper, an absolute must for all politicians, was scheduled for that evening. Gillett was a community of about nine hundred people, and the nearest airport was fifteen miles away in DeWitt. It was not uncommon for a thousand people to attend the supper. I had decided that driving the one hundred miles would be hazardous, and flying was out of the question, so I had mentally scrubbed the supper for that evening, though I had not yet notified the sponsors of the event.

About 2:00 P.M., Bill Clinton, then governor, phoned to tell me the county judge in Arkansas County had called to say he had used the county road graders to clear the runway and that it was in fine shape. Bill said, "Why don't we share a plane and go on down?"

I hesitated, but he was insistent, and I finally agreed. As I left our apartment to go to the airport, Betty said, "You and Bill Clinton both need a saliva test." She was right.

It was dark when we got to the airport. I was accompanied by a woman who had just recently joined my staff as an agricultural aide, and Clinton had a state trooper with him. It is impossible to distinguish a mountain from a valley when flying over a snow-covered landscape, especially at night. The pilot, fearing some snow may have melted during the day and refrozen when the sun went down, wanted to land as close to the end of the three-thousand-foot runway as possible. What he didn't know was that the county road graders had pushed a lot of snow to the end of the runway, creating a six-foot-high snowbank. The snowbank had thawed somewhat during the day and, as the sun had set, refrozen into an iceberg.

Clinton was in the middle of a story when the nose wheel hit the iceberg. It made a terrifying noise, and the plane shuddered. While we were all startled—no, terrified—we suddenly went careening across the pasture next to the runway. We finally came to rest in the pasture with the nose wheel collapsed and the propellers bent double. I yelled, "Open the door, Bill! This thing is going to catch on fire."

Before he could respond, the trooper quickly reached across him and unlocked the door. We all piled out and started running through the snow to escape the plane. As we ran, Bill said, "Boy, I bet we never lose another vote in Gillett." Stark terror suddenly turned to humor.

Cindy Edwards, my aide, was the coolest of all. She had never flown in a small plane before, and I surmised she thought they always landed that way. Strangely, our hosts, waiting at the terminal, had seen the lights of our plane as we came in for the landing but never came to check on us, though it took about twenty minutes to walk to the terminal. I was stunned by the picture of the plane on the front page of the paper on Monday morning. It was virtually demolished.

·   ·   ·

In my twenty-four years in the U.S. Senate, the "world's greatest deliberative body" was seldom deliberative. However, on one very rare occasion it was a deliberative body in the finest sense, and I was involved. The issue was not monumental, but it was important and memorable to all who happened to be watching C-SPAN or were in the Senate chamber that evening. A significant piece of our history would have been lost forever but for the outcome.

It was 9:00 P.M. on October 8, 1988. The debate was about whether we should preserve 542 acres of land where a part of the Second Battle of Manassas (Bull Run, as it was called by the Union) had been fought. It even contained the site where Robert E. Lee's headquarters had been located during the battle.

Princeton history professor James McPherson was my mentor and had previously come to Washington at my request to have lunch with as many senators as I could round up, which turned out to be about twelve to fifteen. Professor McPherson, who had just completed his widely acclaimed history of the Civil War, *Battle Cry of Freedom*, told the senators that one of the major reasons Second Manassas was historically important was that the Confederacy believed France and England would recognize it if it could win an important battle close to Washington. Sadly for the Confederates, their decisive win at Manassas was still not enough to sway Britain and France. They wanted more. Thus, the subsequent Confederate incursion onto northern soil at Antietam.

The acreage in question had been purchased by a Virginia developer named Til Hazel, who intended to build a shopping mall, condos, and homes on the property. The shopping mall was to be built on the precise site where Lee's headquarters had been located during the great battle.

When John Warner, senior senator from Virginia, and I began our debate, there were about fifteen to twenty senators on the floor. And while that was well above normal, what was abnormal was that they were attentive and actually listening to the debate. It was a propitious hour, because when the Senate has evening sessions, senators not involved in floor action go out to dinner and check the Senate floor when they return to see what's going on and find out when the session is likely to adjourn for the night. Then they usually go to their offices or their "hideaways," as their Capitol offices are called. In this case, however, when they checked the floor, their interest was piqued by the obvious drama unfolding and the quietude on the floor. They began to take their seats and listen. None of them had any preconceived ideas about the issue, which was unique in itself. I had two or three charts showing the progression of the battle and tried to make it a gripping hour-by-hour story.

By the time the debate ended around midnight, there were perhaps seventy senators still listening with rapt attention. My most convincing point to the senators was that the Civil War was the defining period in our two-hundred-year history, when we became, once and for all, a unified nation, and I didn't want to take my grandson to this battlefield someday, have him ask, "Granddad, where was General Lee's headquarters?" and have to respond, "Up on that hill where the shopping mall is located." We could not mindlessly allow such a precious part of our heritage to be lost forever.

Senator Warner wanted the government to keep 80 acres and allow the balance to be developed. I wanted to keep all 542 acres. Before the debate began, Senator Warner and I had a gentleman's agreement that neither of us would move to table the other's proposal or engage in any parliamentary maneuvers. We would allow each other to have straight up or down votes on our respective proposals.

My proposal was voted on first, and when the vote was announced, I had won, fifty to twenty-five. Senator Warner then requested and was granted permission to withdraw his amendment. The "Third Battle of Manassas" ended in a victory for the North and South.

Why do I make so much of this one debate? Because senators came to the floor unaware of the issue, with no predilection one way or the other. The leaders of both parties had left everyone to vote his or her own conscience. The senators made up their minds based solely on what they heard in the debate, a rare thing then and today. I am not sure I would have had the courage to undertake this battle had I known the ultimate cost to the government for the 542 acres would be one hundred million dollars. It could have been purchased seven years earlier for two million dollars, but we felt we couldn't afford it.

.   .   .

The most politically volatile issue I faced in my twenty-four years in the Senate was the vote on the Panama Canal treaties. I voted for the treaties knowing that should I have a fairly well-financed opponent in 1980, I would surely be defeated on that one vote. For three weeks prior to the vote, my office received three thousand calls and letters a day, 99 percent of which were in opposition to the treaties. That was ten times more calls and mail than I ever received on any issue before or after. My pollster said my vote cost me 10 percent of the vote in my race in 1980, 5 percent in 1986, and 3 percent in 1992. Senator Sam Nunn of Georgia voted aye, and in 1978, when he ran for reelection, there were signs all over Georgia that said, "We used to have a Senator, now we have Nunn."

The Panamanians were livid over the possibility that the treaties might be rejected. Not only was handing the canal over to the Panamanians morally correct—Senator Hayakawa of California had said that "we stole it fair and square"—but we would have had to maintain a sizable military presence there forever to keep the canal open.

Perhaps the most courageous vote I ever saw cast was by Senator Henry Bellmon, an Oklahoma Republican and former governor. He spoke for only a minute or two shortly before the vote, saying he would vote for the treaties because he "thought we should treat the Panamanians the way we would want to be treated." Shortly afterward, he announced that he would not seek reelection. Apparently he felt his vote would almost surely destroy any chance he might have had of winning. But his constituents soon forgave him and four years later elected him governor again.

By 1980, America's disenchantment with Congress and the Carter presidency was palpable. The Republicans took control of the Senate for the first time in twenty-six years, and Ronald Reagan became president, a result of the Panama Canal treaties, the failed Iranian hostage rescue, and Reagan's promise to balance the budget by 1984. A friend of mine who was running for justice of the peace in Little Rock told me that as he campaigned door-to-door that year, the most prevalent question put to him was how he felt about the Panama Canal treaties.

A few days after the Panama Canal vote, a parade was about to take place in a small town near Georgia's Atlantic coast. It was a hot, humid day, the majorettes' curls were falling out, and everybody was perspiring profusely. A small, cronish-looking old woman in her late eighties, bent double with curvature of the spine, made a beeline for Wyche Fowler, then a Georgia congressman. Her cane was clicking on the pavement with every other step, and she was obviously agitated. When she reached Wyche, she turned her head up to him and asked in a high-pitched voice, "Are you Talmadge?" referring to Georgia's senior senator, Herman Talmadge.

"No, ma'am, I'm not," Wyche replied.

"Where's Talmadge?" she screeched.

"That man right over there holding the dark coat is Senator Talmadge," Wyche answered, pointing to Talmadge.

Off she went toward the senator, pecking the pavement with her cane. Same question with the same cronish, Wicked Witch of the West voice.

"You Talmadge?"

"Yes, I am, young lady."

"Why'd you vote to give our Panama Canal away?" she demanded.

In a patronizing manner and deep-throated voice, Talmadge said, "Now, young lady, there's some facts about that matter that you may not know."

"Facts my ass," she snorted, then turned and contemptuously went pecking off.

Many years later, at a Democratic Party fund-raiser in Little Rock, a man approached me and said, "I thought you were the best governor this state ever had, and when you ran for the Senate, I did all I could to help. But when you voted for the Panama Canal treaties, I had never felt so betrayed, and when you ran in 1980, I did everything I could to beat you. In 1986, I was still mad, and I worked night and day for Asa Hutchinson. In 1992, my wife and I were having dinner and watching television, and you came on announcing that you would run again. I got to thinking, and I turned to my wife and asked, 'Why have I been so upset about that goddamned Panama Canal?' So, I decided I had been foolish and voted for you again." But it took fourteen years.

•   •   •

In 1975, Jimmy Carter was making plans to run for president and came to Washington to meet with Georgia's two senators, Sam Nunn and Herman Talmadge. Carter was apparently making the point to them that they should all be more nationally oriented Democrats rather than southern Democrats. After Carter finished his arguments, Talmadge, in his classic southern drawl, said, "Now, Jimma, I'll go along with that as far as I can, but when the water starts coming over the deck, it'll be every rat for himself."

At about the same time, the two senators also attended a Carter speech on foreign policy that Talmadge thought a bit too high toned. As they left, Sam asked Herman how he liked the speech. Talmadge replied, "Sam, I've always said you've got to throw the corn where the hogs can get to it."

．　　　．　　　．

On my trip to the Soviet Union my first year as governor, we had exited on Aeroflot via Bucharest, Romania, where we met with President Ceauşescu, a soft-spoken dictator who, several years later, was executed in an uprising. On the flight, I was seated next to a gentleman who introduced himself as Dr. Ion Rosculescu. He spoke French, and while I didn't speak it, I knew enough that we could write short snippets back and forth. He was an anesthesiologist and taught at the University of Craiova.

We shared stories about our families. He had a wife, son, and daughter, and he was obviously anxious to make our visit more than a onetime pleasantry on an airplane. He was excited about our meeting and saddened as we parted at the Bucharest airport. We exchanged addresses, and he insisted that we stay in touch.

Shortly after my return home, I received some small, native, handcrafted mementos from the doctor for my daughter. My letter of thanks was answered immediately with a letter sent through a friend in Switzerland, pleading for help in getting him and his family out of Romania. I called the State Department, which offered no help other than suggesting that I respond however I chose. I chose to write inviting Dr. Rosculescu to come to Arkansas and be our guests at the Governor's Mansion. He circulated the letter with every Romanian official he thought might help, but it was futile.

We continued to correspond after I went to the Senate, and in early 1976, I sent him an invitation to be my guest at the U.S. bicentennial celebration in Washington. He wrote back saying he had tried every possible avenue and had utterly no hope of being allowed out of the country.

On a moonlit night in July 1979, the doctor's son, also Ion, now twenty-eight years old, made his way from Craiova to the Danube River, put his clothes in a plastic bag, tied the bag around his waist, and began swimming toward Yugoslavia. The Danube was over a mile wide at that point, but Ion intended to swim to a small island in the middle of the river, rest, then swim the rest of the way.

He made it to the island, but when he waded ashore, roosting waterfowl started flying, making enough noise to attract a Romanian patrol boat, which sped toward the island with searchlights sweeping its shoreline. Ion immediately jumped back into the river from the opposite side of the island and again started swimming toward Yugoslavia as strongly and frantically as he could. He swam underwater when the searchlights came near. The police in the patrol boat fired several shots in his direction. He ultimately managed to elude his pursuers and, utterly exhausted, staggered onto the Yugoslav shore, where he rested long enough to get his breath, then proceeded down a country lane until he came to a field with several large haystacks. He crawled under one and slept soundly until noon. He then started walking and presumably hitching any kind of ride he could to get across Yugoslavia until he reached Trieste on the Italian border. There he was picked up by the police, questioned, and imprisoned. After two weeks in prison, a prison guard came to his cell one night around midnight, opened the cell door, and told him he was free to go. Ion was understandably frightened and reluctant to accept the offer, feeling he would surely wind up with a bullet in his back. However, his unquenchable thirst for freedom overcame his fear of death, and he took off running for his life. Miraculously, no shots were fired.

He finally reached Rome, where he was picked up on a vagrancy charge and put in jail, then shortly transferred to a displaced persons center. He was asked his destination, and he said, "America." When asked if he knew anyone in America, he proudly announced, "I know U.S. senator Dale Bumpers."

Not quite true, but . . .

The Italian authorities called the Romanian Church offices in Rome, who promptly called their counterpart in New York, who promptly called me. I told them that if they could get Ion to the United States, I would try to care for him until some arrangement could be made. A few days later, as I stepped off the elevator on the second floor of the Senate Dirksen Building, my receptionist was waiting. "Ion Rosculescu is standing in the hall opposite our office," she said.

His father had written to tell me Ion had disappeared and that if he showed up at my office, I would have to be the bearer of terrible news: Ion's mother had died. After our greeting in the hall, I took him into my office, seated him, and began relating the bad news. He was unshaken, telling me his mother had been ill for a long time. We spent the day together, and he recounted his harrowing experiences. That evening, he returned to New York and its branch of the Romanian Church.

Ion subsequently enrolled in Rutgers University but soon dropped out to take a job caring for an elderly woman. I stayed in touch with him, and about a year later he came to my office with a couple of men, whose aims were not clear. What was clear was that Ion's friendship with me was obviously important to them. They left, apparently disappointed, never having gotten around to fully stating the purpose of their visit.

Dr. Rosculescu remarried shortly after his wife's death. Two years after Ion arrived in America, he called to tell me his father and stepmother, Daisy, were in New York visiting him. They had gotten permission to visit based on their agreement to leave their daughter behind. They arrived in Washington two days later. They stayed with us, and Betty and I arranged tours, took them to lunch in the Senate dining room, and introduced them to other senators, with young Ion doing the interpreting.

Their departure was a tearful one, all of us knowing we might never see one another again. But the story continues.

Ion never came to Washington again, and we conversed on the phone only two or three times. After about two years, there was nothing but silence. Neither his father nor I heard from him. His father began sending urgent pleas for help in locating him, and we began to make inquiries with the New York City and Syracuse Police Departments. By then he had changed his name to John Ross, but the police never found a trace of him. Ion has not been seen or heard from since, except for one phone call his father received years later. Ion was vague, refusing to reveal his whereabouts or tell his father where he had been; he urged his father not to try to find him, though he suggested he would call again. He never did—a terrible ending to a story of one young man's ordeal to gain his freedom.

.			.			.

One day in the late 1970s, while back home in Charleston and having lunch with my in-laws, I received a call from the president of a major natural gas utility company that served northwest Arkansas. He told me he had just learned that thirty-four thousand acres of Ft. Chaffee lands, a short ten miles from my home and surrounded by dozens of producing gas wells, had been leased for gas drilling to Texas Oil and Gas Company for one dollar per acre. Ft. Chaffee had never been leased before because the law, until then, prohibited leasing of military reservations. After the Arab oil embargo in 1973, Congress decided we needed to become more energy self-sufficient and voted to open military installations to drilling for oil and gas. There were two methods, other than competitive bidding, under which federal lands could be leased. One was by lottery, and the other was by someone simply nominating a tract of land. In the case of Ft. Chaffee, Texas Oil and Gas told the Bureau of Land Management they would like to lease thirty-four thousand acres. At that point, the bureau told Texas Oil and Gas they would have to get the U.S. Geological Survey to issue an opinion that the thirty-four thousand acres was not on or over a "known geological structure"—in other words, that it didn't look as though the acreage had any oil or gas under it. It took the Geological Survey about two days to issue such a finding, though, as I said, there were producing gas wells in every direction as far as the eye could see. A casual observer who didn't understand how incompetent government could be would have quite reasonably assumed money was being paid "under the table," but it was all quite legal. So, thirty-four thousand acres of mineral rights, obviously rich in natural gas, was magnanimously granted to Texas Oil and Gas for the princely sum of thirty-four thousand dollars, one dollar per acre. I have never been as outraged, and I raised hell on the Senate floor and in the Energy Committee. The whole thing was both legal and bizarre. Later, Arkansas Louisiana Gas Company, Arkansas's biggest gas utility, which had long since been interested in leasing Ft. Chaffee, challenged the sale in court and won, and the sale was set aside. The lands were subsequently leased on a competitive basis. The same thirty-four thousand acres brought forty-three million dollars. Some of it brought nine thousand dollars per acre. After years of introducing amendments to repeal this archaic, outrageous system, I finally succeeded in getting rid of both the lottery and the system of nominating mineral rights for sale at one dollar per acre.

·   ·   ·

Prior to the U.S. invasion of Iraq in 1991, the Senate had engaged in a long acrimonious debate. The final vote, which approved the invasion, occurred on a Saturday afternoon. The vote was 52 to 47. I had not spoken during the debate, but voted against, and spoke immediately following the vote.

About three days later, I received a beautiful heartrending letter from a woman in Philadelphia, who had watched the speech on C-SPAN, telling me how inspired she had been by my words, and that she had cried as I spoke. She concluded by saying, "I think my husband operated on your daughter many years ago at Boston Children's Hospital." It had been twenty-five years. She wanted to know how everything turned out. She was the widow of Dr. Don Matson, who had so brilliantly saved Brooke's life in 1966. I, too, was moved to tears.

·   ·   ·

On October 21, 1998, I made my farewell address on the Senate floor, a customary practice when one is leaving. I had dreaded the last day the Senate would be in session. I hadn't planned to speak, but my staff insisted, so I scribbled off a few notes in my office and headed for the Senate floor. It was fully as difficult as I had anticipated.

As January 3, 1999, drew nigh and I prepared to take my leave, senators were very gracious and seemingly sincere in expressing their genuine sadness and regret at my departure. It doesn't take much effort for a senator to believe very complimentary things said about him.

In one's early years, almost everything he hears or reads is new. The shallowest idea or what would otherwise be considered questionable information is ingested as gospel if one has not yet had enough experience, read enough, or been taught enough to intelligently analyze and question new information or theories.

In twenty-four years, I heard many powerful, unassailable arguments on proposals, and I also heard a voluminous amount of sophistry, compelling but specious arguments.

Sometimes the eminently correct side of an argument can be very complex and difficult to explain in an understandable way, and the wrong side of the same issue may be both easy to explain and wildly popular. That's when bad laws are made.

As the years went by, less and less information was new, fewer and fewer arguments were fresh, and the repetitiveness of the old arguments became tiresome. I was becoming almost as cynical as my constituents. I knew it was time to leave. Thomas Jefferson once said that every man should change jobs every ten years.

Three years after leaving, I spoke to a Chamber of Commerce banquet in one of Arkansas's largest cities. In my humorous introductory remarks, I posed this question: "Do you know why you always thought I was more liberal than you were?" I answered the question, "Because I was." They laughed uproariously. But a few years previously, it not only would not have been funny, it would probably have been fatal.

As I sat for interminable hours listening to sometimes brilliant, sometimes banal, inane arguments, I constantly reminded myself, especially in the latter cases, "he or she was sent here by the people." It was a wakeup call to me that that's what our constitution, which I fought assiduously to protect, provides for, and it has worked. There were countless times when I wondered what James Madison would have thought.

The Senate has some brilliant members, and some who are not so brilliant. Some are effective because other members like them or respect them, or both, but unless a senator is chairman of a committee, being effective is a very difficult chore. Partisanship has taken on an odious connotation, and it may indeed be shriller now than ever. But we shouldn't lose sight of the fact that we have two political parties so people will have choices. If everybody agreed on everything, it might be a tranquil society, but it would surely be a dull one and certainly not necessarily a good one. We should remember that we find strength in our differences. I used to point out that we would have been in a helluva mess if every man had wanted to marry Betty.

Only 1,864 men and women have ever been privileged to serve in the United States Senate. It is a small fraternity. The Senate is small enough to allow very close friendships and great camaraderie, but it is mostly lost the day you leave. Your interests diverge, you don't see one another regularly, and your senate friends become those with whom you served but are also ex-senators.

I went to work the day after leaving the Senate, as director of a Massachusetts Avenue think tank called the Center for Defense Information. CDI, as it is commonly called, deals with defense issues and peripherally with foreign policy. I had been in the job less than two weeks when I was suddenly and unexpectedly thrust into a major role in the impeachment trial of Bill Clinton.

Chapter 17

The President Calls

I returned from a trip to Arkansas at about 4:00 p.m. on Sunday, January 18, 1999, two weeks after leaving the Senate. I walked into the kitchen, where Betty was having an obviously convivial telephone conversation with someone.

"Wait a second, Tom," she said. "Dale just walked in." She whispered, "It's Tom Harkin," as she handed me the phone.

Tom Harkin, a Democrat from Iowa, was and is one of my best friends and an excellent senator. We talked for twenty minutes about how I was enjoying life beyond the Senate, whether I was enjoying my new job, and how things were going in the impeachment trial. Finally I said, "Tom, you're very kind to call. We need to stay in touch. I'll call you about lunch soon. Give Ruth my love."

"Wait," he said, almost panicky. "I haven't told you what I called about."

He then proceeded to outline a grandiose plan for me to make the closing argument, or what we thought would be the closing argument, in the impeachment trial of President Bill Clinton. The chances of the president being convicted never seemed high, but the story had dominated the news for months.

The American people had been alternately bored and riveted to their TV screens. The polls had consistently shown that a majority of the American people opposed the president's impeachment by the House of Representatives and now they opposed his conviction by the Senate. The fact that Republicans were willing to fly in the face of popular opinion was a testimonial to the intensity of their hatred of Clinton, along with their fervent but erroneous belief that they could bring public opinion around.

The House had impeached the president on two of the four articles of impeachment recommended by the House Judiciary Committee, chaired by Congressman Henry Hyde of Illinois. The trial, which began in the Senate on January 14 on those two charges, had been going on for four days with thirteen select members of the House Judiciary Committee serving as prosecutors and the White House counsel, headed up by Charles Ruff, defending the president.

The four articles of impeachment considered by the House of Representatives had been carefully crafted to allow a few Republican members who were feeling some political heat from back home the opportunity to oppose two, or even three, of the four articles. That would prove to their constituents that they had pondered each article carefully and concluded that while two of the articles were unarguable, the other two didn't quite measure up as impeachable offenses warranting removal of the president. Such tactics are not uncommon. It's called "covering your ass."

The presentations by the prosecutors had become repetitious and boring. All one hundred Senators were required by Senate rules to be in their seats during what was rapidly becoming a trial to determine how long their posteriors could endure the torturously uncomfortable Senate seats. (My staff thoughtfully purchased my Senate chair and presented it to me as a going-away present when I left the Senate. I put it in my office at home and have sat in it perhaps three times.)

I told Harkin I not only thought the idea was ill conceived, but that if it did make sense for a former senator to return for such a task, that senator should be George Mitchell, former Senate majority leader from Maine. George is thoughtful and persuasive and had been a superb majority leader. He would obviously command more attention and respect than I would.

"More important," I said, "Bill Clinton and I have been friends for twenty-five years, we're from the same state, we've appeared together at political and social functions hundreds of times, and I simply wouldn't be credible. Nobody would value my thoughts on this whole affair."

"That's just the point," Tom replied. "You can say things you know from personal knowledge about the president that nobody else can say. And George Mitchell would be precisely the wrong person to do this. He's great, but he necessarily alienated a lot of Republicans when he was majority leader. He had to battle with them too many times, and they're not yet in a forgiving mood."

"Have you run this by the president?" I asked.

"Well, yes, he knows about it." His tone didn't convey the image of an enthusiastic president.

"What does he think?"

"He thinks it's a good idea."

Knowing the president as I did, I knew he would never say it was a "bad idea" or that "Bumpers is not the right guy for the job." The more I begged off, the more persistent Tom became. I finally agreed to think about it and that we would talk again later.

When I hung up, Betty asked, "What was that all about?"

"Oh, Tom Harkin has this crazy idea. . . ."

I told Betty it was an idea headed nowhere and that I couldn't imagine Bill Clinton signing off on such a plan. I felt certain I had heard the last of it.

I began to think of ways to bag this idea should it develop strength, so I decided to call Vice Admiral Eugene (Gene) LaRoque (ret.), founder and chairman of the board of the Center for Defense Information. CDI, a twenty-seven-year-old organization that had been run almost exclusively by former military

officers, enjoyed an excellent reputation, especially among people who thought the United States consistently spent too much
money on the military. Perhaps the CDI board would object.
After all, we were a nonprofit, nonpartisan, tax-exempt organization, supported mostly by Democrats, although there were some
Republicans.

I related the late developments to Gene and sought his opinion on whether he thought it might adversely affect CDI and
whether the board would likely object. He said he would check
with a few board members and report back. Unhappily, he
quickly reported back that none of them objected. As a matter of
fact, most of them thought it would be good publicity for CDI.
Most CDI supporters were opposed to the whole impeachment
process.

I then called George Mitchell, who told me he had indeed
been sought for the job but said he had declined because he had
such a heavy agenda, which included travel, and couldn't possibly
prepare for it adequately. He said he had told the president he
should ask me to do it.

Monday, the day following my conversation with Senator
Harkin, was Martin Luther King's birthday, a national holiday. I
went to the grocery store around noon, and when I returned,
Betty said, "Bill Clinton is desperately trying to find you."

That was the first time I had thought anything would ever
come of Harkin's idea. But now I knew that if the president made
the request, I would have to have a plausible, compelling excuse
not to honor it; simply thinking it was not a good idea and
wouldn't work would not suffice. I hadn't confided to Harkin that
I was totally bereft of ideas as to what I would say that had not already been said many times. I could argue that it would be virtually impossible to make a speech that would actually change
votes, but that was a given. I could argue that I was very busy in
my new job, that I wouldn't have time to prepare and certainly
not enough time to familiarize myself with the minutiae of the
trial. I had not previously immersed myself in the details of the

trial—such as who had hidden, or simply stored, the gifts; who had said what to whom; and in what context had everything been said. I was utterly at sea, lost as to how I might make a difference. On the positive side, I would have an opportunity to express my feelings on a much wider stage about what I considered the tawdry Starr investigation; the innocent lives that had been destroyed, financially and mentally; and the humiliation and ridicule my beloved home state had endured. When speaking to mostly out-of-state groups meeting in Arkansas, Senator Pryor and I would express our pleasure at seeing them and then add, "As a matter of fact, we're honored to have anyone visit us that isn't here under subpoena."

I waited for almost two hours, pondering what I would say to the president in what would obviously be one of the most important decisions I would ever make. When I returned his call, we discussed various aspects of what had transpired in the trial thus far and how certain senators might vote. I was surprised by the urgency of his plea that I accept this role. Though I knew Mitchell had declined the offer, I thought another try might work, so I repeated the argument I made to Harkin that George Mitchell would be an eminently better choice. I felt the president wouldn't want me to think I was a second choice, which I already knew, but his immediate response was, "He won't do it."

I then went through the litany of excuses I had given Harkin about my lack of credibility because we were from the same state and had been political allies and personal friends for twenty-five years. The president reiterated Harkin's line that those were precisely the compelling reasons I should do it. Finally I said, "Well, I could say that we've been together hundreds of times in both private and public, and that I had never seen you conduct yourself in a manner that didn't reflect the highest credit on yourself, your family, the state, and the nation."

He said, "Damn! I like that a lot."

We continued the discussion for a while without my having to agree to the request. We did agree that such a speech should be short—twenty to twenty-five minutes. I also said that while I didn't think such a speech would change a single mind, it could, if sufficiently persuasive and compelling, have the effect of slowing the momentum for both calling witnesses and pursuing a full-blown trial with all the details that would be involved. It might also fortify the opinion among most Americans that Bill Clinton should not be convicted.

Before terminating the conversation, the president said, with a plea that was sincere, full of pathos, and ultimately irresistible, "If you just don't feel you can do it, I'll understand, but I really need you." I told him I would do anything to help, but what I didn't tell him was that I would never forgive myself if I undertook this monumental task and it came a cropper. My mother's Irish genes were warning me once again that the headlines would be BUMPERS BOMBS. I was obsessed with visions of what I believed had been a fairly respectable twenty-four-year Senate career being torpedoed by one lousy, highly visible failure.

I asked the president for a few hours to think it over and requested that he call back that evening, which he did at around 9:00 P.M. The discussion was little different from our earlier conversation, but he was more insistent. Finally, I told him I would seclude myself for two or three hours in my den and see if I could come up with a broad outline of what I felt might be effective. As we terminated the conversation, he reiterated, "If you don't feel you can do it, I'll understand, but, man, I really need you."

I told Betty not to interrupt me or call me to the phone. I went to the den and sat and meditated for about twenty minutes without writing a word. Slowly and surprisingly, my mind became flooded with ideas. An outline began to take shape, and I started to write feverishly. I felt I could make one unassailable point that would create strong empathy and that had been totally neglected. It was the human element: Bill, Hillary, and Chelsea were, after all, human beings who cried, lost sleep, bled, hurt, and suffered terrible mental anguish just as every normal human being would. One could only guess at the depth of their unending agony over the preceding years, enduring bizarre accusations from Hillary's murdering Vince Foster to suggestions that the president, while governor, had played a role in the death of two young boys in Arkansas who were run over by a freight train. Their critics knew no bounds. I did not know Chelsea well, but as I had watched her grow up and mature, she impressed me as a remarkable young woman whose countenance, stability, maturity, intellect, and easy manner telegraphed a kindness, gentility, and sensitivity that was both appealing and rare for a young woman her age. The president once told me during the early years of his presidency how he got up at 6:00 every morning so he could spend time with Chelsea before she had to leave for school and how much their visits meant to him in the quiet of early mornings before the hurly-burly atmosphere of the White House set in. And Chelsea obviously fully reciprocated her parents' devotion. Every family in America could relate, to one degree or another, to the trials and tribulations, so much a part of the human drama, that the Clintons had experienced. Every family could relate to and empathize with the unrelenting pain that the president, the First Lady, and Chelsea had been enduring for years as one investigation followed another, with millions of words written daily about them, some true, some patently false. Even though some of the president's pain had been self-inflicted, the unending and relentless drumbeat of accusations and investigations was without precedent. The whole thing had become byzantine. Where were the elements of forgiveness and redemption, the very foundation of Christianity? The Falwells, Robertsons, and other televangelists were the harshest critics of the president and the most unforgiving of all. These three people had been treated as though they were unfeeling robots. I felt sure these reminder points would resonate well with a public that had not been called on to think differently, regardless of their opinion about the president's conduct. America's compassion needed to be tapped. I also knew that almost every member of the Senate was a father or mother and would also relate to these points. And who among those who would be seated in that august chamber was without sin? Finally, I strongly believed the constitutional issue was overwhelmingly in the president's favor, and that point had not been made in a clear and understandable way that ordinary Americans could understand.

As I reflected quietly on all those things that night, I also reflected on the history of those days in Philadelphia almost 212 years before, when Madison, Adams, Hamilton, Mason, Morris, and the other Framers of the Constitution debated the justification for removing a president from office. Marital infidelity or denying a marital infidelity was certainly never discussed as a reason to remove a president. Even for those who believed the president had committed perjury by denying the affair, the point needed to be made that there is perjury and then there is perjury. None of the offenses even came close to the definition of treason, bribery, or other "high crimes and misdemeanors," terms clearly understood in Philadelphia.

By midnight, I had developed and become comfortable with a broad outline. Not only was I comfortable with it, I had begun to relish the thought of defending the president. I slept well, and the next morning I called Steve Richetti, who was head of the Congressional Relations Office at the White House, and told him to tell the president I would be honored to speak in his defense. It was Tuesday morning, January 20, and the schedule called for me to speak on the following afternoon, so I had only the rest of Tuesday and Wednesday morning in which to prepare, but I also had a full-time job. In addition, I was scheduled to sit at the White House counsel table in the Senate on Tuesday afternoon. The Senate was proceeding at a snail's pace, much slower than had been anticipated, so, happily, I was rescheduled to speak Thursday afternoon, which gave me badly needed additional time. Steve and I also agreed the speech should be no longer than twenty-five minutes.

In my twenty-four years in the Senate, I probably spoke no more than twenty to twenty-five times from a prepared text, and then only to introduce bills. I never felt uncomfortable speaking from a text, I just never felt such speeches were nearly as effective as speaking from notes. But there is a problem in speaking from notes, or with no notes, and that is that one's grammar is never perfect, verbs and nouns don't always agree, and it isn't unheard of for a sentence to end with a preposition. In the Senate, we were allowed to "clean up the *Record*"—that is, go into the recorder's office and edit our remarks to make them more readable and grammatically correct. I didn't get a chance to edit the impeachment speech in the *Congressional Record*, but I have taken the liberty of making a few corrections in this book to be certain both the intent and substance are clear. In one or two cases, the recorder also misunderstood a word.

As I prepared for my role in the impeachment trial, I knew that all the senators would be in their seats and that the press and visitors galleries would be packed. Seasoned as I was, and accustomed as I was to the Senate chamber, it was an awesome setting to contemplate.

Few Americans understood in the beginning that an article of impeachment is simply a charge, much like a "count" in an indictment returned by a grand jury. The Constitution provides for the House to vote first on the articles of impeachment and then send those that receive a majority vote to the Senate, where the actual trial takes place. Conviction on either of the two charges would have mandated the removal of the most powerful man in the world from the office to which he had been duly elected. In our 210-year history, it had never been done and had been undertaken only one time, when Andrew Johnson was tried and acquitted by one vote. The Constitution made it crystal clear that removal of the president should be only for the gravest of crimes.

On Tuesday evening, Carl Levin, senator from Michigan, called to give me a detailed account of a portion of Monica Lewinsky's grand jury testimony. I told Carl that I didn't have time to absorb all the nitty-gritty details and their meaning.

He kept saying, "Wait. Just listen a minute, will you? Just hear me out."

I stopped protesting long enough to let him tell me about Bill

Clinton buying a small carved bear while on a trip to Vancouver, British Columbia, to meet President Boris Yeltsin. He later gave it to Monica Lewinsky. It was not only an interesting gift, it pointedly demonstrated how fast and loose the House Judiciary Committee had played with Monica Lewinsky's grand jury testimony to totally distort what had actually happened. The story enabled me to make it sound as though the House Judiciary Committee was willing to go to any extremes to win. It was the only assistance I received from another person, except for an article Senator Chris Dodd faxed me, written by a constitutional scholar, that was exceptionally clear, cogent, and helpful.

I spent Tuesday afternoon on the Senate floor at the White House defense table with Chuck Ruff, Bruce Lindsay, and Cheryl Mills from the White House Counsel's Office and David Kendall, Greg Craig, and Nicole Seligman, all outside counsel with the Washington firm of Williams and Connolly. As we milled around before the Senate convened, I was subjected to a lot of good-natured ribbing by former colleagues. It was all in good taste and relieved some of the tension. Texas senator Phil Gramm offered to vote with me if I would cut the speech to ten minutes. Chris Dodd said that if the speech exceeded twenty minutes, I would lose his vote. I told Fred Thompson of Tennessee, with whom I had a warm and humorous relationship, that I had the case on a contingent fee basis and I was willing to "deal." He pulled his coat back, indicating he was "wired," and said, "Would you repeat that, please?" And so it went. Everyone asked if the microphone cord was long enough, because I had a reputation for walking up and down the aisle the full length of my speaker cord when I spoke in the Senate, stopping only when the cord stopped me. I detested being tethered to my desk, and I certainly didn't want to be lassoed to a podium that was much too small anyway, barely big enough to hold my notes.

The press had gotten word of my anticipated role even before I agreed to appear, and my presence on the floor confirmed it. They interviewed a number of senators about me and their thoughts about my selection to close the White House side of the debate. The responses were all complimentary, that I was well liked and respected and they looked forward to my appearance and applauded the president's judgment in seeking my assistance. The Republicans were as kind as the Democrats, and one Republican senator with whom I had not had a particularly close relationship said, "The president couldn't have chosen better." It was all very reassuring. The afternoon's proceeding was not particularly interesting, and I was spending time that could have been spent much more profitably working on my own speech. I concluded that Chuck Ruff was an exceptionally brilliant lawyer. Two days later, I concluded the same about David Kendall, who preceded me and who masterfully cataloged the president's defense.

After immersing myself in the speech for several hours Tuesday night, I pretty much finalized the first half and had developed an outline of the second half. Steve Richetti and Lanny Breuer, another young lawyer in the White House Counsel's Office, came to my office on Wednesday noon to go over it with me. I told them I wasn't finished with it and added, "I hope you like it because I'm in no mood to change it."

Steve, Lanny, my former Senate chief of staff, Mary Davis, and I sat around a huge conference table in my office. I asked them not to interrupt me, but rather to make notes on criticisms and suggestions. When I finished they offered neither. I felt from observing their reactions that they were satisfied—so far.

Suddenly, Steve asked if I could stretch the speech to an hour or more. I was stunned, because we had all agreed that the speech should be no more than twenty-five minutes and that was the time frame toward which I had been working.

"I thought we had all agreed that brevity was to be the hallmark of my appearance."

Steve said, "I know, but if you finish too soon, there's the fear that Lott will attempt to get a vote on whether the Senate should call witnesses, and the Democrats don't want to vote on that or anything else at that point. You'll deliver the closing argument, and we want that to be it."

I said I would do my best, but that the length should be predicated to some extent on how attentive the senators were.

That evening, while I was trying to finalize my thoughts on the second half of the speech, the phone rang and it was Steve.

"Chuck Ruff says we may have a problem," he began.

"What kind of problem?"

"Well, you know, once members of Congress leave, they are barred by law from contacting another member about any pending business in the Congress for a period of one year."

I knew the rule well, and I immediately realized the magnitude of the problem. I assumed that it would probably mean the end of my participation. Before I could respond, Steve said, "Not to worry. We have several slots at the White House that are exempt from this prohibition. They're all nonpaying, but we can put you in one of those."

"Fine," I said.

"Senator . . ." He paused and then went on, "These slots require you to take a drug test."

"Bad news, Steve, I ain't takin' a drug test."

On hindsight, I don't know why I was so testy. But all this, combined with suddenly requesting a one-hour speech, was beginning to grate on my nerves. After four years as governor and twenty-four years in the Senate, that I would have to take a drug test in order to walk back on the Senate floor seemed an absurdity. I conjured up visions of what the debate had been like on the Senate floor when that law was passed. "If we're going to require blah, blah, blah to take a drug test, then the White House staff certainly ought to prove they're drug-free." I knew exceptions couldn't and shouldn't be made just because the trial was so important. Still, it was irritating. We hung up without a resolution of the problem. Before I could get really steamed about it, a woman from Steve's office called about 11:00 P.M. to say I wouldn't have to take a drug test after all. What she failed to add was "immediately" or "before the speech."

I took the drug test two weeks after the speech. About a month later, I received notice that I was drug-free. About eight months after the speech, I received notice from the White House that I had been terminated from my job.

The press ritualistically stood outside the Senate wing of the Capitol every day, shouting questions at the players as they came and went and getting impromptu interviews when they could. It was a cameraman's dream. Shortly after lunch on Thursday afternoon, Mary Davis and I drove into a remote parking spot across from the steps on the Senate end of the Capitol. We walked to the Senate "tunnel" from the opposite side from where the reporters and cameras huddled. I didn't want to be interviewed and especially didn't want to shout answers to shouted questions, because I couldn't think of anything I could say in that setting that would be appropriate to the gravity of the matter that brought me there.

The bantering of the previous Tuesday continued as we milled around the Senate floor, waiting for the afternoon session to convene. I thought I would be tense, but the familiarity of the setting where I had spoken hundreds of times was comforting. The chief justice of the Supreme Court, William Rehnquist, gaveled the Senate to order, and David Kendall was recognized to begin the closing arguments.

His arguments were comprehensive, sequential, and persuasive. He was very methodical.

At the conclusion of his remarks, the majority leader was recognized:

"Mr. Chief Justice, I ask unanimous consent that we recess the proceedings for fifteen minutes, but that senators be prepared to resume at five minutes after four, because we have to hear the eloquence of one of our former colleagues."

When the senators returned from the recess and were seated, the chief justice intoned, "The Chair recognizes Mr. Counsel Bumpers to continue the presentation in the case of the president."

The press and visitors galleries were full. Admission was by

ticket only. All the senators were in their seats except Paul Well-
stone. Paul had told me during the recess that his back was "killing" him and that he simply could not sit any longer. It was 4:10
P.M., Thursday, January 21, 1999. I rose from my seat at the defense counsel table, walked to the lectern, which was barely big
enough to hold my notes, and pinned the microphone (thimble-
size) to my lapel.

The text of the speech is reprinted in the Appendix.

Chapter 18

An Indescribable Moment

The speech lasted fifty-eight minutes. It "listened" better than it reads. My former colleagues were uncharacteristically attentive, but that in itself was not totally reassuring as to what they were thinking. However, only one senator signaled to me with his eyes, head, and body movements that he wasn't buying anything I was saying. As many speeches as I have made in my public career, I have rarely been absolutely certain of how well my words were being received, but in this senator's case, I was certain. The attentiveness of an audience is usually a good indicator, but not always. It doesn't necessarily mean they are agreeing with you. I was absolutely certain the guy with the snarl on his face was contemptuous of everything I was saying, and yet he bounded out of his chair at the end of the speech, grabbed my hand, and told me it was the best speech he had ever heard.

After Majority Leader Trent Lott announced the Senate schedule for the following day, he asked that the Senate stand in recess. I was surprised and immensely pleased by the number of senators who came to the well of the Senate to shake hands and make complimentary remarks. Two were shedding tears. There were as many Republicans as Democrats, if not more. Senators

Roth, Hutchison, McConnell, Chafee, Thurmond, and other Republicans were all lavish in their comments. It was an immensely gratifying and emotional experience. While several senators were still waiting to shake hands, an aide from the cloakroom came to tell me Senator John Glenn was on the phone, calling from Paris. I told the aide to ask him to call back in twenty minutes, which he did.

"Bumpers," he said, "I never thought I would stay up until midnight to hear you make a speech."

John and I had gone to the Senate together and left together. He may be the most consummately decent man I have ever known.

I had another scheduled speech that evening to a group of lawyers, and by the time I got home it was 10:30 P.M., and I was spent. Betty was out of town, and when I walked in, the phone was ringing. It was the president, who was profuse in expressing his gratitude.

I turned on the evening news and heard Senator John Chafee say he thought all senators would have to "reconsider their positions in light of Senator Bumpers' speech." It was a high compliment from a man I had always greatly admired and whom I considered a close friend. I had thought all along that he was one vote I might influence. He subsequently voted no on both articles of impeachment. His untimely death ten months later shook me as no other senator's death had in my Senate career.

I had expected to be deluged with hate mail, because Clinton was a lightning rod for "haters." It didn't happen. Of the thousands of letters I received, no more than forty to fifty could have been classified as hate mail. They were almost uniformly excessive in their praise, and a few, the most cherished ones, were from people who said they had strongly favored conviction of the president but I had changed their minds.

Gratified as I was, I didn't want this one speech to be all I would be remembered for in my twenty-four-year tenure in the Senate. I had made many speeches that I considered better than this one, but almost always to an empty chamber and an indifferent media. My good friend Sander Vanocur said on *Larry King Live* that the best political speech he had ever heard was one I made in Atlanta in 1983 at a "cattle show" when I was considering a run for the presidency. I was immensely flattered by Sander's statement, but I don't remember much about the speech, nor had I saved the notes from which I spoke.

The success of a senator on any big issue depends on whether he or she can capture the attention of the press, but reporters are largely indifferent to issues that, no matter how important, hold little interest to the public and, therefore, to their editors.

There were many times when I knew that if an issue could be debated to an attentive public, the outcome would be wholly different. Disinterest by the press on an issue often allows politicians to cast irresponsible votes, knowing their constituents will not likely know or care and that they won't be held accountable.

Two weeks after the speech, the Senate, after agreeing not to call witnesses, voted forty-five ayes and fifty-five nays on Article of Impeachment Number One. It charged the president with perjury and providing false testimony before a grand jury in the Paula Jones sexual harassment lawsuit and providing false testimony in both the Paula Jones case and his relationship with Monica Lewinsky. The count was twenty-two votes short of the two-thirds majority required to convict, so the president was, therefore, acquitted.

On the second article, alleging the president had obstructed justice in an attempt to delay, impede, cover up, and conceal evidence in the Paula Jones sexual harassment lawsuit, the vote was fifty ayes and fifty nays, seventeen votes short of the required two-thirds to convict. The president was, therefore, acquitted. The nation breathed a sigh of relief, and the Senate returned to its normal duties.

In my speech, when pointing out members of the Senate who were genuine war heroes, I was guilty of one unforgivable omission. Senator Max Cleland of Georgia, the gentlest, kindest soul in the Senate, who sat directly across the aisle from me, had lost both legs and one arm in Vietnam. I had no more than left the Senate chamber when I realized I had failed to mention Max. He was most forgiving when I called to apologize, as I knew he would be, but I will never forgive myself.

The fact that neither Miss Doll nor Dad could be in the gallery during the climax of my public career left me unbearably saddened. I was perhaps even sadder that Dad couldn't accompany me to the federal courthouse that houses the Court of Appeals for the District of Columbia, where eighteen months after the impeachment speech, I went to be sworn in as a member of the D.C. Bar.

Federal courthouses are like airports. All entrances are filled with metal detectors and guards with handheld scanners. This was an unusually busy afternoon, and the lines of people waiting to go through the detectors were long. As I walked through, I was inadvertently looking down and suddenly realized I had set off the beeper. I looked up, and immediately in front of me was a black man about six feet four inches tall and perhaps sixty years old. He was staring at me with an inscrutable look. He had his scanner in hand, and I assumed he wanted me to "spread-eagle" in order to be scanned. Instead he said, "Senator Bumpers?"

"Yes."

He paused a moment and then, "You know, I cried when you said you wasn't going to run no more."

"That may be the highest compliment I have ever received," I said.

He paused a few seconds more and then said, "Would you give me a big hug?"

I said, "I would be honored to give you a big hug."

It was an indescribably gratifying moment that, Dad and I would agree, made it all worthwhile.

Appendix:
Address to the United States Senate

The following speech, given on January 21, 1999, during the impeachment trial of President William J. Clinton, is from the *Congressional Record*.

Mr. Counsel Bumpers. Mr. Chief Justice, distinguished House managers from the House of Representatives, colleagues, I have seen the look of disappointment on many of your faces, because I know a lot of people thought they were rid of me once and for all. (Laughter.)

I have taken a lot of ribbing this afternoon. But I have seriously negotiated with some members, particularly on this (Republican) side of the aisle, about an offer to walk out and not deliver this speech in exchange for a few votes. (Laughter.)

I understand three have it under active consideration. (Laughter.)

It is a great joy to see you, and it is especially pleasant to see an audience which represents the cumulative size of all the audiences I had over a period of twenty-four years. (Laughter.)

I came here today for a lot of reasons. One was that I was promised a forty-foot cord. I have been shorted twenty-eight feet. Chris Dodd said he didn't want me in his lap, so I assume he arranged for the cord to be shortened. (Laughter.)

I want to especially thank some of you for your kind comments in the press when it became known that I would be here to close the debate on behalf of the president.

I was a little dismayed by Senator Bennett's remark. He said, "Yes, Senator Bumpers is a great speaker, but he was never persuasive with me because I never agreed with him." (Laughter.)

I thought he could have done better than that. (Laughter.)

You can take some comfort, colleagues, in the fact that I am not being paid, and when I finish, you will probably think the White House got its money's worth. (Laughter.)

I have told many audiences that during twenty-four years in the Senate, I went home almost every weekend and usually returned about dusk on Sunday evening. And you all know the plane ride into National Airport, when you can see the magnificent Washington Monument and this building from the window of the plane—I recently told students at the University of Arkansas and at Hendrix, a small liberal arts college at home—after twenty-four years of that, literally hundreds of times, I never failed to get goose bumps.

The same thing is true of this chamber. I can still remember as though it were yesterday the awe I felt when I first stepped into this magnificent chamber so full of history, so beautiful. And Tuesday, as I returned here after only a short three-week absence, I still felt that same sense of awe I felt the first time I walked into this chamber.

Colleagues, I come here with some reluctance. The president and I have been close friends for twenty-five years. We fought many battles back home together in our beloved Arkansas. We tried mightily all of my years as governor and his, and all of my years in the Senate when he was governor, to raise the living standard in the delta area of Mississippi, Arkansas, and Louisiana, where poverty is often unspeakable, with some measure of success, though not nearly enough.

We tried to provide health care for the lesser among us, for those who are well off enough that they can't get on welfare, but not making enough to buy health insurance. We have fought above everything else to improve the educational standards for a state that for so many years was at the bottom of the list, or near the bottom of the list, in income, and we have stood side by side in efforts to save beautiful pristine areas in our state from environmental degradation.

We even crashed a twin-engine Beech Baron trying to get to the Gillett Coon supper, a political event that one misses at his own risk. We crashed this plane on a clear evening following a twelve-inch snowstorm the preceding day. It was a small rural airport. The nose wheel hit a snow pack and collapsed as we landed, and we skidded off the runway and sailed across a snow-covered pasture. We jumped out—jumped out—and ran away unscathed, to the dismay of every budding politician in Arkansas. (Laughter.)

The president and I have been together hundreds of times at parades, dedications, political events, social events, and in all of those years and all of those hundreds of times we have been together, both in public and in private, I have never one time seen him conduct himself in a way that did not reflect the highest credit on himself, his family, his state, and his beloved nation.

The reason I came here today with some reluctance—please don't misconstrue that, it has nothing to do with my feelings about the president, as I have already said—but it is because we are from the same state, and we are longtime friends. I know that necessarily diminishes to some extent the effectiveness of my words. So if Bill Clinton the man, Bill Clinton the friend, were the issue here, I am quite sure I would not be doing this. But it is the weight of history on all of us that brings me here, and it is because of my reverence for that great document which you have heard me rail about for twenty-four years, that we call our Constitution, the most sacred document to me next to the holy Bible.

These proceedings go right to the heart of our Constitution where it deals with impeachment, the part that provides the gravest punishment for the president, even though the Framers said they were putting it in to protect the public, not to punish the president.

Ah, colleagues, you have such an awesome responsibility. My good friend, the senior senator from New York (Patrick Moynihan), has said it well. He says a decision to convict holds the potential for destabilizing the office of the presidency. And four hundred historians signed a letter to senators expressing their views that the charges against the president were not grounds for impeachment. I know some have made light of those historians, saying they are just friends of Bill.

Last evening I went over that list, many of whom I know, among them C. Vann Woodward. In the South we love him. He is the preeminent southern historian in the nation. I promise you, he may be a Democrat, he may even be a friend of the president, but when you talk about integrity, he is the walking personification, exemplification, of integrity.

Well, colleagues, I have heard many adjectives to describe these proceedings—historic, memorable, unprecedented, awesome. All of those words, all of those descriptions, are apt. And to those I would add the word *dangerous*, dangerous not only for the reasons I just stated, but because it is dangerous to the political process. And it is dangerous to the unique mix of pure democracy and republican government that Madison and his colleagues so brilliantly crafted and which has sustained us for two hundred and ten years.

Mr. Chief Justice, this is what we lawyers call "dicta." This costs you nothing. It is extra. But the more I study that document, and those four months at Philadelphia in 1787, the more awed I become. And you know what Madison said—the brilliance was in its simplicity—he simply said: Man's nature is to make other people dance to his tune. Man's nature is to abuse his fellow man sometimes. And Madison said the way to make sure that the majorities don't abuse the minorities, and the way to make sure that the bullies don't run over the weaklings, is to provide the same rights for everybody. And I had to think about that a long time before I delivered my first lecture at the University of Arkansas last week. And it made so much sense to me.

But the danger, as I say, is to the political process, and dangerous for reasons feared by the Framers about legislative control of the executive. That single issue and how to deal with impeachment was debated off and on for the entire four months of the Constitutional Convention. But the word *dangerous* is not mine, it is Alexander Hamilton's—brilliant, good-looking guy— Mr. Ruff quoted him extensively on Tuesday afternoon in his brilliant statement here. He quoted Alexander Hamilton precisely, and it is a little arcane. It isn't easy to understand.

So, if I may, at the expense of being slightly repetitious, let me paraphrase what Hamilton said. He said the Senate had a unique role in participating with the executive branch in appointments; and, two, it had a role—it had a role—in participating with the executive in the character of a court for the trial of impeachments. But he said—and I must say this and you all know it—he said it would be difficult to get a, what he called, well-constituted court from wholly elected members. He said passions would agitate the whole community and divide it between those who were friendly and those who had inimical interests to the accused, namely, the president. Then he said—and these are his words— the greatest danger was that the decision would be based on the comparative strength of the parties rather than the innocence or guilt of the president.

You have taken a solemn oath, you have taken a solemn oath to be fair and impartial. I know you all. I know you as friends, and I know you as honorable men and women. And I am perfectly satisfied to put this trial in your hands, under your oath.

This is the only caustic thing I will say in these remarks this afternoon, but the question is, how do we come to be here? We are here because of a five-year, relentless, unending investigation of the president, costing fifty million dollars, with hundreds of FBI agents fanning across the nation examining in microscopic detail the lives of people—maybe the most intense investigation not only of a president, but of anybody ever.

I feel strongly about this because of my state and what we have endured. So you will have to excuse me, but that investigation has also shown that the judicial system in this country can and does get out of kilter unless it is controlled. Because there are innocent people—innocent people—who have been financially and mentally bankrupted.

One woman told me two years ago that her legal fees were ninety-five thousand dollars. She said, "I don't have ninety-five thousand dollars. And the only asset I have is the equity in my home, which just happens to correspond to my legal fees of ninety-five thousand dollars." And she said, "The only thing I can think of to do is to deed my home to my attorney." This woman was innocent, never charged, testified before a grand jury a number of times. And since that time she has accumulated an additional two hundred thousand dollars in attorney fees.

Javert's pursuit of Jean Valjean in *Les Misérables* pales by comparison. I doubt there are many people—maybe nobody in this body—who could withstand such scrutiny. And in this case those summoned were terrified, not because of their guilt, but because they felt guilt or innocence was not relevant. After all those years, and fifty million dollars, Whitewater, Travelgate, Filegate—you name it—nothing, nothing. The president was found guilty of nothing, official or personal.

We are here today because the president suffered a terrible moral lapse, a marital infidelity—not a breach of the public trust, not a crime against society, the two things Hamilton talked about in "Federalist Paper Number 65," which I recommend to you before you vote—but it was a breach of his marriage vows. It was a breach of his family trust.

It is a sex scandal. H. L. Mencken once said, "When you hear somebody say, 'Now, this is not about money,' it's about money." (Laughter.) "And when you hear somebody say, 'This is not about sex,' it's about sex."

You pick your own adjective to describe the president's conduct. Here are some that I would use: indefensible, outrageous, unforgivable, shameless. I promise you the president would not contest any of those or any others.

But there is a human element in this case that has not even

been mentioned. That is that the president and Hillary and Chelsea are human beings. This is intended only as a mild criticism of our distinguished friends from the House. But as I listened to the presenters, to the managers, make their opening statements, they were remarkably well prepared and they spoke eloquently, more eloquently than I really had hoped.

But when I talk about the human element, I talk about what I thought was, on occasion, an unnecessarily harsh, pejorative description of the president. I thought that the language should have been tempered somewhat to acknowledge that he is the president. To say constantly that the president lied about this and lied about that, as I say, I thought that was too much for a family that has already been about as devastated as a family can be. The relationship between husband and wife, father and child, has been incredibly strained, if not destroyed. There has been nothing but sleepless nights, mental agony, for this family for almost five years, day after day, from accusations of having Vince Foster assassinated on down. It has been bizarre.

I didn't sense any compassion. And perhaps none is deserved. The president has said for all to hear that he misled, he deceived, he did not want to be helpful to the prosecution, and he did all of those things to his family, to his friends, to his staff, to his cabinet, and to the American people. Why would he do that? Well, he knew this whole affair was about to bring unspeakable embarrassment and humiliation on himself, his wife whom he adored, and a child he worshiped with every fiber in his body and for whom he would happily have died to spare her or to ameliorate her shame and her grief.

The House managers have said shame, an embarrassment, is no excuse for lying. The question about lying—that is your decision. But I can tell you, put yourself in his position—you have already had this big moral lapse—and ask yourself what you would do. We are, none of us, perfect. Sure, you say, he should have thought of all that beforehand. And indeed he should have, just as Adam and Eve should have, just as you and you and you and you and millions of other people who have been caught in similar circumstances should have thought of it before. As I say, none of us is perfect.

I remember—Where is Chaplain Ogilvie? The chaplain is not here; too bad, he ought to hear this story. This evangelist was holding this great revival meeting, and at the close of one of his meetings he said, "Is there anybody in this audience who has ever known anybody who even comes close to the perfection of our Lord and Savior, Jesus Christ?" Nothing. He repeated the challenge, and finally, a little guy in the back held up his hand. "You, sir. Are you saying you have known such a person?" He nodded in the affirmative. "Stand up." He stood up and the evangelist asked, "Tell us. Who was it?" He answered, "My wife's first husband."

Make no mistake about it, removal from office is punishment. It is unbelievable punishment, even though the Framers didn't intend it to be punishment. Again, they said—and it bears repeating over and over again—they said they wanted to protect the people. But I can tell you this, the punishment of removing Bill Clinton from office would pale compared to the punishment he has already inflicted on himself. There is a feeling in this country that somehow or other Bill Clinton has gotten away with something. Mr. Leader, I can tell you, he hasn't gotten away with anything. And the people are saying, "Please don't protect us from this man. Seventy-six percent of us think he is doing a fine job; sixty-five to seventy percent of us don't want him removed from office."

Some have said we are not respected on the world scene. The truth of the matter is, this nation has never enjoyed greater prestige in the world than we do right now. I heard Carlos Menem, president of Argentina, a guest here recently, say to the president, "Mr. President, the world needs you." The war in Bosnia is under control. The president has been as tenacious as anybody could be about the Middle East peace process, and in Ireland, actual peace. And maybe the Middle East will make it. And he has the Indians and the Pakistanis talking to each other as they have never talked to each other in recent times.

Václav Havel said, "Mr. President, for the enlargement of the North Atlantic Treaty Organization, there is no doubt in my mind that it was your personal leadership that made this historic development possible." King Hussein: "Mr. President, I've had the privilege of being a friend of the United States and presidents since the late president Eisenhower, and throughout all the years in the past I have kept in touch, but on the subject of peace, the peace we are seeking, I have never, with all due respect and all the affection I held for your predecessors, known someone with your dedication, clear-headedness, focus, and determination to help resolve this issue in the best way possible."

I have quotes of Nelson Mandela and other world leaders who have said similar things in the last six months. Our prestige in the world, I promise you, is as high as it has ever been.

When it comes to the question of perjury, you know, there is perjury and then there is perjury. Let me ask you if you think this is perjury: On November 23, 1997, President Clinton went to Vancouver, B.C., to meet with President Yeltsin. And when he returned, Monica Lewinsky was at the White House at some point, and he gave her a carved marble bear he had purchased in Vancouver. I don't know how big it was, but here's the question to Monica Lewinsky before the grand jury, August 6, 1998:

QUESTION: What was the Christmas present or presents that he got for you?

ANSWER: Everything was packaged in the Big Black Dog or big canvas bag from the Black Dog store in Martha's Vineyard and he got me a marble bear's head carving. Sort of, you know, a little sculpture, I guess you would call, maybe.

QUESTION: Was that the item from Vancouver?

ANSWER: Yes.

QUESTION ON THE SAME DAY OF THE SAME GRAND JURY:

QUESTION: When the president gave you the Vancouver bear on the twenty-eighth, did he say anything about what it means?

ANSWER: Hmm.

QUESTION: Well, what did he say?

answer: I think he—I believe he said that the bear is the—maybe
  an Indian symbol for strength—you know, to be strong like
  a bear.

question: And did you interpret that to be strong in your decision to continue to conceal the relationship?

answer: No.

The House Judiciary Committee report to the full House, on
the other hand, knowing the grand jury subpoena had requested
gifts, says that giving Ms. Lewinsky more gifts on December 28
seems odd. But Ms. Lewinsky's testimony reveals why he did so.
She said that she "never questioned that we would not ever do
anything but keep this private, and that meant to take whatever
appropriate steps need to be taken to keep it quiet."

Yet the House committee report says: "The only logical inference is that the gifts, including the bear symbolizing strength,
were a tacit reminder to Ms. Lewinsky that they would deny the
relationship, even in the face of a federal subpoena."

She just got through saying "no." Yet the House report says
that "yes" is the only logical inference. And then the brief that
came over here from the House accompanying the articles of impeachment said, "On the other hand, more gifts on December
28. . . ." Ms. Lewinsky's testimony reveals her answer. She said
that she "never questioned that we were ever going to do anything but keep this private, and that meant to take whatever appropriate steps need to be taken to keep it quiet."

Again, the House says in its brief: "The only logical inference
is that the gifts, including the bear symbolizing strength, were a
tacit reminder to Ms. Lewinsky that they would deny the relationship even in the face of a federal subpoena."

Is it perjury for the House to say the only logical inference is
one thing when the only shred of testimony in the record is, "No,
that was not my interpretation. I didn't infer that"? Yet, here you
have it in the committee report and you have it in the brief. Of
course, that is not perjury.

First of all, it is not under oath. But I am a trial lawyer and I will tell you what it is. It is wanting to win too badly. I have tried three hundred, four hundred, maybe five hundred divorce cases. Incidentally, you are being addressed by the entire South Franklin County, Arkansas, Bar Association. I can't believe there were that many cases in my little hometown, but I had a practice in surrounding communities, too. In all those divorce cases, I would guess that in 80 percent of the contested cases, perjury was committed. Do you know what it was usually about? Sex. Extramarital affairs. But there is a very big difference in perjury about a marital infidelity in a divorce case and perjury about whether I bought the murder weapon, or whether I concealed the murder weapon. And to charge somebody with the first and punish them as though it were the second stands our sense of justice on its head. There is a total lack of proportionality, a total lack of balance in this thing. The charge and the punishment are totally out of sync. All of you have heard or read the testimony of the five prosecutors who testified before the House Judiciary Committee—five seasoned prosecutors. Each one of them, veterans, said that under the identical circumstances of this case, they would never charge anybody because they would know they couldn't get a conviction. In this case, the charges brought and the punishment sought are totally out of sync. There is no balance; there is no proportionality.

But even stranger—you think about it—is that if this case had originated in the courthouse rather than the Capitol, you would never have heard of it. How do you reconcile what the prosecutors said with what we are doing here?

Impeachment was debated off and on in Philadelphia for the entire four months, as I said. The key players were Gouverneur Morris, a brilliant Pennsylvanian. George Mason, the only man reputed to be so brilliant that Thomas Jefferson actually deferred to him; he refused to sign the Constitution, incidentally, even though he was a delegate, because it didn't deal with slavery and he was a strict abolitionist. Then there was Charles Pinckney from South Carolina, a youngster at twenty-nine years old; Edmund Randolph from Virginia, who had a big role in the Constitution in the beginning; and then, of course, James Madison, the craftsman; and Alexander Hamilton. They were all key players in drafting this impeachment provision.

Uppermost in their minds during the entire time they were composing it was that they did not want any kings. They had lived under despots, under kings, and under autocrats, and they didn't want any more of that. And they succeeded brilliantly. We have had forty-two presidents and no kings. But they kept talking about corruption. Maybe that ought to be the reason for impeachment, because they feared some president would corrupt the political process. That is what the debate was about, corrupting the political process and ensconcing oneself through a phony election. Maybe that is something close to a king.

They followed the British rule on impeachment. The British said the House of Commons may impeach, but the House of Lords must convict. And every one of the colonies had the same procedure—the House and the Senate. In all fairness, Alexander Hamilton was not very keen on the House participating. But here is the sequence of events in Philadelphia that brought us here today. They started out with the word *maladministration*, and Madison said, "That is too vague; what does that mean?" So they dropped that. They went from that to *corruption*, and they dropped that. Then they went to *malpractice*, and they decided that was not definitive enough. And then they went to *treason*, *bribery*, and *corruption*. They decided that still didn't suit them.

Bear in mind one thing: During this entire process, they were narrowing the things for which you could impeach a president. They were making it tougher to impeach. Madison said, "If we aren't careful, the president will serve at the pleasure of the Senate." And then they went to treason and bribery. Somebody said that still is not quite enough, so they went to treason and bribery, and George Mason added "or other high crimes and misdemeanors against the United States." They voted on it, approved it, and on September 10 they sent the entire Constitution to a committee they called the Committee on Style and Arrangement, which was the committee that would draft the language in a way that everybody would understand it, that is, that it would be well crafted from a grammatical standpoint but would not change their intent. That committee, which was dominated by Madison and Hamilton, dropped the words *against the United States*. And historians will tell you that the reason they did was because the words were redundant, because that committee had no right to change the substance of anything. They would not have dropped those words if they had not felt they were redundant. Then, for good measure, they added, and we can always be grateful, the two-thirds majority requirement.

This is one of the most important points of this entire presentation. First of all, the term *treason and bribery*—nobody quarrels with that. We are not debating treason and bribery here in this chamber. We are talking about other high crimes and misdemeanors. And where did "high crimes and misdemeanors" come from? It came from the English law. They found it in English law under a category which said "distinctly political offenses against the state."

Let me repeat that. They added "high crimes and misdemeanors" because they took it from English law, where they found it in the category that said "distinctly political offenses against the state."

So, colleagues, please, just for one moment, forget the complexities of the facts and the tortured legalisms—we have heard them all brilliantly presented on both sides. And I am not getting into that. But ponder this. If "high crimes and misdemeanors" was taken from English law by George Mason, which listed high crimes and misdemeanors as "political" offenses against the state, what are we doing here? If, as Hamilton said, it had to be a crime against society or a breach of the public trust, what are we doing here? Even perjury in concealing or deceiving an unfaithful relationship does not even come close to being an impeachable of-fense. Nobody has suggested that Bill Clinton committed a political crime against the state.

So, colleagues, if you are to honor the Constitution, you must look at the history of the Constitution and how we got to the impeachment clause. And, if you do that, and you do that honestly, according to the oath you took, you cannot convict—you can censor Bill Clinton, you can hand him over to the prosecutor for him to be prosecuted, but you cannot convict him. And you cannot indulge yourselves the luxury or the right to ignore this history.

There has been a suggestion that a vote to acquit would be something of a breach of faith with those who lie in Flanders Field, Anzio, Bunker Hill, Gettysburg, and wherever. I did not hear that. I read about it. And, incidentally, I think it was Chairman Hyde who alluded to this and said those men fought and died for the rule of law.

I can remember a cold November 3 morning in my little hometown of Charleston, AR. I was eighteen years old. I had just gotten one semester in at the University of Arkansas when I went into the Marine Corps. I was to report to Little Rock to be inducted. My, it was cold. The drugstore was the bus stop. I had to be in Little Rock by eight o'clock to be sworn in. And I had to catch the bus down at the drugstore at three o'clock in the morning. So my mother and father and I got up at two o'clock, got dressed, and went down there. I am not sure I can tell this story. And the bus came over School House Hill. I was frightened about going. I was quite sure I was going to be killed and only slightly less frightened that Betty would find somebody else while I was gone.

When the lights of the bus came over the crest of School House Hill, my parents started crying. I had never seen my father cry. I knew I was in some difficulty. Now, as a parent, I know he must have thought he was giving not his only begotten son, but maybe both of his begotten sons. Can you imagine? You know that scene. It was repeated across this nation millions of times.

Then, happily, I survived that war, saw no combat, but was on my way to Japan when it all ended. I have never had a terrible problem with dropping the bomb. It has been a terrible moral dilemma for me, but there were estimates that we would lose as many as a million men in that invasion.

But I came home to a generous government which provided me, under the GI Bill, an education in a prestigious law school, which my father could never have afforded. I returned to practice law in my little town for eighteen years and loved every minute of it. I didn't practice constitutional law, and I knew very little about the Constitution. I did study constitutional law in law school, Mr. Chief Justice, but it was very arcane to me. And trying to read the *Federalist Papers*, de Tocqueville, all of those things that law students are expected to do, it was tough for me, I confess.

So after eighteen years of law practice, I jumped up and ran for governor. I served as governor for four years. I guess I knew what the rule of law was, but I still didn't really have much reverence for the Constitution. I just did not understand any of the things I am discussing and telling you. No. My love for that document came day after day and debate after debate right here in this chamber.

Some of you may have read an op-ed piece I did a couple of weeks ago when I said I was perfectly happy for my legacy to be that during my twenty-four years here I never voted for a constitutional amendment. And it isn't that I wouldn't. I think the Framers were mistaken in not giving you fellows (House members) four-year terms. (Laughter.)

But you are about to cause me to rethink that one. (Laughter.)

The reason I developed this love of the Constitution is because I have seen Madison's magic working time and time again, keeping bullies from running over the weak, keeping majorities from running over minorities, and I think about all the unfettered freedoms we have. The oldest organic law in existence has made us the envy of the world.

Mr. Chairman, we have also learned that the rule of law includes presidential elections. That is a part of the rule of law in this country. We have an event, a quadrennial event, in this country which we call a presidential election, and that is the day when we reach across this aisle and hold hands, Democrats and Republicans, and we say, "Win or lose, we will abide by the decision." It is a solemn event, a presidential election, and it should not be undone lightly or just because one side has the clout and the other one doesn't.

And if you want to know what men fought for in World War II, for example, or in Vietnam, ask Senator Inouye. He left an arm in Italy. He and I were with the president at Normandy on the fiftieth anniversary of D-Day, but we had started off in Anzio. Senator Domenici, were you with us? It was one of the most awesome experiences I have ever had in my life. Certified war hero. I think Senator Inouye's relatives were in an internment camp while he was fighting for the United States. So ask him, what was he fighting for? Or ask Bob Kerrey, Congressional Medal of Honor winner, what he was fighting for. You would probably get quite a different answer. Or Senator Chafee, one of the finest men ever to grace this body and certified marine hero at Guadalcanal, ask him. And Senator McCain, a genuine hero, ask him. You don't have to guess. They are with us, and they are living, and they can tell you. And one who is not with us in the Senate anymore, Robert Dole, ask Senator Dole what he was fighting for. Senator Dole had what I thought was a very reasonable solution to this whole thing that would have handled it fairly and expeditiously.

The American people are now and for some time have been asking to be allowed a good night's sleep. They are asking for an end to this nightmare. It is a legitimate request. I am not suggesting that you vote for or against the polls. I understand that. But nobody should vote against the polls just to show their mettle and their courage. I have cast plenty of votes against the polls, and it has cost me politically a lot of times. This has been going on for a year, though.

In that same op-ed piece, I talked about meeting Harry Truman my first year as governor of Arkansas. I spent an hour with him—an indelible experience. People at home kid me about this because I very seldom make a speech that I don't mention this meeting. But I will never forget what he said: "Put your faith in the people. Trust the people. They can handle it. They have shown conclusively time and time again that they can handle it."

Colleagues, this is easily the most important vote you will ever cast. If you have difficulty because of an intense dislike of the president—and that is understandable—rise above it. He is not the issue. He will be gone. You won't. So don't leave a precedent from which we may never recover and almost surely will regret.

If you vote to acquit, Mr. Leader, you know exactly what is going to happen. You are going to go back to your committees. You are going to get on with your legislative agenda. You are going to start dealing with Medicare, Social Security, tax cuts, and all those things which the people of this country have a non-negotiable demand that you do. If you vote to acquit, you go immediately to the people's agenda. But if you vote to convict, you can't be sure what is going to happen.

James G. Blaine was a member of the House when Andrew Johnson was tried in 1868, and twenty years later he recanted. He said, "I made a bad mistake." And he said, "As I reflect back on it, all I can think about is that having convicted Andrew Johnson would have caused much more chaos and confusion in this country than Andrew Johnson could ever conceivably have created."

And so it is with William Jefferson Clinton. If you vote to convict, in my opinion, you are going to be creating more havoc than he could ever possibly create. After all, he only has two years left. So don't, for God's sake, heighten the people's alienation, which is at an all-time high, toward their government. The people have a right, and they are calling on you to rise above politics, rise above partisanship. They are calling on you to do your solemn duty, and I pray you will.

Thank you, Mr. Chief Justice.

About the Author

DALE BUMPERS was born and reared during the depths of the Great Depression, in the miserably poor town of Charleston, Arkansas, population 851. He was twelve years old when he saw and heard Franklin Roosevelt, who was campaigning in Arkansas. Afterward, his father assured him he, too, could be president.

After suffering a financial disaster and personal tragedies, he ran for governor, starting out with 1 percent name recognition and $50,000, mostly borrowed from his brother and sister. He served four years as governor and then twenty-four years in the Senate.

Two weeks after leaving the Senate, the president of the United States called him with an urgent plea to make the closing argument in his impeachment trial.

This book is a remarkable saga of poverty, personal tragedies, and financial reversals, but ultimately and most important, it is a story of Dale Bumpers, the only lawyer in town, keeping faith with his father.

About the Type

The text of this book was set in Janson, a misnamed typeface designed in about 1690 by Nicholas Kis, a Hungarian in Amsterdam. In 1919 the matrices became the property of the Stempel Foundry in Frankfurt. It is an old-style book face of excellent clarity and sharpness. Janson serifs are concave and splayed; the contrast between thick and thin strokes is marked.